Families, violence and social change

Issues in Society
Series editor: Tim May

Current and forthcoming titles

Zygmunt Bauman: *Work, Consumerism and the New Poor, 2nd edn*
David Byrne: *Social Exclusion, 2nd edn*
Graham Crow: *Social Solidarities*
Mitchell Dean: *Governing Societies*
Gerard Delanty: *Citizenship in a Global Age*
Steve Fuller: *The Governance of Science*
David Knights and Darren McCabe: *Organization and Innovation: Guru Schemes and American Dreams*
Nick Lee: *Childhood and Society*
David Lyon: *Surveillance Society*
Linda McKie: *Families, Violence and Social Change*
Graham Scambler: *Health and Social Change*
Graham Scambler: *Sport and Society: History, Power and Culture*
Piet Strydom: *Risk, Environment and Society*

Families, violence and social change

LINDA McKIE

Open University Press

Open University Press
McGraw-Hill Education
McGraw-Hill House
Shoppenhangers Road
Maidenhead
Berkshire
England
SL6 2QL

email: enquiries@openup.co.uk
world wide web: www.openup.co.uk

and Two Penn Plaza, New York, NY 10121-2289, USA

First published 2005

A catalogue record of this book is available from the British Library

ISBN 0335 21598 X (pb) 0335 21599 8(hb)

Library of Congress Cataloging-in-Publication Data
CIP data applied for

Typeset by YHT Ltd, London
Printed in Poland by OZGraf S.A. www.polskabook.pl

This book is dedicated to Uncle Eric, Dad and Daniel.

Contents

Series editor's foreword

The social sciences contribute to a greater understanding of the workings of societies and dynamics of social life. They are often, however, not given due credit for this role and much writing has been devoted to why this should be the case. At the same time we are living in an age in which the role of science in society is being re-evaluated. This has led to both a defence of science as the disinterested pursuit of knowledge and an attack on science as nothing more than an institutionalized assertion of faith with no greater claim to validity than mythology and folklore. These debates tend to generate more heat than light.

In the meantime the social sciences, in order to remain vibrant and relevant, will reflect the changing nature of these public debates. In so doing they provide mirrors upon which we gaze in order to understand not only what we have been and what we are now, but to inform ideas about what we might become. This is not simply about understanding the reasons people give for their actions in terms of the contexts in which they act, as well as analyzing the relations of cause and effect in the social, political and economic spheres, but about the hopes, wishes and aspirations that people, in their different cultural ways, hold.

In any society that claims to have democratic aspirations, these hopes and wishes are not for the social scientist to prescribe. For this to happen it would mean that the social sciences were able to predict human behaviour with certainty. This would require one theory and one method applicable to all times and places. The physical sciences do not live up to such stringent criteria, whilst the conditions in societies which provided for this outcome would be intolerable. Why? Because a necessary condition of human freedom is the ability to have acted otherwise and to imagine and practice different ways of organizing societies and living together.

It does not follow from the above that social scientists do not have a valued role to play, as is often assumed in ideological attacks upon their place and role within society. After all, in focusing upon what we have been and what we are now, what we might become is inevitably illuminated. Therefore, whilst it may not the province of the social scientist to predict our futures, they are, given not only their understandings, but equal positions as citizens, entitled to engage in public debates concerning future prospects.

This international series was devised with this general ethos in mind. It seeks to offer students of the social sciences, at all levels, a forum in which ideas are interrogated in terms of their importance for understanding key social issues. This is achieved through a connection between styles, structure and content that is found to be both illuminating and challenging in terms of its evaluation of topical social issues, as well as representing an original contribution to the subject under discussion.

Given this underlying philosophy, the series contains books on topics which are driven by substantive interests. This is not simply a reactive endeavour in terms of reflecting dominant social and political pre-occupations, it is also pro-active in terms of an examination of issues which relate to and inform the dynamics of social life and the structures of society that are often not part of public discourse. What is distinctive about the series is an interrogation of the assumed characteristics of our current epoch in relation to its consequences for the organization of society and social life, as well as its appropriate mode of study.

Each contribution contains, for the purposes of general orientation, as opposed to rigid structure, three parts. First, an interrogation of the topic which is conducted in a manner that renders explicit core assumptions surrounding the issues and/or an examination of the consequences of historical trends for contemporary social practices. Second, a section which aims to 'bring alive' ideas and practices by considering the ways in which they directly inform the dynamics of social relations. A third section then moves on to make an original contribution to the topic. These encompass possible future forms and content, likely directions for the study of the phenomena in question, or an original analysis of the topic itself. Of course, it might be a combination of all three.

Social scientific research often brings to public attention the widespread nature of particular social phenomena that otherwise remain hidden. The result may be one of discomfort, particularly when those issues reach into what is held to be the private realm of human affairs. Yet, as historical research has taught us, this is a shifting sphere of activity and one in which the affairs of government have become increasingly interested on the grounds of protecting the rights of individuals. Nowhere, in terms of the ambivalent reactions that is raises among the public and governments in general, is this process more evident than in the sphere of family affairs. Add to this the violence that may be manifest within these relations and the reaction is even more uncertain and at times, contradictory.

Linda McKie takes us through thinking about families, violence and social change and in so doing provides us with a comprehensive and vivid picture of issues associated with incidence, reasons, effects, policies and reactions. In the process of these discussions, she never leaves us without seeing the ways in which thinking about these issues and subsequent policies not only have unintended consequences, but ones which can work to favour particular dominant views to the detriment of those who are the actual victims of violence. In relation to the uncertainty that surrounds the definition of violence, for example, she notes that many definitions focus on physical to the exclusion of psychological, violence. Further, that violence takes place at many levels, from the intimate to the institutional and societies condone certain forms, or even render them invisible due to an unwillingness to admit of its existence.

In terms of the existence of violence in extreme situations and their effects upon different groups, terrorism and genocide are features of our contemporary existence. Nevertheless, whilst it is important to note that violence takes place against both sexes, the abstract idea of equal rights mixes with a sexual contract which as it moves into the private domain of the family, becomes a 'fraternal contract' that discriminates against women and children and whose effects fluctuate according to age. The result can be appalling atrocities in the private realm, conducted in the name of experiencing 'shame' and saving 'honour' and 'status' in the public realm. In the face of this, where the security and privacy to which all should expect to be entitled may be found, varies. Taking us through a comparison of countries that are democratic and are seen to be civilized, Linda McKie explores a fundamental question: how can there be so much domestic violence?

The challenge of an engaged and critical social science is to explore the relations between myths and incidence and not to turn away from an exploration of causes in order that we may produce better understandings. Linda McKie does just that in this study and explores the dimensions of our collective existences that many will find uncomfortable. Yet all too often our gaze is turned away from those places where violence is perpetrated in favour of those spaces where there is less apparent uncertainty about the implications of intervention. We can see this in the rise of CCTV in urban areas which then focuses on particular ways of seeing social problems and their apparent solutions. Behind the closed doors of the domestic sphere, there is much to celebrate about our lives together. Behind those same doors, however, there are also forms of behaviour that no civilized society should expect to tolerate. By exploring these issues, Linda McKie has done a great service to an improved understanding. Those politicians, professionals and policy-makers who hesitate in the face of a public opinion that oscillates, should read this book, as should all those who are concerned to reduce violence in the family.

Acknowledgements

Achieving a balance between interaction and the solitude necessary for writing leaves friends, family and colleagues with the task of anticipating when and where human contact is possible, and might even be appreciated. Being able to spend two extended periods of writing on North Uist consolidated my love of the Western Isles – people and place – and allowed for dedicated time to write. Thanks to Norma Neill and Neil Johnson. Back on the mainland, Margaret Black, Sue Gregory, Liz Jagger, Nancy Lombard, Arbory McNulty and Daniel Wybrow read and commented on earlier versions of the chapters; this was much appreciated. Many thanks folks!

Colleagues in the School of Law and Social Sciences, Glasgow Caledonian University, and the Centre for Research on Families and Relationships, offered practical and moral support. Sophie Bowlby, Debra Hopkins, Bill Hughes, Sarah Morton, Marsha Scott, Fran Wasoff and Nick Watson offered inspiration through our work on older women and domestic violence, and the ethics of care. Colleagues in the USA, in particular Sharon Best and Theresa Montini, guided me through the breadth of research sources in Pennsylvania and Washington. Jeff Hearn, Liisa Husu and Leena Ruusuvuori helped me in numerous ways, not only through a critical engagement with policies and services, but through the strength of their work in contesting and reimaging gender and social relations.

Last but not least, Auntie Ella, and my daughter Laura, kept up my spirits. They asked how I was progressing so often that if they had received £5 for every enquiry they would have been able to go on a long haul holiday for several weeks!

Thanks to everyone for gauging my need for refuge in isolated islands and other locations, followed by flurries of academic engagement and social involvement in the universities, cafés, bars and gyms of Edinburgh, Glasgow, Helsinki and Washington.

Finally, thank you to Mark Barratt (Open University Press/McGraw-Hill), Jonathan Ingoldby (Copy Editor) and Tim May (Series Editor for Issues in Society). Mark demonstrated great patience when I could not resist yet more changes to the manuscript. I was guided through the editing stage of production by Jonathan, who took great care to ensure consistency. Tim gave unstinting support and encouragement. Thanks Tim for your advice and energetic dialogue on sociological work and ideas.

I, alone, am responsible for the contents.

Introduction

> Violence pervades the lives of many people around the world, and touches all of us in some way. To many people, staying out of harm's way is a matter of locking doors and windows and avoiding dangerous places. To others, escape is not possible. The threat of violence is behind those doors – well hidden from public view.
>
> (World Health Organization 2002: vii)

This book is primarily concerned with charting and analysing violence that takes place 'behind closed doors', as manifested in abuses perpetrated among adults known to each other. I offer a review of empirical, theoretical and policy studies on the interaction of gender, violence and families. As a result of this review I assert that in most post-industrial societies, physical and psychological violence between adults known to each other, through current or previous intimate relationships, continues to be cloaked in opacity. This is especially the case when it comes to addressing the wider social practices and policies that seemingly silence or sanction violence in families.

Despite the prevalence, and implications, of violence among adults in families, major dimensions and consequences of this violence have received limited attention in policy, practice and research. Certainly, many people in gender and women's studies, and in social and legal services, have worked tirelessly to achieve recognition of this violence, and to develop services. However, much of this work has concentrated upon those who are experiencing or have survived violence. Risk assessment, containment and management have formed a spine in the response of many organizations, governments and agencies to violence among adults in families. All too often the focus is upon the agency of those who are experiencing, or have survived, violence, with the premise that their removal from the place, or relationship, in which violence takes place must take precedence. Securing and ensuring safety is important. Nevertheless, to continue to frame the issues in this manner offers limited attention to the broader social, cultural and economic contexts that appear to sanction and silence violence in families. Thus, although the available evidence charts the prevalence of violence in families, strategies and theories tend to focus upon containment rather than social practices. Recent shifts in welfare policies and spending have exacerbated these trends. For me there is a broader question to address: 'what sort of process, mechanism, agency, and so on' (Benton and Craib 2001: 185) does violence in families have as its consequences?

In this book I draw upon a range of studies and theories. In many aspects of theoretical work, greater attention has been paid to war, civil unrest and conflict, and increasingly to the global impact of terrorism, than to domestic violence. Given the breadth of media coverage and outlets, these are forms of violence that take place in highly visual and audible ways. Further, they do present issues for everyday consideration, ranging from national and international concerns about inter-state and intra-movement conflicts, to the implications for civilians and military who find themselves in localities of conflict. Here, I seek to work across the meta-narratives of elements of the mainstream theories (Giddens 1994; Ray 2000; Besteman 2002), and the apparently specialized, generally empirical work on gender, age and violence (Hester *et al.* 1997; Hearn 1998; Allan and Crowe 2001; Stanko *et al.* 2002; Hague *et al.* 2003). I argue that there is much to gain from a synthesis, drawing across these broad, and in places, discrete and somewhat specialized, areas of work on violence (Young 1997; McNay 2000; Eagleton 2003).

Most of us consider families, and family living, as a major aspect of our lives. While paid work receives increasing prominence as a source of both income and identity, many of us cite our families and relationships as the major and most satisfying aspect of our lives. Every family has it ups and downs, as do personal and intimate relationships. As we get on with our everyday lives, anticipating and planning futures, the emotions of, among others, love, care, companionship, frustration and anger may become evident. Talking about the past and exploring ideas for the future provides pillars to a sense of familial solidarity, continuity and history. Our roles, responsibilities and relationships in families give us a sense of place and belonging. Thus the schisms caused by violence among adults known to each other have implications for those directly involved, for those in the immediate vicinity and for society in general. Yet it is not unusual to hear suggestions that there is something atypical or dysfunctional about the perpetrator and survivor; surely any perpetrator must be evil and look so (whatever that looks like) and, as for those experiencing violence, were they to blame in some way?

The overwhelming burden of violence is borne by women and is perpetrated by men known to them. This is the notable trend in violence among adults known to each other. Although data demonstrates that women can be violent towards their male partners and that violence occurs in same-sex relationships. More commonly known as domestic violence, this violence is evident across all social classes, ethnic groups and communities. Studies have considered why men are violent to a current or former partner and have offered explanations, including and interconnecting, a history of violence in the family, alcohol and drug abuse and discord within the relationship. Further, low income and inequitable distribution of resources in households places pressures on relationships that can promote stresses and strains leading to physical and psychological violence (World Health Organization 2002). Inequalities between men and women proffered through religious or cultural norms, governmental legislation or the workings of services and agencies, escalates the risk that violence will be sanctioned and individualized. For example, the recognition and insistence that universal human rights must be protected can apparently be diluted when it comes to tackling the murder of women by male relatives (Glover 1999). When these murders concern the reputation of families ('honour killings'), they may be explained as tragic but reflective of cultural differences and traditions. I would argue we cannot turn a blind eye to the intersection of gender, families and violence that results in women becoming the markers for cultural and religious propriety.

The arrival of children promotes the adoption of more traditional gender roles in parenting and family life. The relationship between mother and child is one that is imbued with idealized notions of nature, love and family life across most cultures and countries. Despite increased opportunities for men to challenge ideas on parenting and masculinity, studies conclude that women continue to have a primary role in care about, as well as care for, children and others in families, not least their partners (Baxter 2000; McKie *et al.* 2004). Presumptions about families and gender roles therein place particular responsibilities upon women, which can make leaving a violent relationship difficult. Further, income differentials between the sexes and access to, and the costs of, childcare can also pose barriers. The social meanings and practices attributed to families, home, relationships and parenting can prevent people from speaking about violence, may even sanction violence, and certainly pose barriers to its elimination.

Social change in post-industrial capitalism appears rapid and challenging to family life. Divorce, serial monogamy, solo living and longevity, coupled with later childbearing and extended periods of children living at home, are notable shifts in living and relationship arrangements. In recent years, fathers' rights and responsibilities have been reinforced in a number of countries. Ironically, as domestic violence has gained recognition by most governments and international organizations as a crime, violent men have gained enhanced access to ex-partners through contact with their children. Further, societies in which war, tyranny and civil unrest have ostensibly ceased (e.g. Afghanistan, Northern Ireland and South Africa) demonstrate an increased prevalence of violence against women. These trends in violence and family life are worthy of further analysis and reflection, as governments and societies attempt to manage the everyday and longer-term consequences of violence in families.

Any review and analysis of existing data and ideas must address debates concerned with definitions of key terms, such as 'the family', 'families', 'violence' and 'domestic violence'. Each term is surrounded by myths, whether associated with notions of the functioning and 'good' family, or the dysfunctional 'bad' family. Families are sanctioned to undertake work crucial to the maintenance of societies, and members of families are afforded roles and responsibilities that can act as a smokescreen to violence (Card 2002). Given these challenges, this book seeks to develop new ways of thinking about, and approaches to the analysis of, families and violence by reflecting on the framing of the problem of violence and families. The current emphasis on the individual experience and consequences of violence promotes an averted gaze from questions about who perpetrates violence, where, when and why. This averted gaze shifts the emphasis away from the need to examine and address broader meanings and practices of families, gender and violence. The privacy associated with home and family has reinforced the idea that violence in families only involves those in close proximity to it and that analysis and solutions should be at an individual or familial level.

Exploring existing research it is evident that violence in intimate relationships takes place over long periods of time, often many years, and has a lasting impact upon those who experience and witness it. Services seek to offer a sense of security and build upon trust between women and professionals. Yet we live in a society where images of violence abound, especially images of violence against women or violence used to seemingly protect women and children. Thus, welcome developments in legislation and services to address the impact of gendered violence in families must be set alongside the array of films that glorify violence, often in the name of good triumphing over evil, so as to secure a safe family life; for example, the *Die Hard* series.

There are a number of excellent studies of gender and violence (e.g. Hearn 1998; Ehrenreich and Hochschild 2002; Mason 2002; Moran *et al.* 2004) and theories on violence and conflict (Ray 2002). My own research background is in the study of gender, age and domestic violence. I have not studied childhood or child abuse. The study of childhood has emerged as a topic for theoretical and research work (Lee 2001), with recent work considering children's perspectives on domestic violence (Mullender *et al.* 2003). My task is to draw across these seemingly specialized areas of work and illuminate the value to theorists, researchers, policymakers and practitioners of this synthesis. So the parameters of this book are set: in short to work across the breadth of work on violence, and violence among adults known to each other, in the context of social, cultural, political and economic change.

I became involved in researching violence against women when asked to attend a meeting of the Domestic Violence Forum in Grampian, Scotland. To situate myself, I was a 40-something white woman who was brought up in Belfast during the worst of 'the troubles'. During those years I witnessed acts of violence and the impact of long-term civil unrest on everyday social and political practices. The consequences of bombs, shootings and acts of intimidation, combined with the day-to-day fear of encountering violence, made me keen to leave and avoid similar conflicts. People might be shot in their own homes but violence was perpetrated in ways that were largely designed to achieve local and international coverage in the media. These were violent acts that took place in a public arena.

By the time I came to work in Aberdeen in the mid-1990s, at the University of Aberdeen, Department of General Practice and Primary Care, I was a researcher in health and illness and keen to avoid any overt association with violence, especially violence in Ireland. The Irish situation seemed an intransigent one. However, an ongoing concern for human rights led me to participate in a meeting of the domestic violence forum. The coordinator requested an input from the medical school and Health Board, given concerns about what appeared to be a limited availability of general practitioner (GP) services for those residing in local women's refuges. At this meeting it became evident that a range of public and social agencies were trying to address the needs of women working through the process of disclosing their experience of violence and its consequences. While maternity services were active in these developments, general practice was grappling with a range of policy changes. Further, there appeared to be a focus on the treatment of the physical and psychological symptoms that result from violence with apparent ambivalence by some family doctors. I built up an impression that for some GPs, violence in families was an event that they thought could be treated and patched up.

Participating in the meeting of the domestic violence forum led to a proposal for a research project on GPs' experiences and perceptions of the process of women disclosing domestic violence (McKie *et al.* 2002). The doctors who took part in interviews all identified domestic violence as evident in their work, but to varying degrees. While they accepted a wide definition of physical and psychological abuse, they found it easier to work with physical symptoms. Doctors were concerned about the time taken for any given consultation. Some suggested that it could be stressful for them and patients in the waiting room if a woman chose to disclose violence towards the end of the time allotted for a consultation. Further, an analysis of data suggested that some doctors hold views that question the motives and agency of the women experiencing violence rather than those of perpetrators. Some commented, 'if they want to stay in a violent relationship there's not a lot I can do but patch them up'. Yet most contended that violence in families should be addressed. However, many felt ill-equipped and ill-informed to manage any disclosure of violence. Questions or comments that might promote the disclosure of domestic violence were more likely to be posed where children were known to be present, suggesting that women without children were less likely to receive help from primary care services.

The findings from this research were presented at a national conference on research in primary care, alongside a presentation from a project on the experiences of women who had been or were in violent relationships of using health services. Subsequently, colleagues across these projects combined with the Queen's Nursing Institute for Scotland, the Women and Children Unit of the Department of Health at the Scottish Executive and a range of women's and health organizations to develop guidelines for healthcare workers in Scotland (Queen's Nursing Institute 2003; Scottish Executive 2003). This national project ran parallel to the designation of local coordinators for developments in policy and practice in domestic violence in health services. Research findings were beginning to impact on policy developments and a much broader appreciation of the issues. Further, in 2003 I joined a research team that undertook a literature and policy review on older women and domestic abuse (Scott *et al.* 2004).

There are other welcome initiatives. For example, in Scottish schools projects on violence are included in curricula. However, monitoring and evaluation suggests that the views of some teenagers, both male and female, are accepting of violence against women. National advertising campaigns draw attention to violence but these appear to have a limited impact. Nevertheless, these developments, projects and campaigns are imperative, and do require continued and increased financial, practical and professional support. However, these activities could only ever constitute a baseline from which to operate as they act to raise awareness, enhance disclosure and offer support for those choosing to leave. They remain predominately focused on the individuals experiencing or witnessing violence. I began to reflect: were those of us working in research and service developments on domestic violence merely creating a patchwork quilt that addressed the immediate consequences of violence but did little to tackle ambivalent attitudes towards violence against women? Statistics in Scotland suggest that around one in four women experience domestic violence during their adult life. Violence among current or former partners is not such an unusual occurrence. It seemed as if violence towards women by men known to them, especially in the context of families, was marginalized from broader debates on violence, conflict and families.

Structure of the book

In line with other books in the Issues in Society series, this book comprises three parts. Part one, 'Families, violence and society' has three chapters. The overarching aim of this first part is to identify and assess key concepts and terms. Having established that violence among adults in families is not an irregular occurrence, Chapter 1 offers a review of definitions and theories on families and the changing nature of family life. In the second half of this chapter a similar task is undertaken on the term 'violence'. The processes and impact of social and economic change form the context for this analysis. The chapter closes with a suggested framework for the analysis of families.

Chapter 2 concentrates on theoretical approaches to violence, and gender and violence. The chapter opens with a consideration of studies on gender and violence and then goes on to consider mainstream theories of violence, asserting that the lack of attention to violence in families reflects the taken for granted nature of families, and of violence in families. Explanations of violence have focused upon the threats of violence to cohesion, solidarity and authority but also the potential for the use of violence to achieve freedoms from the exploitation of capitalism. Contemporary theories and ideas have shifted attention to modernity, reflexivity and the interplay of social change. The knowledge of, and yet seeming denial of, violence in families is evident in aspects of theoretical work, social and public policies, and service development and delivery. The gendered workings of power and control are worthy of further analysis.

A critical approach to families, and families and violence, is developed in Chapter 3. Beliefs about, and myths of, families as solidarities, as territories for fusion, reside alongside the evidence of fission through violence. The home, as a place, space and location imbued with meanings, is crucial to the formation of myths about families and the separation of family life from social practices in public spaces. The historical shifts and continuities in meanings and practices illuminate the nostalgia and romance attached to families and the home. The chapter finishes with a call to reclaim and democratize the notion of autonomy which offers a challenge to the opacity of privacy and the home (Young 1997).

Part two, 'Gender, age and violence', comprises two chapters. In the first, the development of policies and politics on domestic violence in Finland, Scotland and Sweden is critically considered. Of particular note is the role of women's organizations in placing violence on agendas for government and organizations. Gender and women's studies provide the evidence and insights to bring violence in families among adults known to each other to the mainstream theoretical agendas. The subsequent chapter considers research on older women and domestic abuse to provide evidence on the double jeopardy of gender and age.

The final part of the book explores theoretical debates within social sciences. It is asserted that future work on the topic of families and violence must consider the social and family practices – the 'lifeworld' that surrounds and informs violence and violations. The gendering of violence does not mean that all women are victims, and all men potential perpetrators. Rather it allows the recognition and analysis of data and hegemonic trends in our social and cultural lives. Societies and social sciences have a challenge if they are to address the averted gaze all too evident in many aspects of the analysis, theorization and policy work on violence in families.

Nevertheless, we must address this challenge and offer further insights and ideas to inform global responses to violence, and thus aid in the development of a safer world for all.

PART ONE

Families, violence and society

Your family, my family, their family

⊙————————————————

Introduction

The Mochrie family lived in a five-bedroom house in a quiet cul-de-sac located in a middle-class suburban housing estate in South Wales. Robert Mochrie appeared to be a successful businessman, his wife Catherine had recently completed a degree, they had been married for 23 years and had four children aged 10 to 18. Outwardly they seemed a settled family, not demonstrative or publicly affectionate but apparently 'ordinary' or 'normal'. In 2000 Robert Mochrie murdered his wife and four children. After the murders he tidied up the house and attempted to clean the bloodstains that were the result of his battering his eldest daughter to death. He then wrote a note for the milkman cancelling deliveries for a few days, left a message that his younger daughter would not be on the school bus for that week, sent a text message cancelling a meeting his wife had with a friend later that day, let the cat out and set the family dog loose. After this he committed suicide. The police described the murders as 'methodical', 'controlled' and 'managed'. Robert Mochrie made sure no one else was involved or interfered and he was so successful that it was some 11 days after the murders before the badly decomposed bodies were discovered. There was no note and no apparent motivation.

This is an extreme and horrific case and the deaths of this family made headlines in the press and other media for several weeks. A white, middle-class family, seemingly happy and self-sufficient, this case spurred an in-depth investigation by a journalist and more recently a one-hour TV documentary (Toolis 2002; Channel 4 2003). It would seem that many of us are fascinated by these deaths; why on earth would this man murder his family and then commit suicide? No one will ever know the full story, but after the discovery of the murders it became evident that Robert Mochrie was facing financial ruin, a situation he hid from family members and friends. Those stresses, coupled with psychological strains and a history of marital tensions emerged, as family and friends pieced together their knowledge and experiences of the marriage and household life of the Mochries. An apparently contented, happy, suburban family was anything but. However, the nature and depth of tensions remained elusive until the discovery of the bodies.

What happened is known in official circles as 'family annihilation' and in Britain it is estimated that similar killings take place about every six to eight weeks. Most of these cases receive minimal coverage in the press and other media. The tragedy of the Mochrie family was that behind those closed doors the family hid from each other (never mind friends and neighbours) mental health issues, a history of affairs and high levels of collective debt. Commentators concluded that Robert Mochrie became despondent about financial failures and, having maintained a 'secret self' within the marriage by not sharing his mental health concerns, he was isolated and saw no means of escape. We can never be sure of his motivations but this case drew attention to the secrets and lies that reside in some families, and which would seem to be factors in extreme violence.

Each year in Britain there are around 800 murders. Approximately 70 per cent of female victims are killed by their partner or other family member, and a parent murders 90 per cent of child victims. By contrast, a relative commits only 20 per cent of the murders of adult men. These are gender and age patterns of extreme violence that are largely repeated across the globe. Women and children are more likely to be killed by those they know, often immediate and intimate members of the family. A larger proportion of men are killed by strangers.

While intimacy seems to frame much violence, the threat of violence is a very obvious expression of power and oppression. The weight of evidence demonstrates that men predominate across the spectrum of violence. Global trends follow patterns illuminated in, for example, the USA and Australia, where 90 per cent of those arrested for murder and manslaughter are male, and rape is overwhelming by men on women (Connell 2000: 214). Not all men are violent: 'though most killers are men, most men never kill or even commit assault' (Connell 2000: 215). So not all men are violent but violence appears to be an accepted part of masculine repertoires that on occasion, such as war, is promoted and sanctioned by the state. Few governments or service providers overtly accept or seek to address the gendered nature of violence. After all, if governments wish to use armed forces to attack certain groups or countries and/or act in the defence of the country it requires citizens, predominately males, to accept orders to fight. The strong links between masculinity, violence and states are evident in many forms of the media, as well as military and defence policies.

Murders of children by parents, of an adult by a partner, current or ex, or of older people by relatives, are acts of extreme violence. Much more common are acts of physical assault, psychological abuses and economic control within families. These can include slapping, punching, kicking, assault with a weapon, sexual acts that degrade and humiliate women and are perpetrated against their will, rape, and mental and emotional abuses including controlling behaviour, resources and contact with others. More often than not the experience of 'violence' encompasses a combination of physical and emotional abuses. Children are often witnesses to, and may be subjected to, some, or all of these abuses. Other family members may also be perpetrators. On occasion, abuses may be committed in the name of family honour, and to ensure continued male control of the household and family image. The effects of domestic abuse include physical injury, poor health and psychological problems. In addition to the fears experienced by the victims of violence, children and other family members will also be stressed and frightened through the knowledge of, and witnessing of, abuses.

If these abuses were committed outside the home, and involved strangers, they would lead to prompt intervention and sanctions from legal, criminal and other services. A review of the printed and visual media, and governmental policies, illustrates a focus on crime and violence in public and work places. Less attention is paid to the location and context in which women and children are most likely to experience violence, namely the family. Violence in families remains the violence addressed after tackling acts committed in public spheres.

It is a central aim of this book to interrogate aspects of research, policies and services that focus upon those experiencing violence. Often, and inadvertently, this focus results in the containment of, rather than a challenge to, violence against women. Why do debates continue to emphasize the agency of those who experience violence with the oft-repeated cry, 'If it was that bad they'd leave!' Here I wish to engage with the 'dual mandate' of social scientists, namely to engage in the 'development of general, abstract (in a sense, neutral) knowledge and the methods of pursuing such knowledge' in addition to a concern 'with what is going on, with the times and news, whether in some particular phase of their own times or of some past time' (Hughes 1971: 452).

The aim of this chapter is to set the scene for the book as a whole by offering definitions, statistics and commentary on families and violence, especially the gendered nature of violence. The chapter opens with a consideration of debates and research on defining families. The absence of violence in many studies of family life and relationships is noted and considered. The second part of the chapter considers definitions of violence. The role of international organizations, governments and social movements is reviewed. In the final section, issues concerned with establishing levels of violence are considered and a summary of recent data on the experience and costs of violence is presented.

Defining families

Defining what the term 'family' means raises a raft of issues. Families are essentially about solidarities and these are created and pursued through blood ties, marriage and intimate relationships such as parent, child, grandparent and grandchild (Crow 2002). In the twenty-first century there are both continuities and diversities in forms and experiences of families. The notion of families and the lived experience of families remains an enduring one for everyday human existence, memories of the past and anticipations of the future (Silva and Smart 1999). Families are premised upon notions of kinship and assumptions about obligations and responsibilities between relatives and intimate partners, all of which constitute an accepted part of what we should do in families (Finch and Mason 1999: 300). Introducing individuals as wives, husbands, partners, mothers, fathers, daughters or stepbrothers positions them in specific sets of relationships, roles, expectations and responsibilities.

Regardless of previous, current or anticipated living arrangements, most of us will consider 'our family' central to self-identification. Obligations between spouses, cohabiting partners, grandparents, parents and children are often the strongest we encounter. However, there is no easy nor straightforward relationship in the judgements and activities people undertake in supporting and working within families (Cheal 1991: 141; Finch and Mason 1999: 310). There remain implicit ideas, and empirical evidence, that adult women have stronger obligations to their kith and kin than men. This is certainly the case with regard to caring and domestic tasks where it is not unusual to hear debates start off with a discussion of 'parents' and slowly shift to a debate on the activities and concerns of 'mothers'.

Families are places of activity and discourses; of communication, noise, change, reminiscence and anticipation (Morgan 1996; Bernardes 1997; Jamieson 1998; Berthoud and Gershuny 2000; Allan and Crow 2001). What happens in families also involves silence and not 'just in the sense of quietness, but in the sense of what is unspoken' (Hearn and Parkin 2001: 3). Many dimensions of family life persist through accommodations about who does what and when, and these are often reached in silence. Activities and roles are not actively discussed and (re)negotiated, but rather presumed and based on certain claims to roles within families – for example, the statement 'because I am your husband' can be used to diminish challenges from a wife. There are points in time and topics which family members will actively discuss, and negotiate roles and responsibilities that become 'family strategies'. Often these are concerned with the organization of time, care and resources – for example, getting children to and from childcare or school (Wallace 2002). Thus 'accommodations', whether reached through conversation or in silence, concern matters of gender, age and dependency, caring, intimacy and identities. These rest on assumptions about who is responsible for and/or undertakes tasks and organizational work in families (McKie *et al.* 2002).

Ideologies are not just a set of abstract ideas but are expressed in everyday actions and images (Barrett 1980), and these are implicated in all sorts of accounts of families. They can include calls for the continuance of gender-based inequalities, gendered practices in childrearing, criticisms of same-sex relations and the silences that continue to surround aspects of violence in families. There exists an ideology of 'familism' (Dalley 1996) which 'allows us all to deceive ourselves into believing in our own normality by creating and sustaining an image of the family' (Bernardes 1997: 33). Ideologies that imbue families with ideas of sanctity, security, nurturing and intimacy can result in some unpleasant aspects of family life becoming invisible. Abuse or unhappiness in families may be screened out in our search for these idealized notions (Bernardes 1997: 31).

Families change and mould around shifts in gender, ethnicity, demography, economic opportunities and social norms. One notable example of changes in relationships and childbearing is reflected in recent statistics from the UK on the birth of babies (www.statistics.gov.uk). Over 40 per cent of babies are now born to parents who are not married. A century ago the equivalent figure was less than 4 per cent. The percentage of children born outside marriage has grown markedly in the last 30 years. Further, despite the UK having the highest rate of teenage pregnancies in western Europe, the mean age of women at first pregnancy has risen from the early to late twenties.

There is a large body of historical and contemporary work on social change, social traditions and social cohesion that illuminates the continuities and diversities in the lives of families (Durkheim 1976; Weber 1978). Prior to the industrial revolution, families were bound together by necessity and tradition, kin, family and neighbours worked to enhance the chances of survival. Often lives were brief and bleak but relationships offered intimacy and support that tended to concentrate on the survival of children and other family members. With industrialization, changes in the organization of families, especially the separation of paid work and home, made possible new forms of privacy and an enhanced focus on intimacy in the immediate family grouping. Marriage was romanticized, and it is the case that over the last two centuries the potential for personal and sexual fulfilment through heterosexual partnerships has been emphasized. In many societies childhood has become a definable stage with the attainment of adulthood apparently offering completeness (Lee 2001: 21). Young people increasingly choose to marry for love and the potential to develop their own households. With increasing longevity the concept of old age has evolved (Phillipson 1998).

Lest this brief résumé of the history of social change and family life paints too positive a picture, there were, and remain, inequities in gender, age, ethnicity and income evident in any analysis of family life. The possibilities for sexual intimacy and expression were structured by the inequities between men and women, adults and children, rich and poor. The notion of the 'double standard', originating from the social and sexual norms of

Victorian times, extolled the virtues of monogamous marriage while child, domestic and other forms of sexual and physical abuse were not uncommon (Jamieson 1998). Aspects of the law, and interpretations of religious writings and thought, promoted the idea that men should have authority over women and children. Despite changes in the law and the promotion of the human rights of individuals regardless of gender, the 'double standard' is still evident in cultural representations of, and discourses about, families. For example, both men and women will more readily forgive an adulterous man than an adulterous woman. Women continue to carry the burden of being the symbolic focus for the sanctity of family and sexual life.

Older age is now associated with activity and many years of life post childrearing, albeit that these years can also be characterized by gender differences, economic hardship and declining familial contact and social networks (Arber and Ginn 1995; Phillipson 1998). Longevity is a phenomenon that demonstrates the success of enhanced living conditions and public health services. However, growing older and living longer poses a number of issues for most societies, not least of which are the provision of adequate income and care. Attitudes towards age and ageing differ across the globe. For example, broad trends may be observed in Japan and the USA. Despite evidence of some shifts in the former country, family priorities in Japan continue to emphasize support for older relatives from children and family members. It is not uncommon for households to comprise three generations. In the USA, older age tends to be marked by independent couple households with the heterosexual couple being most common. Support networks are often drawn across friends, neighbours and, to a lesser degree, family, whereas in Japan support is sought first and foremost from adult children. There are clear familial channels and expectations for seeking support in Japan. By contrast, in the USA, where independence is highly rated, sources for support may be blurred across various groups and service options, often involving payment (Cheal 2002: 40–1). Of course, there are differences across ethnic groups in both countries but drawing out these broad trends illuminates the consequences of cultural, historical and economic contexts for family relations and later life.

Imagining families

There is a wide variety of family types. Nevertheless, in post-industrial societies, the so-called 'nuclear family' continues to be prevalent in the many discourses and policies on families. Currently, the nuclear family comprises parents, not necessarily married but co-habiting, in employment, and with dependent children. The focus in much debate is upon the heterosexual adult couple rearing children, even though such families are now in the minority. Images in advertising vacillate between portrayals of the nuclear family with limited, and somewhat cynical, presentations of changing gender roles. Occasionally there is a nod of recognition for diversities in race, ethnicity, sexuality and age groups. There are attempts to promote ironic notions of social change through images of gender role reversal, with many promoting the apparent inability of men to undertake domestic tasks or deal with emotions. This use of irony and humour does little to enhance the potential for gender parity. Regardless, the dominant image of families is one of a cohesive group, based around an adult heterosexual partnership and children, with parents ensuring economic stability and social cohesion.

Many images of, and discussions about, families conjure up thoughts of security, warmth and intimacy. Yet for a notable number of people 'family' forms a context for experiences of fear, intimidation and violence. Violence in families takes place between immediate family members, intimate partners and also wider groups of relatives, family and friends. Until the late twentieth century, much of this violence was ignored and silenced, even accepted as a 'natural' part of family life. These silences, active or forced, reflect the location in which much of this violence takes place – the privacy of the home – as well as the continued mystic idealization and sanctity afforded to family life. Today there are numerous examples of research, campaigns and services that seek to chart and address violence in families. Of particular note is work by campaigning and service groups, for example, Women's Aid, and the growth of international initiatives such as the work of the United Nations on the elimination of violence against women.

Even with this growth in campaigns, initiatives, legislation and services, violence in families is still considered by some to be unusual, even atypical. This runs contrary to available evidence. In a review of 48 population-based surveys from around the world, between 10 to 69 per cent of women reported being physically assaulted by a male partner at some point in their lives (World Health Organization 2002: 15). Even allowing for the range in responses, and the different ways in which surveys were designed and data collected, it would be fair to conclude that violence perpetrated by intimate male partners is not uncommon. The recognition that violence does take place among adults in families can provoke discourses in which perpetrators are spoken of as abnormal or unstable, and in some way visibly different. Those experiencing violence may also experience the frustration of other people that they choose to remain in relationships where violence is evident: 'Why do they stay?' Just as families are imbued with some ideas that have limited grounding in evidence and experience, so too is violence in families. If, as is suggested by a number of studies, around one in four women in the UK experience domestic violence at some point in their adult lives then there are clearly many people, generally men, who use violence to achieve a range of outcomes, not the least of which are dominance and control in adult relationships (Scottish Executive 2000; World Health Organization 2002).

Despite the available data, and the implications of these, much of the policy and service work on domestic violence, and many public debates, focus upon the victim and the potential for them to leave a violent relationship or situation. Important as it is to support someone who wants to leave a violent relationship, there are a number of wider social and economic issues to consider, including:

- The gendered nature of much of this violence. While both men and women can be violent it is overwhelmingly men who are violent to spouses, partners, children and other relatives.
- Gender and age inequities in caring responsibilities and resources that make leaving a violent relationship a difficult and even dangerous choice for women, children and dependent adults. For example, a woman may not have the income to rent or purchase another home, and leaving may involve a change in schooling for children, taking both mother and child out of known networks that can offer support.
- The direct and indirect impacts of violence may take place over a long period of time. These impacts have a negative effect on the self-perceptions, self-esteem and networks of those experiencing violence. Older people can find it especially difficult to leave violent relationships.

An ideal type? The absence of violence

Families have been described and explained as a social institution. Idealized versions of family life are based on presumptions about knowing your place 'rather than through mutually negotiated knowledge of each other' (Jamieson 1998: 22). The term 'the family' generates thoughts and ideas that can be both comforting and disturbing. Certainly the family has become a concern for a range of groups including social work, psychology, legal and health professionals. Identifying and working on violence, distress and dissatisfaction in families is now firmly on the agenda for training, policy and practice issues, for these and many other professionals and organizations. And so it should be. A range of groups, most notably Women's Aid and other non-governmental organizations, have built campaigns and programmes on a recognition of the prevalence of violence against intimate partners in all countries, all cultures and at every level of society.

Commentators have been concerned with the promotion of the family as a stable organic unit, capable of emotional and physical support for all members. After the Second World War this notion of the family as a 'system' had a profound impact on popular images, ideas and policies. By linking roles and responsibilities in families to economic requirements for a current and future workforce, welfare services could be tailored to support those families that adhered to this model. This concept of the nuclear family was based on marriage, a relationship premised upon monogamy between heterosexual adult partners (Parsons 1943, 1949). The marriage relationship began to take superiority over other social and familial commitments. It was also reinforced as the core relationship for the bearing and rearing of children. Support came from a number of quarters including various religions, political theories and parties, and social policies. Child-rearing, many argued, was the major fulfilment of the adult relationship. Further, the home achieved a prominence not just as the location for co-residence of immediate family members but also as a physical haven from the outside world. The maintenance of the home, and needs of family members, were to be met through the employment of one or more of the adults outside the home.

This notion of the family as a system promoted the differentiation of sex roles. Husbands and fathers were considered 'breadwinners', and wives as mothers, unpaid carers and domestic workers who provided emotional support for family members. An instrumental and expressive divide was viewed as the adaptive capacity required for the needs of market economies. These views provided a justification for the dichotomy between the private (home and family) and public (employment and civic activity) (Van Every 1995: 5). Families that did not conform to, or seek to achieve this model, were considered disorganized. This tendency to 'disorganization' was seemingly more prevalent among lower class households. Mutuality and solidarity among immediate family members was emphasized, along-side the promotion of an individuation of the family unit. To achieve a stable nuclear family supported through policies, discourses and services, necessitated families, and family members, to be moulded to meet the needs of industrialization. Such ideas diverted attention from the mosaic of family forms and experiences evident across industrial and agrarian economies (Murdock 1949: 10).

The strong link proposed between maternal care, and the mental health and well-being of both mother and child had implications for roles and responsibilities in families (Bowlby 1952, 1965). The need for, and importance of, a mother's love for the infant child was promoted as being just as important as food, shelter and material well-being. In the years following the publication of these ideas, juvenile delinquency and anti-social behaviours involving children and young people were said to emerge from poor socialization in families. The role of mothers became a focal point for debate. With a growing number of women entering or returning to the labour market before their children started formal education, mothers were not always at home for the end of the school day. Regardless of childcare arrangements, these children were termed 'latchkey kids'. This phrase became synonymous with poor parenting, especially mothering. A number of psychological and social psychological theories emerged that sought to explain violence and crime in industrial societies as arising from maternal deprivation and poor parenting in the early years (Sroufe and Fleeson 1986). There was an assumption that children were better off spending time with their mothers, particularly in their early years, regardless of the quality of parenting by fathers or mothers. This placed particular emphasis upon mothers and children, with increased surveillance of their activities in and outside the home. Some psychological explanations remain relatively uncritical of the workings of gender, social and economic changes in families. These, and other explanations, coupled with societal pressures on families to conform to certain roles and images of the cohesive and supportive network, reinforced shame and stigma among those experiencing or witnessing violence (Schneider and Schneider 1994).

By the 1960s, governments in industrialized countries were concerned with what was thought to be the breakdown of family life. There was uneasiness about the changing role of women, increasing divorce rates and the apparent increase in the delinquency of young people (Spinley 1953; Fyvel 1961). Alongside these concerns was a recognition of the continued popularity of marriage, and the potential for a companionate adult relationship to form a sound basis to family life (Gorer 1955; Titmuss 1958). Enhanced welfare policies led many to be optimistic about the family's ability to adapt to social and economic change while other studies demonstrated continued economic, social and gender divisions (Spinley 1953; Townsend 1954; Dennis *et al.* 1956; Coates and Silburn 1971). These are debates and concerns that remain current, albeit with differing emphases.

Marxist analysis offered particular ideas on the relationship between social class, the economy and, ultimately, the family. These also ascribed gender roles in families, and in a largely uncritical fashion (Marx [1867] 1970). The family was explained and understood with reference to its relevance for capitalist production: 'the family is created in the image provided by the corporation' (Smith 1973: 21). The relationship between economic production and family life necessitated a separation of family life (private) from the processes of production (public). These divisions ascribed women and children to economically dependent roles with highly problematic economic consequences when death or separation resulted in family breakup. Contemporary Marxist feminist perspectives have critiqued social relationships and economic structures, arguing that a limited analysis of gender leads to narrowly framed understandings of families that promote the male breadwinner model (Delphy and Leonard 1992: 105).

More recent debates on divorce and lone parenting have ranged from concerns about parenting in same-sex relationships to the sexual and parenting role models provided by lone or partnered parents (Young 1997: 103). Heterosexual partnerships and parenting continue to be favoured and promoted through a number of discourses, policies and services. These are promoted over and above the other family forms that can offer nurturing and security. Lone parent or same-sex families can be considered to be inferior forms of family life by some commentators, and to be avoided as a location for parenting, regardless of the levels of violence or discontent that are evident in heterosexual households (Cheal 2002: 135–6). There have been notable shifts from general berating of the lone parent family in previous decades to an emphasis on families that are socially cohesive, embedded in local communities, and practicing a lifestyle that limits the need for state intervention (Barlow *et al.* 2002: 115). However, while proclaiming moral tolerance, most governments and cultural references continue to promote the ideal as children living with heterosexual parents supported by wider kinship and friendship networks. Parenting, by same-sex parents, remains a controversial area for many governments, services and groups, as shown in current debates on same-sex marriage. The differing international and national approaches to legislating on same-sex marriages illuminates the breadth of attitudes to sexualities, gender and the family.

Social and moral phenomena are intertwined, and never more obviously so than with families. While few people would now argue that mothers should not participate in education, training and employment, childcare arrangements for young children continue to come in for particular scrutiny and comment. Economic changes, and the impact of these on families and households, have not resulted in the anticipated changes to relationships – namely, greater equality in private as well as public spheres of life. Rather, wives/mothers do a 'double shift' in so far as they undertake more than their fair share of domestic labour in addition to paid work (Hochschild 1990). It would appear that there is a 'stalled revolution' in which women's entry into paid employment has not been matched by changes in men's behaviour in domestic work (Lupton and Barclay 1997; Baxter 2000; Sullivan 2000). Gender is a political, economic and social project that creates tensions and difficulties in domestic and other spheres of life (Holter 1995). Rather than imply a simplified or static notion of gender roles, and of femininities and masculinities, 'doing gender' is a 'complex, and powerfully effective, domain of social practice' (Connell 2001: 18).

Changing families: descriptions and explanations

Contemporary trends in family life illustrate continuities and diversities. These are not simply shifts in response to macroeconomic and social forces; they also demonstrate the ways in which individuals and family members are active in shaping domestic life (Allan and Crow 2001: 9). Consider an analysis of the first three studies of national birth cohorts in Britain. These respective studies included participants born in the years 1946, 1958 and 1970. As longitudinal studies they provide information on a number of aspects of family life from the early years to mid-adulthood (Ferri *et al.* 2003). The most striking trend is in attitudes and behaviours towards relationships and the postponement of marriage and parenthood. Cohabitation is now the most common form of first partnership (Ermisch and Franceconi 2000). Divorce, repartnering and serial monogamy are increasingly common with 'little evidence that failed relationships are a disincentive to repartnership or remarriage' (Ferri and Smith 2003: 105).

As noted earlier, the mean age for first birth has risen from the early twenties in the 1980s, to the late twenties in the early twenty-first century. These trends are linked to educational attainment with many women graduates not having their first child until into their thirties (Bynner and Egerton 2001), and for this group the number of births has declined. A growing number of women are choosing not to have children. Women with few or no educational qualifications are rather more traditional. Often they form partnerships within a few years of leaving school and, if they do, parenthood follows soon after. Most European countries, Britain and the USA continue to have high levels of teenage pregnancy (Coleman and Schofield 2001). Thus despite higher economic and occupational aspirations there remain patterns of transition into relationships and parenting that are indicative of social class differences.

An increasing number of children experience change in their immediate family structures, and so do grandparents. The formation and reformation of families has led to social (rather than biological) parenting and diverse caring relationships. Family breakdown is a process rather than an event (Ferri *et al.* 2003) and this process of change causes emotional, social and economic stresses. It is estimated that one in eight children in Britain will experience life in a stepfamily and debates continue on the longer-term implications of family changes for children's health, well-being and educational attainment (Berthoud and Gershuny 2000; Ferri *et al.* 2003).

A recent study of family roles, values, work orientations and lifestyle preferences concluded that there is a:

> crucial distinction between personal preferences and public opinion attitudes, between what people choose for themselves and what are thought to be good general rules for society as a whole. It is perfectly possible for people to believe that women are just as able as men and can perform equally competently in any occupation and yet personally choose to be full-time homemakers or secondary earners who give priority to their families.
>
> (Hakim 2003: 257–8)

That the relationship between personal beliefs and personal choices is complex is evident in the decisions many people make about work-life activities. Secondary earners in households continue to be overwhelmingly female, and most are mothers. This may be through choice, as suggested by Hakim (2003), or as a result of structural barriers such as limited access to good quality, affordable childcare. Further, there remains a 'continuing strong conviction in modern societies that women's family responsibilities, particularly those involving young children, must come first' (Hakim 2003: 3). In households where adult partners work in professional jobs there is evidence of greater equality in tasks and more negotiation on family matters. However, even in these households women continue to undertake a greater proportion of domestic labour (Berthoud and Gershuny 2000; Ferri *et al*. 2003: 146). For example, in addition to the day-to-day paid and domestic work, there are a myriad of tasks associated with 'family labour' such as planning for, and managing, celebrations and anniversaries. The organization of these tasks remains, first and foremost, in the domain of women in families (Benn 1998).

Data from the *British Social Trends Survey* in 2003 (National Statistics 2002) found that 43 per cent of adults aged over 24 had grandparents alive and almost 90 per cent of people over 60 were grandparents. Nearly two thirds of these grandparents saw their grandchildren (defined as aged 16 or under) at least once a week. With the work commitments of parents, and relationship breakdown, many grandparents are involved in practical and emotional support for their children and grandchildren. Yet of all those surveyed, 63 per cent considered that ensuring a decent standard of living for older people was largely the responsibility of government. This finding suggests that reciprocity in support and care may be increasingly difficult due to employment and care commitments on the part of adult children that leave limited time and resources for grandparents. Those in mid-life can find themselves sandwiched between two generations with their attendant calls upon economic, social and family resources. Families of different ethnic minority origins may currently demonstrate lateral branches of family networks and larger than average sized households, but these patterns are changing too and moving, albeit slowly, towards this model of 'beanpole families' of several generations alive though not living in the same household.

The suggestion that we are moving into an era of the beanpole families is an interesting one, and appears to be borne out by a review of available evidence. Beanpole families are those of multiple generations that include older people and fewer children. Lateral family connections appear to have slimmed down and with a growing number of people living into their eighties and nineties, there are often families of four generations. In the UK the average life expectancy is 81 for men and 84 for women. In a decade or so the proportion of people in the population aged 65 and over is predicted to be greater than those people aged 16 and under. In 2001 there were 9.1 million people aged 65: an increase of 51 per cent since 1961. These are dramatic changes to the composition of populations and these trends are strikingly similar in most other post-industrial societies. However, somewhat different demographic trends are evident in sub-Saharan Africa and societies in which HIV and AIDS have torn apart family structures. The illness and death of many adults has left young and old with limited economic and social support.

Defining violence and violation

People form families, families are collectives formed of people, and the relationships therein reflect material and social differences. These relationships and groupings play a critical role in social and economic processes (Brannen and Wilson 1987; Cheal 1999). Families and familial relationships are focal points for the transmission of knowledge and the formation of ideas on violence (McKie and Jamieson 2003). There can be complex and contradictory reasons for knowing about, and yet ignoring, violence in families (Cohen 2001). The potential departure of an adult and parent from intimate and familial relationships leads to emotional, social and economic losses. State intervention in families has allowed certain attempts at the assessment and study of violence – for example, legislation to outlaw child abuse and neglect. Ironically, this enhanced role for the state appears, in the view of some commentators, to have lifted the responsibility from neighbours and relatives to question any evidence or suspicions of violence. Despite reforms and interventions, policies and related services have tended to downplay the significance of the patterns of gender, age and violence. The focus is upon the need to mediate violence so as to limit wider challenges to the supposed sanctity of the family.

Reflection upon a range of definitions of violence highlights the manner in which organizational, academic and legal discourses debate and contest what is included and excluded. Violence is a complex and contested term (Arendt 1970; Hearn 1998; Hatty 2000), and debates on its definition and the processes associated with it can become reified – the human beings involved in immediate and sustained acts and experiences of violence seem to become lost. It has been argued that these very debates have made it easier to ignore or silence violence in families (Renzetti et al. 2001; World Health Organization 2002). Certainly the contested nature of the term violence reflects 'the process of the reproduction of and indeed opposition to violence' (Hearn 1998: 15).

The failure to agree a definition works to the benefit of abusers and reinforces the ad hoc manner in which policies and services respond (Kelly 1999). There is no agreed definition of domestic violence between nations, nor within the UK: legal, police and related services work with a range of definitions. This means that the collection of data on prevalence and incidence is highly problematic, thus making concerted policy and service development complex and potentially difficult (Weldon 2002). It is accepted that domestic violence, and most other forms of violence in families, is likely to be under-reported, and levels of violence higher than they are estimated to be on the basis of current data. Certainly it has taken much work on the part of the autonomous women's movement through global, national and local activities to continue to tackle men's authority over women and children, as it is manifested in much of the violence in families and relationships.

Despite studies charting the material, reflexive and varied nature of experiences of violence, many policies and services continue to favour interpretations that emphasize physical rather than psychological acts of violence (Renzetti *et al.* 2001; World Health Organization 2002). Research with children and young people found that while many children will say that they know what domestic violence means, there is confusion, with most definitions differing from those accepted by statutory bodies (Mullender *et al.* 2003: 16). Children and young people find it easier to define the physical dimensions (punching/hitting) than psychological abuse. By concentrating on the physical, many other forms of violence can become obscured, in particular how the workings of power relations underpin and are evident in violence in families. Many definitions favour what can be seen – the physical injuries and symptoms. Further, much research that seeks to document violence (e.g. crime surveys) concentrates on specific acts (common assault, robbery and damage to property) with the assumption that crime will take place predominantly outside the home. From this narrow starting point, child protection legislation and services broaden out definitions to include neglect and emotional abuses that continue to occur; psychological acts are considered and it is recognized that they can take place over many years and in various places. However, even in child protection work, intervention on the basis of neglect and emotional abuse remains problematic.

Physical violence, and the broader processes of psychological violation and abuse, are social phenomena. Definitions must include the varied forms of 'opaque' as well as obvious physical violence; in particular, the long-term impact of power disparities (Bessant 1998). Nevertheless, the debate on definitions remains heated and largely ungendered, with limited consideration of imbalances in power in relationships.

Aiming to capture the multidimensional nature of violence, Ray (2000: 145) proposes that: 'violence refers to diverse behavioural forms and multiple levels of analysis. It may range from local and unregulated to orchestrated and controlled behaviour. Violence breaks through moral prohibitions but may be legitimated with elaborate normative systems'. Again, this definition offers possibilities but also poses problems. What are moral prohibitions and normative systems? Societies seek to regulate certain types of behaviour, not least of which are behaviours which result in violence to the person and which take place in public spaces. The nature of violent behaviours and activities, and the process of regulation, is constantly under review by campaigning groups, governments and international organizations. Violence can be narrowly defined as pointless aggression. However, at times there may be positive uses of aggression; for example, the need for violence to secure the safety of victims of abuse and violence, and to ensure the enforcement of laws (Denfeld 1997: 7; Moran *et al.* 2004). True, today few societies condone physical violence unless acts are considered to be self-defence or sanctioned through membership of the police, armed forces or the growing industry of security companies. Even in ambiguous situations, laws, both national and international, and accepted social and moral norms, can and do challenge what may be considered excessive use of force; for example, complaints in the media and from pressure groups that the police were heavy-handed in monitoring an anti-war demonstration. In debates on moral prohibitions on violence, the emphasis is upon the obvious; on what is visible and quantifiable in public spaces. The focus on violence in public spaces encourages an emphasis on physical acts, as well as locating violence and violation outside the space of the home and family life.

As discussed earlier in this chapter, violence in the context of intimate and familial relationships is under-reported and often veiled by concerns with potential challenges to the realm of the private. In contrast, evidence demonstrates that in most societies violence among young men that occurs in public spaces is a major political and social issue. Social institutions can be violent, often on behalf of the state, operating through a range of agencies such as the police, welfare and health services. International and inter-community violence impacts on families, as do continued offerings of violent films and images that simplify ideas of good and evil, men and women, and heterosexual relationships.

Violence may be defined from several standpoints: the violated, the violator, those dealing with violence and those who observe violence. These perspectives may overlap as well as compete. The prominence given to any one perspective (or definition) reflects the shifting nature of power, domination and oppression. Changing perspectives and definitions also reflect historical changes in attitudes, not merely to violence and families but also individual rights. For example, just over a century ago the labour of children was considered crucial to economic and family fortunes and child prostitution was not unusual. However, in the early twentieth century, the presumed vulnerability and dependency of children led to moral and legal prohibitions on their employment. 'Stranger danger', and latterly abuses by parents, became concerns and these also resulted in legal and policy interventions. Similarly, in many countries, attitudes to and legislation on marriage and divorce have changed in ways that now offer women equal rights. However, the workings of legislation and related services continue to illuminate the unspoken and taken for granted manner in which women and men are framed as partners and parents with attendant gendered roles and responsibilities. Ultimately, social relations are historically and contemporaneously underwritten through economics and gender (Hearn 1998; Connell 2002). The resulting inequities are considered by many to be immutable. Violence in families connects people and structures in a manner that is 'both material and discursive' (Hearn 1998: 15).

International organizations, governments and social movements

International organizations play a major role in violent conflicts between and within nation states but perhaps less so with violence in families. Many governments, policymakers, practitioners and social movements have tended to focus on the definition of the World Health Organization (1996) that includes a range of acts that are said to constitute violence. From the narrow base of physical acts, this definition has expanded to include acts of fear and intimidation (World Health Organization 2002: 5): 'The intentional use of physical force or power, threatened or actual, against oneself, another person, or against a group or community, that either results in or has a high likelihood of resulting in injury, death, psychological harm, maldevelopment or deprivation'. This is a definition that includes both violence and violations, and physical and psychological dimensions. However, three points are worthy of note. First, the definition avoids any reference to the context of violence (the place or the relationships). Second, the word 'intentional' is open to debate: acts of violence in families may not be seen as intentional but as culturally determined norms (e.g. punishing a child, chastising a wife, withholding economic resources from an older relative so as to maintain inheritance for other family members). Finally, acts of violence need to be recognized as such by a third party; for example family members or friends, a legal authority or social service recognition that what has happened is violence. Without these criteria, acts of violence can remain framed as misdemeanours or misunderstandings. However, while many governments have adopted the definition of the World Health Organization, the interpretation of this varies across countries and governments (Weldon 2002).

Despite data on the prevalence of violence in intimate and familial relationships, nation states tend to emphasize civil strife, wars and violence in public places. It could be argued that governments need to prioritize the continued security of the nation state and population, although these goals may be used as a means of retaining or developing undemocratic forms of government. Further initiatives by governments do not follow the patterns that might be anticipated. For example, some countries that have strong international reputations for work on human rights and peacekeeping have not always prioritized activities to tackle the gendered nature of domestic violence (Weldon 2002: 208). This is further considered in Chapter 4 in which the evolving nature of policies and services in Finland, Scotland and Sweden are discussed.

The World Health Organization (2002) also offers a typology of violence. Originating from an international body, this typology carries some authority across the globe. It is a broad definition that includes a range of acts and victims. The typology of violence includes family and intimate partner violence alongside community violence under the broad heading 'interpersonal violence' (World Health Organization 2002). This reflects the interrelated role of families, communities and individuals, offering a link between the potential origins and conduct of ethnic conflicts and the role of families in both these and intimate violations. Yet the category 'interpersonal violence' might be critiqued as being too broad, incorporating many discrete forms of violence.

Families, relationships and communities can be powerful forces in forging identities, sometimes constructed around grievances that may be powerful forces in ethnic violence. In ethnic conflicts, violence becomes embedded in social relations, erupting when 'historical grievances are reproduced' (Ray 2000: 156) through rituals and other forms of public remembrance (Hinton 2002). The role and positioning of women can become symbolic for ethnic identity, making rape (and the systematic use of rape) a weapon against both the individual woman and the ethnic group to which she is deemed to belong. While families can become places for the engendering of ethnic violence they also constitute spaces and places in which violence takes place. Sometimes, that violence against women is both physical and repressive in so far as their positioning as moral symbols places them in a double jeopardy of violence from men known and unknown to them.

Legal definitions in post-industrial societies are 'somewhat more restrictive' (Hatty 2000: 46). For example, definitions of violence between adults are largely based on 'physical force applied to another person, contrary to that person's will'. The emphasis is on the corporeal experience and for legal purposes it remains the case that physical boundaries, and physical violence, are paramount. More recently, in response to cases of stalking and harassment, legal systems have extended definitions to include psychological harm, but again the focus tends to be on violence between those with little knowledge of each other. The law continues to distinguish between intra-familial and extra-familial violence perpetrated by men (Collier 1995). The former is presumed to be relatively non-threatening and the latter to be potentially destructive. This distinction reflects interweaving associations that underpin gender relations: public/private, work/ home and dangerous/safe. These are manifest in the workings of legal services and the courts, and it continues to be difficult to achieve convictions among adults known to each other, especially for psychological violence.

Historically, legal concerns were with violence among males in public places, a problem that appeared to mirror increasing urbanization. In contrast, the so-called 'family man' was cast as respectable, responsible and economically active. Thus legal definitions and functionalist theories on families often ran parallel to each other, reflecting strong ideas and laws to promote the nuclear family with the 'family man' at the head. Violence between men and women in relationships illuminates instabilities in boundaries between, on the one hand, the family/adult man and on the other, the violent/abusive man. Likewise there are instabilities in boundaries between notions of supportive and protective family members and those who shield knowledge of the violent, abusive partner, parent or relative.

The requirement, therefore, is for definitions that address the workings of power within violent relationships and activities (and the patriarchal basis of much of this power), and which have the potential to provoke debates. Some examples include:

- 'emotional, psychological, sexual, physical and/or material damage' (Stanko 1994: xiv);
- 'that which violates or causes violation, and is usually performed by a violator upon the violated'. Violence may be sexual, physical, verbal, cognitive, emotional, or representational and may also include the 'creation of conditions of violence, potential violence, threat and/or neglect ... [and] can be dramatic, subtle, occasional or continuous' (Hearn 1998: 42–3);
- patriarchal terrorism: 'a systematic use of violence as well as economic subordination, threats, isolation, and other control tactics against a relationship partner' (Johnson 1995);
- 'intimidation, interrogation, surveillance, persecution, subjugation, discrimination and exclusion that lead to experiences of violation' (Hearn 2002: 18).

In summary, definitions of violence are historically, socially and culturally constructed. Some forms of violence are often missing from sociological and policy concerns, as are the broad and pervasive impact of patriarchy, capitalism and nationalism, evidenced in, for example, psychological abuses. By contrast an interesting example of the impact of social change on competing definitions of domestic violence is the decision by the Scottish Executive (the government body in Scotland) to replace the word 'violence' with 'abuse' and include the 'gender' basis to this violence in the definition. Women's groups were strong advocates for changes to legal and societal definitions and for these to recognize and admit the psychological, economic and social aspects of violence; to consider oppression and power inequities (Mullender 1997; EVA 2001). Activists proposed the adoption of the term abuse rather than violence as it was felt to better explain the breadth of violence and violations. On the basis of the work of the Partnership Group on Domestic Abuse, the Scottish Executive (2000: 5) adopted the following definition:

> Domestic abuse (as gender-based abuse) can be perpetrated by partners or ex-partners and can include physical abuse (assault and physical attack involving a range of behaviour), sexual abuse (acts which degrade and humiliate women and are perpetrated against their will, including rape) and mental and emotional abuse (such as threats, verbal abuse, racial abuse, withholding money and other types of controlling behaviour such as isolation from family and friends).

This definition coincided with a programme of work sponsored by the Scottish Executive to work across agencies and groups: 'domestic abuse is a complex and wide-ranging issue encompassing many areas of Government policy' (Scottish Executive 2003: iii). A government-wide strategy evolved and a range of agencies and professions came into contact with this definition, drawing some interesting reactions.

During work with a multi-agency group to develop an information resource for health workers in Scotland it became apparent that for many the word 'abuse' appeared to soften the realities of violence. Rather than placing an increased emphasis on psychological abuses and traumas, for some the word generates a sense of violence that is ongoing at levels that may be tolerated or easily hidden from services. Further, the association of the word abuse with child abuse left some with the idea that domestic abuse is also best positioned in the arenas of social and legal services. I cite these responses to the term domestic abuse to draw attention to the complex and unintended consequences that may follow from any change of terms and definitions. Further, no matter how much we debate definitions, categories and policies, the *interpretation* of policies remains problematic. Many people argue that there is much to be gained from the strategic, multi-agency approach adopted in Scotland, but despite the existence of a national strategy, many health and social workers admit they are unsure about their role when violence in families, especially domestic violence, becomes evident.

Establishing levels of violence

The taboos, and sense of shame, surrounding violence in families inhibits reporting. We only know what people are prepared to share with others about their families, and in the telling of these experiences 'people often draw upon public stories to reinterpret and make sense of their own lives' (Jamieson 1998: 156). In many countries and contexts there are innumerable cultural and policy pressures for people to adhere to specific notions of family life; of support and intimacy achieved through mutual living and nurturing arrangements. Stories, ideas and lives interweave, diverge and change.

When violence comes to the attention of services and practitioners some (e.g. doctors, nurses, teachers) consider it best not to record incidents. This may result from a number of concerns. Healthcare professionals might consider that the recording of violence in records could challenge the confidentiality of other family members, or pose a further threat to the safety of the person and their dependants. It may lead to an engagement with services that results in the break-up of families; something most doctors actively seek to avoid. A few consider that the disclosure of violence adds to their workload in ways they resent or find frustrating. Many have limited knowledge, or confidence, about what to do next (McKie *et al.* 2002).

Cultural attitudes and assumptions about family life, and professional boundaries and roles, do have a bearing on the reporting of violence. More often than not, the strongly held notions of families as being the best place in which to bring up children, achieve intimacy and grow older, reinforce tendencies to under-report violence. Further, many working in services and government fear public reaction to interventions in families, especially if an intervention proves ill founded. These fears, combined with other concerns, lead to an averted gaze in so far as violence may be seen but ambivalence results in limited (or, indeed no) engagement with this knowledge.

As noted earlier, violent acts include physical, sexual and psychological dimensions and generally involve deprivation or neglect. In the World Health Organization's (2002: 7) typology of violence it may be self-directed (suicide, self-harm, self-abuse), interpersonal (familial, partner or community) or collective (social, political and economic). However, typologies, which generally offer seemingly straightforward categories, rarely offer insights into the possible motivations and the wider social processes in operation around, and through, acts of violence: 'Different forms of violence are understood very differently' (Hearn and Parkin 2001: 86).

Information about these motivations may be gained through individuals, agencies in the statutory and voluntary sector, community and government records and studies, population-based and other surveys and academic and specific studies. Many governments and international organizations collect data that describe the types, levels and impact of violence. Major sources of information include data on mortality, morbidity and crime. Collection of data involves a range of services and organizations. Mortality data are considered reliable, even though there is an emphasis upon the *immediate* causes of death. These data can monitor changes over time, across countries, and identify groups and communities at risk of violent acts (World Health Organization 2002: 7). However, a note of caution: these data cannot record the ongoing patterns of abuse that many women murdered by men known to them will have gone through.

Research in Scotland found that on average a woman will be assaulted by her current or ex-partner around 35 times before reporting it to the police or a family doctor. Building up trust and security is critical to disclosure (Henderson 1998; Home Office 1999; Department of Health 2000). In the first instance women are much more likely to discuss abuse with female friends and relatives, fearing judgement or stigma from those outside immediate friendship or family circles (Mitchell and Hodson 1983; McWilliams and McKiernan 1993). Leaving the family will have economic and social consequences and the thought of these can present further barriers to disclosure (Henderson 1998). These concerns are rarely captured in current forms of data collection and records. Often the needs of an organization or research project are paramount when the collection of information is organized. Thus data are likely to be partial in that the long-term patterns of violence, relationships and intimacies are rarely recorded.

Medical records will include symptoms, diagnosis and treatment, and may include information on social and economic factors, but rarely will these records contain detailed long-term histories of familial and intimate relationships and the long-term workings of these. The process of collecting information, who asks what, when and where, has important implications for what is collected, documented and disclosed.

In the global context it is estimated that in the year 2000, 1.6 million people died as a consequence of self-inflicted, interpersonal or collective violence. This constitutes an age-adjusted rate of around 29 deaths per 100,000 population. Suicide accounts for almost 50 per cent of these deaths; just over 30 per cent are homicides and 18 per cent are war-related. The vast majority of these deaths, 91 per cent, take place in what may be termed low- to middle-income countries. There are notable variations. In the Americas and some African regions, homicide rates are nearly three times greater than suicide, while in the European region suicide rates are more than double those of homicide (World Health Organization 2002). Non-fatal violence is harder to chart as not all incidents lead to contact with services. What is known is often generated from population-based self-reported survey data. Given taboos surrounding the reporting of violence in families, these results will almost certainly under-represent the number and nature of incidents.

In the USA, the 1998 Commonwealth Fund Survey of Women's Health found what the researchers termed 'disturbingly high' rates of violence and abuse during women's lifetimes. Of those surveyed, one third of women had experienced physical abuse, with 3 per cent reporting abuse in the last year – a figure that represents more than 3 million women in the USA. As in the UK, violence and abuse rates varied little by location, race, ethnicity or education. Again as in the UK, 'while women living on low incomes tend to be at higher risk from various types of violence, rates remain high across the income spectrum' (Commonwealth Fund 1999: 1). All those who experienced violence were significantly more likely to state they had a range of health problems, some of which were related to, or exacerbated by, violence.

Sexual violence is especially difficult to quantify given sensitivities and pressures in many cultures and religions. In some countries, if a victim reports rape to family members or the police it can result in death (a killing committed on the basis that it would limit damage to male/family honour) or exclusion from a community (tainted goods). Any survivor can find themselves in a situation of double jeopardy; that is, of suffering physical and psychological injuries from sexual violence, but subsequently unable to speak out for fear of further indignities and violations from relatives who feel family honour has been compromised (Card 2002: 130).

Some governments have become concerned with the costs associated with policing and managing interpersonal violence. These costs place particular hardship on those with least options to protect themselves and to leave violent relationships. The social and economic costs are hard to calculate but the toll of injuries, mental health problems, misery and family breakdown is massive. Studies sponsored by the Inter-American Development Bank concluded that, expressed as a percentage of gross domestic product (GDP) in 1997, healthcare expenditure arising from violence was 5 per cent in Colombia, 4.3 per cent in El Salvador, 1.9 per cent in Brazil and 0.3 per cent in Venezuela. Recent studies on the costs associated with domestic violence have sought to assess these for the economy in general, and a range of services. Data from Finland suggests costs of €9 million per annum, excluding indirect impact such as managing and overcoming emotional traumas. In Scotland, work on costs is ongoing but in one study it was estimated that between 87,000 and 136,000 general practice consultations per year are related to domestic abuse and its consequences (Young 1995). Work in the Borough of Hackney estimated the annual costs of domestic abuse just for that one part of London as approximately £5 million per annum (Stanko et al. 1998).

Summary

The aim of this chapter has been to introduce definitions and debates on key terms: namely, families, family life and violence. While the tragic story of the Mochries is an extreme example of violence in families, it does illustrate how we can know, and yet not know, partners, relatives, friends and neighbours. The Mochrie family was also notable as their deaths generated media coverage on the secrets and lies that may underpin stresses and strains in families. Much of the ongoing, everyday violence in families – the slaps, punches, kicks, intimidation and control of income and networks – receives limited attention in the media and many aspects of government and society more generally.

Global trends follow patterns with 90 per cent of those arrested for murder and manslaughter in 1998 in the USA and Australia being male. Rape is overwhelming by men on women (Connell 2000: 214). Women can be violent too, but research demonstrates that men use violence in relationships to achieve control, often through generating ongoing fears of violence and intimidation. Not all men are violent and 'most men never kill or even commit assault' (Connell 2000: 215). When violence occurs in relationships, governments or service providers may accept the gendered nature of the violence but rarely seek to tackle gender inequities within which the privacy of family and home life are imbued. Further, there are strong links between masculinities and violence in many aspects of the media, military and defence services.

Families are about solidarities and people working collectively to achieve everyday and longer-term sustenance and emotional support. At times they are tense, difficult and even violent places to be. While the nuclear family continues to be a commonly adopted and adapted model for childrearing, any analysis of families demonstrates a variety of arrangements for parenting and intimate relationships. The formation, breakdown and reformation of families is not unusual. Dramatic increases in lone parenting and solo living among younger and older age groups add to the shifting experiences of how we choose to live as we grow up and grow older.

Families are diverse and our experiences of them vary. We now live in more complex and web-like networks of partnerships, generations, step-relatives and grandparents. Many of us continue to feel obligations to care and experience the delights and drudgery of this. Perhaps we are less connected through marriage and more likely to value friendships than in previous decades. And while solo living is on the increase among young and old, most of us are not isolated from familial and social networks. We still value and cherish relationships with others, whether or not we happen to reside with them.

Violence in families is dealt with in many policies and services. That acknowledgement, while welcome and worthy of much more support, is partial. The focus is on those experiencing violence and not wider individual and societal responsibilities to tackle this ultimate experience of power and patriarchy. The ongoing and prevalent levels of abuse in families are presented as seemingly *out there*, somewhere in the ether of society – sometimes silenced, often muted – and hopefully not in *my* family or *your* family. The contested and competing nature of definitions combined with problems of documenting levels of violence adds to the challenges for any analysis.

2

Violence in families

Introduction

Agencies and governments acknowledge that violence takes place in families. Yet all too often violence in families is considered, or framed as, a 'misdemeanour' that takes place between adults at times of tension or stress. Many see it as being a matter of concern or action by those in the intimate relationships and family networks affected, and not by police or legal services (Card 2002: 142). Until extreme acts of physical violence take place, that may indeed involve the police, many family members, neighbours and friends will look the other way. Perpetrators may be ignored as irredeemable, while those experiencing violence may be encouraged to leave regardless of their social, economic or psychological well-being. The violence in families, from which individuals and societies often avert their gaze, would generally attract statutory intervention if it happened in public spaces.

Those who look away from violence in families are aware of the contradictory emotions evoked by witnessing or suspecting violence in this context. All of us experience arguments with partners and members of our families. Sometimes disagreements take place in view of others, and on occasions the pressures and tensions of family life become evident to those outside the immediate family group. In these situations we do not welcome the intervention of anyone else; feelings of embarrassment can mingle with questions about the right those outside the family have to intervene in intimate and familial relationships. Few of us are brave enough to act if we see a woman who appears to be intimidated, frightened or even being dragged along a street by a man she seems to know. We are unsure about what we should say or do and, as a result, become uneasy about intervening. After all, we are certainly not experts in tackling violence.

Thoughts of intervention may also make us fearful for our own safety. An averted gaze from this violence is created and reinforced through notions of privacy in, and around, families and relationships.

Most countries have laws allowing for statutory intervention in families where child, domestic or elder abuse is suspected, and this is considered an appropriate area for the involvement of governments and those concerned to protect the rights of the vulnerable and others to safety, dignity and respect. These laws and related services vary and it is beyond the remit of this book to consider them in any detail. The general trends in legislation and services in Scotland are mirrored in governmental responses elsewhere. Of note is the tightening of laws to enable police to act to offer protection from persistent and ongoing acts of violence and intimidation. The potential to remove the perpetrator from the family home is also a welcome development. However, laws and services tend to be generic with little reflection upon, or appreciation of, the diversity of backgrounds, age, cultures and ethnicities.

In some ways it may be comforting to feel that violence in families is distant from our everyday experiences and that, if severe, then there are professionals who can intervene. While certain groups and practitioners are sanctioned to intervene in families, intervention tends to be exceptional. When there is no evidence of extreme physical violence or psychological abuse, concerns can be expressed that interventions in families take place too often and are generally needless. By the time physical violence is extreme it is more than likely that much psychological damage and distress will have taken place. Violence in families takes place, remains under-reported with a continued focus on those least able to act – namely, those who are experiencing or have survived violence. These processes of awareness, and yet distance, from violence in families are complex.

While violence in wars, civil unrest and other conflicts is a major element in shaping societies and history, violence in families has received less attention. In this chapter I consider work that has shaped the identification of, and ideas on, violence in families. Families and relationships have critical functions in (re)creating identities and attitudes to familial roles, communities and violence in global, national and civil conflicts. But what of conflicts among those in intimate and familial relationships?

The interweaving of public and private

> No one engaged in thought about history and politics can remain unaware of the enormous role violence has always played in human affairs, and it is at first glance rather surprising that violence has been singled out so seldom for special consideration ... violence and its arbitrariness were taken for granted and therefore neglected; no one questions or examines what is obvious to all.
>
> (Arendt 1970: 8)

> The twentieth century [is one] that will be remembered as a century
> marked by violence.
>> (Mandela cited in World Health Organization 2002: ix)

Academics and commentators have devoted much time and effort to
addressing the origins, rise and workings of totalitarianism, warfare and
conflicts, researching the role of governments, political parties, collective
movements and individuals (Glover 1999; Hinton 2002). Technological
advances have resulted in greater protection for those in military forces but
have, by contrast, led to increased risks of death and injury for civilians.
The 2004 annual report of the human rights organization Amnesty
International asserted that it is a 'dangerous and divided' world (Amnesty
International 2004). Wars and conflicts are evident in every continent.

In North America and Europe, governments have referred to the last 60
years as an era of peace. The absence of war and regional conflicts on the
soil of most of the dominant post-industrial economies has been a notable
point in history. The contradictions posed by ongoing global and national
conflicts in most continents, running parallel to extended periods of stability in dominant post-industrial societies, have been described as the
phenomena of 'war in times of peace'. Against this backdrop, violence in
families is evident across cultures, and all social and economic groups.
Similarly, family life and social change have blended in post-industrial
societies while in other parts of the world families struggle daily to survive.

Growing tensions between Judaeo-Christian and Islamic cultures and
governments have formed a context to recent conflicts and acts of terrorism. It is the increased threat from terrorism that is exercising a range of
governments as they seek to retain power and security, and maintain
cultural and economic stability. Governments are engaged in a so-called
'war on terror'. In the name of achieving security of the state and its
people, some governments have utilized and supported technological
developments to survey the movement of citizens and residents, most
evidently at airports, train and bus stations. Most of us seem happy to
submit to increasing controls on our movements and scrutiny of our
identities if this is the price of safety.

But what price might we be prepared to pay for the safety of our families
and ourselves when the state scrutinizes identities in search of ethnic and
other groups for the purposes of their annihilation? In Nazi Germany the
systematic use of violence involved both military personnel and civilians.
Hannah Arendt spent much of her career reflecting on the relationship
between violence perpetrated and sanctioned by the state, and the individual. Born in Hanover, Germany, in 1906 into a Jewish family, Arendt
has been described as a 'deeply paradoxical figure' (Baehr 2000: vii). In the
post-war years she became a notable political and philosophical theorist and
was often at odds with academic feminism. She emigrated from Germany
in the 1930s, and while working on behalf of Zionism, she opposed an
Israeli state. Arendt wrote a number of major essays that contributed much

to post-war debates on desegregation, civil rights, the nature of evil, totalitarianism in Nazi Germany and the legacy of the Holocaust.

Totalitarianism is a system in which violence, or the threat of violence, imbues every aspect of life and in recent times has occurred in circumstances when the private and public interweave: 'Corruption and perversion are more pernicious, and at the same time more likely to occur, in an egalitarian republic than in any other form of government. Schematically speaking, they come to pass when private interests invade the public domain, that is, they spring from below and not from above' (Arendt 1951: 338). When private interests coincide with those of government and wider powerful interests that inform mass culture, then the prospects for totalitarianism and genocide become heightened. Such shifts are underpinned by mass conformists; by 'job holders and good family men'.

In Nazi Germany, mass murder bore the hallmarks of the pedestrian – families struggled to survive and safeguard their private lives. Over a series of essays, most notably *The Origins of Totalitarianism* (Arendt 1951) and *Eichmann in Jerusalem: A Report on the Banality of Evil* (1963), Arendt details the banal processes that led individuals, families, communities and states to sacrifice any sense of dignity, honour or ideas on human rights. These were not common criminals and rarely part of a mob, but rather people who in the midst of possible ruination of their private lives sacrificed the lives of others. Societies in which people are dedicated to private interests will lend themselves to the interests of 'party machines and demagogues'. Here we might draw parallels with the analysis of Bauman (1989) who argued that modern processes have facilitated the production of mass death through the combined forces of science, technology and bureaucracy.

These are powerful arguments and yet the role of family practices and families in the everyday creation and formation of violence is less considered (Arendt 1970; Glover 1999; Juergensmeyer 2000; Hinton 2002). Arendt's (1970) analysis concentrates on the interdependence of the private (family world) and public (mass society and the rise of totalitarianism). Her detailed portrayal of Eichmann is of a civil servant who moved through a series of bureaucratic posts, rarely if ever making a decision on his own. This was also his main line of defence when tried for war crimes in 1961. Eichmann bragged about his role and power but the everyday realities for him were of tasks dictated through legal statutes and the ideas of others. In contact with superiors, he never presumed more than he felt his current position allowed. Ever deferential, he was the consummate civil servant, who took his place in the 'final solution', as many so-called ordinary people did. Unfortunately, he proved to be somewhat efficient in undertaking his duties and played a major role in the organization and maintenance of the systems for mass murder.

At times the violence of the totalitarian state is promoted within the family context; for example, the involvement of families in ethnic cleansing encouraged by governmental propaganda or the lack of sanctions. These are forms of violence that are less visible but nevertheless widespread in numerous countries resulting in untold misery across social, religious and ethnic groups (Bringa 2002). We should feel safest in our homes and communities yet this is a context in which members of families can plan and carry out acts of violence against those once considered neighbours and friends; and against intimate partners too.

Domestic violence is evident across the globe regardless of the presence or absence of democratic political systems (Weldon 2002; World Health Organization 2002). This is an important point, for some contend that violence in general, and violence in families, is more likely to be found in societies in which civil unrest and warfare are evident; for example, levels of civil and domestic violence remain high in Afghanistan, Northern Ireland and South Africa. These presumptions form part of the process of the averted gaze to families and violence in so far as they can encourage the idea that violence takes place 'somewhere else'.

Uncovering violence in families

Much of the focus of this book is on violence in heterosexual partnerships as manifested in domestic violence. Despite evidence on the prevalence of male violence to women it can be difficult to propose an emphasis upon the gendered nature of violence in intimate relationships. This results from the assertion that female to male partner violence is not uncommon, and can be frequent, severe and persistent. The Conflict Tactics Scale (CTS), a fixed-format questionnaire survey, asked couples to report violent incidents (Stets and Straus 1990). Respondents were asked to cite the number of times they had used a variety of tactics during a dispute, ranging from calm discussion to the use of a knife or a gun. Rather than conceptualizing violence among couples as potentially evident of the control of one partner by another, the survey did not offer opportunities for an explanation of the context and circumstances surrounding the violence.

In response to criticisms of the lack of attention to context in the survey, researchers claimed that the question 'who started the physical conflict, you or your partner' sufficed (Stets and Straus 1990: 153). In addition, this scale seeks information on physical rather than psychological abuses. The results of this survey suggested that women were potentially just as violent as men, and in certain circumstances would be so. It was argued that violence often originates from the most powerful member of the family through their exercise of control and that this powerful person can be a male or female (Straus *et al.* 1980). Despite criticisms, some commentators argued that the results of the survey provided support for explanations of violence, such as 'she provoked me to do this' (Kurz 1993: 93). Everyday and long-term differentials in power, evident in gendered and age-related experiences of families and relationships, were largely ignored. The prevalence of violence is explained as emerging from the everyday stresses and strains of family life.

By contrast, the coercive workings of power were considered in a number of small-scale qualitative studies. Explanations emerged of the potential for men's control of women through violence (Johnson 1995). Gender is one of the fundamental and organizing principles of society (Dobash and Dobash 1992) and in women's and gender studies there is a concern that the analysis of violence in relationships fails to address the resulting inequities. As a consequence, policies are narrowly conceptualized with services and practitioner work based around ideas that violence is a 'mutual' occurrence between partners (Kurz 1993: 99). Might family violence be an accepted part of relationships for some? If so, perhaps services need to focus upon the extreme cases and accept that violence may always be with us (Kelly 1996: 47). Such an approach has its appeal. It offers the possibility of narrowing the need for interventions by the state and specialist services, thus saving costs. This analysis also limits the potential challenge to the sanctity of the family by positioning low levels of couple violence as not unusual. It places at the margins any need for an analysis of gender and the discursive workings of power in the arenas of the home and relationships.

Why is evidence on the prevalence and gendered nature of domestic violence seemingly ignored, even dismissed? Suggestions that women can be just as violent as men, or that men who are violent are different from other men in obvious ways, can absolve us from the need to analyse and address the everyday workings of patriarchy and power in families (Moran-Ellis 1996). It would seem that violence can be explained in ways that restrict the need for any meta-analysis, and for societal, rather than just family focused, interventions (Cohen 2001: 103).

Reflecting on competing assertions from psychological and familial researchers, and gender and women's studies, Nazroo (1995) interviewed 96 couples about violence in their partnerships. These were couples below retirement age and drawn from the lists of family doctors. Couples that were known by doctors to have experienced marital violence were excluded.[1] Both partners were interviewed separately and asked about acts of physical aggression that they considered were 'non-playful'. For three fifths of couples interviewed, both husbands and wives perpetrated violent acts. However, there were significant differences in the nature of the violence used, and importantly, the impact of violent acts. Focusing upon injurious or intimidating episodes of violence, the balance between husbands and wives changed, and the sample in the study was reduced to 19 men and six women. In these episodes women felt they were unable to protect themselves. They spoke of feeling continuously threatened, as they

---

[1] Refusals were the result of either the partner of the person approached not being interested, or their relationship being so poor that the respondent would not approach his/her partner. This suggests that this sample probably under-represents distant and highly abusive relationships, although both types are evident in the data collected.

did not know when the next episode of violence could occur. Men spoke about episodes of violence in terms that led the researcher to conclude that they used violence as a means of dominating their partners and securing subjugation. Thus, violence on the part of the men represented something quite different and much more threatening than anything the women could perpetrate.

The broad system of social and economic relations that offers and reaffirms men a dominant position is referred to as patriarchy. These social and economic relations are articulated in the everyday and global workings of market and agrarian economies (Walby 1990; Connell 2000). The patriarchal basis to household and workplace relations may change but the interweaving of these creates and promotes myriad dimensions of inequalities (Walby 1990: 21). Experiences interweave across the public and the private, most obviously between home and work. While some suggest that changes in men's involvement in domestic labour are evidence of shifts in the everyday workings of patriarchy and gender relations, change is undoubtedly slow (Sullivan 2000; McKie et al. 2002).

It is possible to differentiate between 'common couple violence', outbursts that occur within relationships in moments of stress, and 'patriarchal terrorism' in which violence is not irregular and is contingent upon the gendered workings of power (Johnson 1995). The term 'terrorism' may seem extreme but it helps to emphasize the ongoing range of physical and psychological violence perpetrated in a context of fear and intimidation: 'The relationships defined by marriage and motherhood trap victims of terrorism in the home. They pose serious obstacles to escape by granting perpetrators enforceable intimate access to victims and extensive control over the knowledge and access of others' (Card 2002: 140).

The basis to many families is marriage or cohabitation, the heterosexual partnership. Marriage is said to be a 'contract' but it differs greatly from other contracts that form the basis to employment or a bank loan (Card 2002: 157). Many of the obligations in marriage and parenting are highly informal and on the ending of the contract (e.g. divorce or separation) obligations do not dissolve as they would when a loan is paid off or a house sold. The debtor paradigm in the example of the loan is a highly formalized one and if obligations are reneged upon the sanctions and consequences are clear. In marriage, the paradigm is one that may be described as a trustee model. Here, a trustee or guardian is expected to 'exercise judgment and discretion in carrying out obligations to care, protect, or maintain' (Card 2002: 156). Given that these intimate relationships are underpinned with the processes of power and the exercise of judgement and discretion, legal and social services may find it 'difficult to hold a spouse, or a parent, accountable for abuse' (Card 2002: 156).

The experience and continuous threat of violence can leave women isolated. It can also encourage feelings that they are responsible for the abuse; that in some way or another they have provoked violence. Yet many women may seek to retain immediate family networks, especially if these provide order and security for children and vulnerable or sick relatives (Allan and Crow 2001: 112).

Policies, practices and movements

These vulnerabilities are reinforced by the complex and often contradictory nature of the manner in which women and their relationships are framed by the state, evident in a number of social and public policies and services. As asserted earlier, gender is a fundamental concept in the organization of societies. There are gendered implications in all policies and the services, even when they may appear to be concerned with matters of relevance to both men and women. Policies that appear to be gender-neutral (e.g. retirement income systems) have notable gender effects. These policies penalize those who do not work full-time for lengthy continuous periods of time. Time out of the labour market to care for others, and potentially combined with subsequent periods of part-time working, leads to limited income in later years. Care work, whether informal or formal, is undervalued.

The main responsibility for the organization, scripting and delivery of care continues to be that of women as partners, relatives, friends and workers. In economies where income is predominantly derived from the labour market, women and families are seeking to combine caring and working. Trends in fertility and longevity have led governments to promote childbearing through taxation and other incentives. These policies are designed and implemented in ways that promote heterosexual relationships, discriminate against same-sex parents and, for mothers, result in limited incomes in later life. While governments enshrine human rights, and many (but not all) defend the rights of women to have control over their bodies, most offer poor income security, especially post-motherhood and in retirement.

Global trends in emigration and immigration, including the migration of refugees and the search for asylum, have drawn out further examples of state policies that are gendered in their interpretation if not in their content. For example, if systematic violence against women is said to result from religious and cultural practices or legislation in other states, judicial systems tend to ignore this as a basis to a claim for asylum. In the UK, government officials and the courts have been slow to recognize domestic abuse, state-perpetrated rape or rape as a war crime as valid reasons for offering asylum. It has been argued that asylum claims are best based upon evidence of state organized torture with an attendant focus on overt physical torture that leaves visible evidence. The legacy of post-colonialism has left sensitivities to allegations of cultural imperialism and the gendered consequences of policies in other countries remain off-stage.

Social movements and international, non-governmental organizations continue to campaign for gender sensitivity in legislation and human rights. Across the globe there are numerous examples of violence against women that are condoned. One example is a recent review conducted by Amnesty International (2004) of the systematic abuse of women and girls in Turkey. Girls are deprived of equal access to education, and women are under-represented in the professions and politics. Forced and early marriage is not uncommon. A study conducted in several provinces in east and south-east Turkey found that nearly half of those surveyed were not consulted about their choice of marriage partner and were married without their consent. Many women forced into marriage were underage. Women who refused, or did not conform to the process of arranged marriage were at risk of physical violence and even death. Abuses documented included beatings, rape, exclusion from the family home and resources and, in extreme cases, women killed or forced to commit suicide.

The police and judiciary in Turkey frequently fail to thoroughly investigate and document violent deaths and injuries to women, making the monitoring of crimes difficult. The failure by the authorities to address violence against women promotes a culture which condones such violence. Some groups attempt to explain the level and nature of abuses as a dimension of traditional practices in which women's sexuality and choices are restricted. The public image of families and family honour has a strong tradition in Turkish life, and this makes it difficult for women to discuss private matters. Reporting abuses of human rights places women in double jeopardy. They run the gauntlet of public scrutiny of their lives and accusations of bringing family honour into ill repute. Rather than being supported to report domestic and sexual violence to the authorities, women have been forced to take their own lives. Men may not agree with these sanctions against women but can come under pressure from others to 'cleanse their family honour'. Failure to do so can affect the whole family through, for example, the loss of livelihood if the family business is shunned.

Underpinning these abuses is discrimination against women in all aspects of life. Turkey has ratified a number of international treaties on human rights and the rights of women, including the Optional Protocol to the United Nations Women's Convention. Legal changes followed and in 1998 the Law for the Protection of the Family in Turkey became law. Considered by many human rights groups to be a generally progressive piece of legislation it is not properly implemented by the relevant authorities, nor backed up by campaigns on the elimination of violence.

The situation of women in Turkey is distressing and has caused a number of national and international groups to offer recommendations on changing policies, practices and attitudes. However, as the Amnesty International campaign '*Stop violence against women*' demonstrates, violence against women is endemic, and even promoted by some governments and religious groups: 'Violence against women is the greatest human rights scandal of our times. From birth to death, in times of peace as well as war, women face discrimination and violence at the hands of the state, the community and the family' (Amnesty International 2004: 1).

The role and behaviour of women are considered strong symbols of group identity and conformity. The common denominator in fundamentalist views is the refusal to accept that there may be more than one way of interpreting a religious tract. Most fundamentalist religious ideas and practices, in both Christian and Islamic sects and communities, emphasize family values with women primarily framed as mothers, wives and daughters. The honour of communities and families is often identified with the control of women's sexuality. Women may accept these constraints given the possibility of achieving a stable family life. But these are not uniformly reactionary responses. Accepting codes of dress and submitting to male family members may offer an outwardly conservative portrayal of femininity. Women may accept male authority to assuage fears and smooth anxieties while moving into public arenas (Ruthven 2004: 125). However, the general trend to the personification and idealization of femininity results in the commodification of women and this is implicated in the systematic use of violence against women in the family and during times of war. Violence, especially sexual violence, attacks the identity and well-being of women, as well as that of the communities or groups in which they reside or are members of. In some cultures women who are attacked may subsequently be killed by male relatives or banished from communities in the belief that they are defiled and thus bring dishonour on males, families and communities.

Global perspectives

Reported levels of violence in families are on the increase (World Health Organization 2002). Today the amount and nature of violence in various aspects of culture (films, TV, magazines, etc.) and institutions (military, police, prison systems) rests alongside state policies that promote humans rights and seek to contain and control violence more generally. The right to free movement of the public in general is said to be under threat from violent crime in public spaces, national and global conflicts and the franchising of global terrorism. Governments introduce legislation that aims to monitor the lives of people and sanction some services, such as security and intelligence services, to use violence.

With ongoing conflicts between states and communities, combined with threats of terrorism, particular ethnic and religious groups are viewed with suspicion. Tackling violence originating from wars and terrorism is a priority for governments and their security and defence agencies. Many governments have increased the level of surveillance they undertake in respect of both their own citizens and often people who are seeking entry to that country. They have done so in support of the so-called 'war on terror' and the search for possible terrorists. This threat to national security has spawned an industry of surveillance. National identity cards, primarily developed to confirm entitlement to benefits and services and establish residency status, are also promoted as an important means of combating terrorism. While these objectives may seem reasonable, two points are worthy of note. A review of available evidence concluded that the relationship between identity cards and the control of terrorism 'appears to be largely intuitive' (Privacy International 2004: 2). Terrorists, such as those involved in the September 11 2001 terrorist attacks, usually gain entry to countries on the basis of tourist visas. Alternatively, they are domiciled in the target country already and this was the case with those who carried out the Madrid bombings in 2004. Further, female citizens and residents are much more likely to experience violence as a consequence of intimate relationships than have any engagement with terrorist violence. Of course in war or periods of civil unrest this would not be the case but combatting terrorism does not address gendered violence in families.

In international law, and most states, men and women are defined as citizens with equal rights, but social and public practices continue to privilege the privacy of family life alongside the continued dominance of masculinities. Sexual and cultural codes seek to define men and women as opposites, avoiding any ambiguities on gender roles and sexualities. Discourses and ideas on gender define women and men in terms of their engagement, or otherwise, with domestic or paid work (Connell 2002: 56). This notion of a social or employment contract is underpinned by a 'sexual contract' (Pateman 1988) – that is, the subordination of women to men in the private spheres of life. This overspills and interweaves with everyday experiences of public life. The sexual contract gives liberal democracies an opacity in which gender parity is said to exist alongside the everyday realities of a 'fraternal social contract' that discriminates against women and girls.

Underlying the workings and patterns of patriarchal relations are the discourses of femininities and masculinities. Gendered identities are rooted across various aspects of social structures and relations. Notions of femininities in many post-industrial societies were moulded historically by ideas about virtue and sacrifice drawn from the Victorian period. At that time, middle-class family life was sanctified in popular culture. Glowing ideas and images of that era remain in many contemporary images of Victorian England (Jamieson 1998: 21). Notions of masculinities are drawn from a broader orientation to the outside world (Walby 1990: 105). Contemporary masculinities are multiple and constructed across different economies, states and cultures. Although a hegemonic form of masculinity ensures that men in general receive a dividend through being male, men and boys have 'a divided, tense, or oppositional relationship to hegemonic masculinity' (Connell 2002: 111). Material, educational and institutional inequalities persist and are hard to tackle, as masculinities are discursive, contested and always changing:

> Imperialism and globalization have created institutions that operate on a world scale. These institutions all have internal gender regimes, and

each gender regime has its gender dynamic – interests, gender politics, processes of change. World-spanning institutions thus create new arenas for gender formation and gender dynamics.

(Connell 2002: 111)

Gendered patterns of exploitation have reached new heights with the sharp increase in the global trafficking of women and children for work in the sex industry, domestic and other forms of labour. These patterns of exploitation affect men, women and children differently. Women and children are more vulnerable to sexual and economic exploitation. In many cases families are involved in exploitation through selling, coercion or encouragement of many women and children to leave their homes in search of an income that might be partially returned to the family (Beale 2003).

The World Health Organization (2002) undertook a review of available evidence on violence and health and the Pan American Health Organization (2000) continues to promote community development programmes to tackle exploitative and abusive attitudes towards women and children. Trans-national agencies and campaigning groups have formed alliances to encourage national action and offer examples of good practice in policies and services (Pan American Health Organization 2000; Connell 2002; World Health Organization 2002). Yet, running alongside attempts to promote dignity and respect, violence (including sexual violence) is glorified and purveyed in many dimensions of the media and culture, from advertising to Hollywood blockbuster films (Jokinen 2000).

A three-year study of men's violence to women whom they know included interviews undertaken on two or more occasions with 60 men, and explored their accounts of what they had done. Interviews sought men's understanding of why they had been violent; the responses of family, friends and state and other agencies; their attitudes to, and relationships with women; what they had done about the violence (if anything); and their plans for the future (Hearn 1998: 12). From the accounts it would seem that in most cases members of families did not directly confront the perpetrator. One man commented, 'our family minds our own business. If he clouts his wife, he clouts his wife. If I clout mine, I clout mine' (Hearn 1998: 189). Family members did offer support to women experiencing violence but men interpreted this as 'a significant inconvenience' (Hearn 1998: 190):

The doing of violence affects the construction – the very recognition – of violence, of what counts as violence. The more that violence occurs, the greater the number of violent occasions or the greater the intensity of violence, the more that violence is likely to be taken for granted. Thus the greater the violence, the less awareness of violence there is likely to be.

(Hearn 1998: 202)

Detailed accounts suggest that perpetrators monitor and control the daily activity of those to whom they are violent. This includes actions such as scrutinizing letters, limiting access to money and other resources, and restricting contact with other family members and friends. Increasingly, abuse of older people, perhaps as a result of tensions concerning care or the securing of inheritance is a cause for concern.

If, over time, men who are violent become less aware of the impact of their violence, by contrast those experiencing violence individualize the experience, assuming they are in some way to blame. Most of those who experience violence are left isolated, with low self-esteem and unsure what to do next (Card 2002). Oppression follows and this is created, recreated, and takes place, in and around family networks and the home. It is extremely difficult to address these violences in ways that do not place added burdens on those actually experiencing violence (Young 1997: 164).

Safety and security

Refuges and services for abused women and children have become important in supporting those who leave violent relationships and families. They also offer a support network and practical assistance (Dobash and Dobash 1992). Provision is limited and few refuges offer more than minimal facilities and comforts. More often than not, to leave a home and go into a refuge leads to a reduced standard of living and ruptures social and educational networks. However, there are many examples of good practices and services that involve women survivors in planning and review. Consultation with women, and working with their experiences and ideas to inform policies and practice are hallmarks of best practice (Hague et al. 2003: 146).

The decision to leave a home, especially when children are involved, is a major and life-changing one. The short-term impact of leaving a violent relationship is likely to include a substantial decline in living standards. This must be set against an enhancement in psychological and physical well-being. Leaving a relationship is a complex decision and likely to be arrived at over a period of time; it is a process rather than an event. I am referring here to the numerous occasions on which women are likely to seek help and advice before feeling confident and able to leave. Many professionals express frustration with this 'process' as a paramount concern is achieving the immediate safety and security of a woman and her children. For many health and social care professionals achieving safety and security is associated with leaving the violent relationship and home. If a woman continues to be part of a violent relationship this may be considered a failure on the part of some professionals. Leaving is never easy. While the perpetrators of violence may be asked to leave the home, it remains the case in most situations that it is those experiencing violence who are expected to leave. It is ironic that in averting our gaze from the causes and implications of violence in families, we draw attention to the most vulnerable – namely those experiencing violence.

Women and children are known to have anxieties and fears about crime, in particular violent crime, that reflect 'fear of men' in general, and in particular, fear of the attitudes and behaviour of men in intimate relationships (Radford and Stanko 1996: 71). Fear of violence in public spaces mingles with fears of attack or abuse from men known to them. And this fear of violence both inside and outside the home is one that shadows, even controls, the lives of many women and children. Often they are expected to take steps to avoid violent situations or control and placate those who are threatening or attacking them.

This individualization of the experience and consequences of violence has encouraged police forces and governments to focus upon the individuals at risk, actively minimizing potential threats. In this thesis violence can be avoided by not going to specific localities, avoiding strangers, not going out at particular times of night and not drawing attention to yourself through dress or behaviour. This strategy places an onus on those who are said to be vulnerable to violence to attempt to prevent such crimes. It also emphasizes risks in public places, reinforcing the myth that most violence takes place outside the home and family context. This leads to contradictions in attitudes, activities and legislation, and marginalizes political debates and policies on violence in families.

All too often, rape continues to be framed by popular discourses, and in many courts, as a crime that achieves enhanced validity when the allegations involve strangers. Allegations that involve those known to each other rarely lead to convictions, especially in the case of rape within marriage or long-term relationships. There is a reluctance among legal services and juries to convict on the testimony of one person against an accused known to the victim without corroboration from others. A narrow focus on a specific act of violence denies the wider context and history of relationships. This may be critical if violence has involved a range of behaviours and threats over periods of time. Further, a woman's sexuality and sexual activities may be scrutinized in a manner that is itself a form of abuse. Changes in the law have sought to address some of these issues through, for example, a detailed review of the practices of the police and other services. While women may find reporting violence less daunting than a decade ago, many express frustration with the lack of action against perpetrators and wider societal attitudes to women and violence.

The practices of safety and security were the topic for a study considered in the book *Sexuality and the Politics of Violence and Safety* (Moran *et al.* 2004). Drawing upon research undertaken as part of the Economic and Social Research Council programme of research on violence (http://les1.man.ac.uk/sociology/vssrp) the authors consider safety and security as a reaction and response to violence. Their data illuminate and inform theoretical and policy developments in political strategies as they explore 'the limits of contemporary political projects of violence and safety more generally' (Moran *et al.* 2004: 3) 'through which lesbians and gay men produce themselves as objects and subjects of violence and safety' (2004: 171). Arguing that violence is often represented in opposition to safety, the authors assert that violence can also be 'for safety and security' (2004: 1). Engaging in violent acts may potentially offer a form of safety and security. This analysis clearly poses challenges to emancipatory and pacifist politics. Violence generates reactionary and conservative responses, resulting in 'unfreedom' in the name of freedom (Brown 1995). Recent strategies on the part of governments to monitor movement across state boundaries with the apparent aim of controlling terrorist activities could be considered an example of policies that promote 'unfreedoms' in the name of achieving safety and security for the 'free' world.

For Moran *et al.* (2004: 3) the uncritical promotion of discourses, services and policies on safety and security are 'one context in which a progressive and emancipatory politics of sexual violence may in fact reinforce modalities of subordination and exclusion'. The boundaries of violence and safety are opaque and interweaving; for example, 'the promotion of home as a location of safety may expose the already vulnerable to further danger' (Moran *et al.* 2004: 172). The political and governmental policies of safety and security seek the attainment of order, and achieving this requires the containment or elimination of violence in public spaces. Common notions of 'order' emphasize social, gender and ethnic divisions in and outside the home. For example, the assertion that if a woman is on her own in a public space late at night then she is placing herself at enhanced risk of attack. This assertion places limitations on where and when women can move around in public spaces. Likewise a gay couple might be criticized if intimidation or violence follows their obvious signs of affection for each other when this takes place in a venue frequented by a predominantly heterosexual clientele.

In these examples there is no engagement with the causes and consequences of violence; rather, those who are 'labelled' as vulnerable must achieve or submit to a social order that fails to address the ambiguities of mobilities, spaces and identities. Here we might consider the need to avoid general notions of good or bad behaviour on the part of those who experience violence. Many agencies and groups, such as security companies, may gain from retaining and promoting an uncritical stance on social 'order' with regards to violence in public places and spaces. Friday night alcohol-fuelled fights between young men are tolerated and actively managed through the work of security staff and the police. There is little recourse to those who promote alcohol linked to images of masculinities. When health officials and pressure groups bring attention to marketing policies on alcohol, there are some who will argue that any curtailment of freedoms to buy and consume alcohol should be resisted. But what of the freedom of those who want to move around city centres on Friday nights without fears for their safety?

Her violence, his violence, their violence

Among many women's groups there is a reluctance to discuss the use of violence by women (Kelly 1996: 35). This may reflect fears that women's use of violence could be employed to misrepresent the incidence, prevalence, nature and implications of violence in intimate relationships. Few would question the overarching trends of violence. Men perpetrate around 90 per cent of the reported acts of domestic violence. This figure is the one on which policies, planning and the delivery of services are based. However, there have been a number of commentators, groups and individuals who have been keen to point out that this leaves around 10 per cent of cases in which women could be the main perpetrators.

Concerns were raised in Scotland during the 1990s. While Scottish police statistics suggested that women perpetrated around 1 in 13 incidents, the Scottish Crime Survey (2000) suggested that men were victims in a third of cases. Pressure from campaigners for men's rights, coupled with a wider concern about apparent contradictions in statistics, led the Scottish Executive to commission a study to review data and undertake research (Gadd *et al.* 2002). Existing statistical data were reviewed. Interviews were conducted with staff in key agencies and with a sample of men who had indicated to the Scottish Crime Survey that a partner or ex-partner had threatened or used force against them. In conclusion the study found that in large part the differences between police figures and those of the crime survey could be explained by:

- Male respondents misinterpreting the focus of the self-completion component of the Scottish Crime Survey, which in turn revealed the varied nature of the experiences of men. For example, in responses some men were referring to property crime and non-domestic assaults rather than domestic violence.
- In comparison to women who experience violence, men are less likely to experience repeat episodes, be seriously injured, or feel fear in their own home.
- During interviews some men freely admitted that they were perpetrators of the violence. There were also some whose description of the violence placed them in the main perpetrator role.

In conclusion, once researchers excluded those who misinterpreted the self-completion questionnaire, only a minority of those men who referred to themselves as 'victims' were actually so. There were men, albeit fewer than anticipated, who reported experiences similar to those of abused women. The report recommended that rather than establishing a new agency or charity to support men experiencing violence, current provision and practitioners might be more sensitive to the issues of gender and violence in relationships *per se*.

The issue of the actual and potential violence of women demands a critical analysis. Without this, any broader analysis of the social problem of violence among intimates would fail those who experience violence, whether male or female. It would also leave the issue to professionals and sections of the media, many of whom continue to underplay men's violence. The small number of cases in which women are perpetrators have been employed as a diversionary topic from the overarching patterns of gendered violence (Kelly 1996: 35).

Women can and do use violence, and strategies of power and control in a range of relationships that can include a range of abuses: 'Although women and girls are the most usual victims, some women abuse both children and husbands, who are reluctant to admit it and who encounter disbelief when they do. Assault is not a function of bodily strength or muscle power but of such things as resentment, lack of scruples, and willingness to use weapons' (Card 2002: 146). Some women, a minority, will use violence (Card 2002). Given the practices of social relations and oppression that weave across the home, workplace and society more generally, violence may be used by women to achieve control in self-defence, or to avoid (further) violence to children or relatives. In many cases women are compelled or cajoled to become involved in violence or to ignore abuses of others (Mathews *et al.* 1991).

Being violent, and experiencing violence, is not confined to one sex. While some women may be violent it is the still the case that 'violence is presented as the antithesis of womanhood' (Denfeld 1997: 11). Women murderers, such as Myra Hindley and Rosemary West, come in for particularly vicious comments. Often these concentrate on the way in which violence is said to challenge their supposedly natural feminine and mothering tendencies to protect children. Maxine Carr, convicted for lying on behalf of her partner (who unbeknown to her, murdered two children), is berated in many parts of the media and described as 'evil'. These examples leave women little room for their own agency. Rather, women convicted of, or involved in, violent crimes are viewed through the gendered workings of social practices and power in intimate relationships.

Young women witness violence inside and outside the home, sometimes at first hand. Verbal abuse in schools, families and on the streets is not unusual and this can be personalized, sexualized and for some will be racist (Burman *et al.* 2001). In a recent study conducted in a range of localities across Scotland, including inner-city, town and rural areas, young women's experiences of violence were sought. The project used a range of methods to elicit experiences and views, including self-completion questionnaires, small group discussions and individual interviews. In the self-completion questionnaire, 10 per cent of the young women described themselves as violent. A similar percentage of young women reported the highest levels of victimization and many of them were also involved in perpetrating much violence. So those on the receiving end of victimization were also perpetrating violence. The home was the most common location in which girls reported using physical violence.

Given the prevalence of violence in the home, marriage and mother-hood can form a backdrop to violent acts. As noted earlier while marriage is a 'contract' the obligations of it tend to be highly informal. Being a parent does have obligations that may be legally enforced but there is no formal entry to parenting. The legal recognition of heterosexual rela-tionships shelters and facilitates violence, fear and intimidation (Card 2002: 160). At the core of marriage and motherhood is intimate access to others and thus intimate relationships can form smokescreens to abuses (Card 2002: 160). While appreciating that most childrearing work is undertaken or scripted by mothers, with attendant stresses and strains, motherhood can become a zone in which violence is ignored or accepted for the sake of retaining so-called family life.

The norms and values that surround and infuse parenting and marriage assert that these are the locations and contexts for the best quality care for young and old. Believing in this diminishes other forms of care regardless of how good these may be. If children represent all of us, in so far as we have all been children, and many of us rear children, then the concern should be to achieve the best form of care. These may not necessarily follow familial relationships achieved through heterosexual partnerships and parenting.

Through violence, 'differences are obscured in the maintenance of unities' and yet these 'unities of men's power are maintained through difference' (Hearn 1998: 217). The workings of power and oppression, through and in masculinities, are discursive and explanations and responses to violence must be multi-faceted and multi-layered, recognizing the web-like and dialectical social processes in operation.

It can be argued that men are violent because they 'are constructed as "men"' (Hearn 1998: 209) and may be 'involved in relations of power and dominance over women' (Hearn 1998: 216). Lest it appear that there is a homogeneity of approaches to violence and gender among men, Hearn (1998: 217), drawing upon his research, suggests there are 'unities and commonalities' and these need to be explored alongside a range of dif-ferences. These unities and commonalities include men who are:

- regularly violent to women *and* men over a lifetime;
- regularly violent *only* to women (or a particular woman) over a lifetime;
- occasionally or less regularly violent to women;
- occasionally violent to women, and possibly to men too;
- violent on a one-off occasion;
- violent to children;
- violent to men, because of their involvement with particular women;
- violent mainly to men, but may also be occasionally violent to women.

Anyone, regardless of gender, age or sexuality can be violent. For some, often men, the experience of actual and cultural representations of violence is much more socially and structurally routine. Within families, violence is also used by men *on* men and thus is a means of maintaining systems of oppression and domination more generally. Further, male on male violence in families is also indicative of tensions and hierarchies among men that are gender based in so far as they create and reflect a male world of expression through the corporeal (Card 2002; Connell 2002).

Summary

For many years the realities of domestic violence were experienced in the privacy of the home and family, and generally denied in public circles. Domestic violence was quite literally out of sight, contained and concealed, and in some communities or cultures it was even normalized. The social construction of legal and police services was premised upon the designation of women as property and the protection of the family as a private space in which the adult male was dominant. Feminist activities in the 1960s, combined with the campaigning work of a number of social movements on human rights and violence, led to changes in the law, related services and wider societal attitudes. Women's and campaigning groups ensured that violence against women was never far from public and political debates. The development of women-only refuges was heralded as practical and symbolic in the recognition of domestic violence. Yet in many societies there remain 'cultural interpretations and neutralizations ... [that] encourage a dulled, passive acceptance of violence: this is what men are like, this is the fate of women, there's no point in telling anyone, these things should be kept in the family' (Cohen 2001: 52).

There has been a shift from the denial of violence in families to acknowledgement, particularly of child abuse and more latterly of domestic violence. This is a sequence that reflects the broad picture in many contemporary post-industrial countries. Nevertheless, acknowledgement of violence has resulted in containment. The slow pace of change in gender roles, and images of violence in various dimensions of culture, interweave to ensure that while there is acknowledgement of violence, attempts to explore and challenge its causes are limited.

Uncovering violence in families has ranged from work on family violence to research based on feminist and pro-feminist perspectives that focus on power and gender differentials. Family violence researchers suggest that violence results from a variety of structural factors, including long hours in work, financial stresses and, more generally, the tensions that may be caused through trying to achieve a balance between the demands of home and work (Kurz 1993). In this school of thought there is a belief that men and women can be equally violent but that women come off worse as they have less physical strength. While noting the prevalence of violence in families, such theories do not reflect upon the institution of marriage and heterosexual partnerships, and the norms promoting male dominance and certain behaviours within families. Views of families as gender neutral and partnerships of equals are not borne out by available evidence. It is unrealistic to assume that perpetrators of violence are obvious to others through appearance or behaviour. Further, there is a strong association, (re)created in culture and the media, that men can and should use violence in a range of circumstances; for example, to protect the family and home in the face of burglars. The ordinary, everyday nature of violence for some draws attention to the discursive and dialectic processes of family life, much of which is taken for granted.

Trends in legislation suggest a toughening of measures to address violence against women. Coupled with the growth in services to support women and children leaving violent relationships these are welcome initiatives. Recognition of domestic violence and the longer-term consequences has led to policies designed to support women staying in the family home. Women do benefit from generic services and policies on domestic violence but these fail to recognize specific issues for a number of groups; for example, older women, disabled women and women from ethnic or religious communities.

An abusive spouse may be asked, 'Why did you do that?' Analysis needs to consider 'violence as a social choice, a clear intention to do harm, for which men are individually responsible':

> The reproduction of feelings of powerlessness and being out of control can easily be one mode of maintaining power and control. And yet while men are certainly engaged, through the doing of violence, in maintaining and elaborating power and control, in another sense some men are also not fully in control of themselves – whether through drink or drugs, through rage, through the lure and excitement of violent movement. That sense of not being in control of themselves is, however, still knowable and to an extent predictable.
>
> (Hearn 1998: 220)

Accounts of violence may include justifications and excuses and many are drawn from cultural repertoires that may prove acceptable; for example, 'I didn't mean that. It was an accident.' Or 'I had to hit her to calm her down. She was hysterical.' Through such accounts perpetrators can aim to neutralize the violence and appeal to well-established ideas that violence is uncontrollable, unpredictable and sometimes necessary, if unfortunate.

3

Families: fusion and fission

Introduction

> There is no virtue in human co-operation in itself. It depends on who
> is co-operating with whom and for what purposes.
>
> (Eagleton 2003: 172)

Relationships and solidarities in families continue to play a crucial role in
our lives. Social and political debates have taken a narrow view on how
families operate, and how they are experienced by those who inhabit them.
There also continue to be strongly held notions of defending your family to
outsiders, coupled with the oft-heard cry of 'blood is thicker than water'. A
so-called haven from the everyday pressures of life, the 'family' can form a
prison that reinforces gender and age inequalities, oppressing women and
children through, for example, domestic and sexual exploitation and
financial dependency (Barrett and McIntosh 1991).

Such prominence is given to family life that non-familial institutions –
for example, children's homes or sheltered accommodation – are perceived
in negative terms, as lesser options, regardless of the quality of care and
relationships they may provide. Family groupings, especially the heterosexual couple with dependent children, reign supreme as the preferred
mode of living regardless of the consequences of the stresses, pressures and
bleaker sides of family life. Within families, solidarities create loyalties that
can provide support in times of need. They can also turn a blind eye to
violence and abuse for fear of any overt challenge to the internal workings
of the nuclear or extended family.

In this chapter I consider the discursive relationship between the micro
workings of family life and the macro influences and factors that both
create and are reinforced by familialism and families. An analytical

framework to explore the workings of families is offered. Commonly-held presuppositions about families are considered. These presuppositions are drawn upon to consider the themes of being in, and belonging to, families; territories and home, and practices and projects (Bourdieu 1996). These are further explored in the section entitled 'Shame and subjugation'. The summary offers a synthesis of key points and material.

Developing a critical approach to families

I have established that the 'family' and 'families' are terms that evoke a range of visions and ideas, of discourses and representations. Notions of the family and families could be said to be in a state of flux. Relationship formation, divorce and childbearing are all shifting dimensions of social life that have a profound impact on the creation, formation and changes in families and households.

Below are some commonly-held presuppositions about families that are worthy of reflection (Bourdieu 1996):

- The language family members use about their family proposes *a unit capable of agency and endowed with feeling and actions*. These discourses appear founded on 'normative prescriptions about the proper way to conduct family relationships' (Bourdieu 1996: 20) and these pre-scriptions include notions of *doing gender*, which while shifting are slow to demonstrate equality. West and Zimmerman (1991) have argued that the *act of performing or not performing specific tasks* can be seen as a continuous demonstration, on a day-to-day basis, of personal gender identity.
- *Exchanges in families are paramount* and these are infused with notions of trust, reciprocity, giving, intimacy and feelings (Morgan 1996; Jamieson 1998). These exchanges are rarely negotiated or verbalized (McKie *et al.* 2001). Often they are improvised, although they draw upon norms and conventions (Jenkins 1996: 71). Exchanges require the sacrifice of one or some for the benefit of others. Often these changes are conducted in silence and on the basis of what is unspoken. For example, presumptions that a mother, as opposed to a father, will or should take a child aged 5 or under to the doctor or dentist.
- Families are viewed as *transcending their immediate members*. The term 'kinship networks' embodies a grouping that goes beyond geographical location and yet is also endowed with commonalities in ideas, experiences and plans.
- Complementary to this, families are seen as having a *separate social universe* inhabited by those in the immediate household, and shared on occasions with other members of the family residing elsewhere. Here we have the idea of the *sanctum*, with doors closed to protect intimacy. The very *privacy* of families has evolved as the notion of a haven from

the troubled, hectic outer world and yet forms the *backstage to life*. The family is a universe where the law and legal system rarely come into play, and then generally only in what are framed as extreme, 'atypical' cases such as child abuse.

- Nevertheless, the social universe of families is grounded in the *'home' as an idea of a place and space* that is permanent and endurable. This universe links to kinship through increasing concerns about property and inheritance. The analogy is the tree – and an increasing number of us seek to identify and explore our family tree.

Activities and relationships in families that are imbued with violence and violations are not exchanges as such – the word 'exchanges' provokes notions of equity between giver and receiver. Physical and psychological violence passes from the perpetrator and is received by another in ways that may demonstrate fear, intimidation, passivity, challenge or self-defence. Often violence and violations take place over time, fluctuating in content and intensity, and those experiencing violence may defend themselves or feel provoked to seek redress through violent acts. Nevertheless the context to this violence is the 'social universe' of families and family life, and the intimacy that frames or is sought through familial relationships.

The presumptions cited above present us with a social world that is a *description* of how many choose to live but it also provides a *prescription* that many feel obliged to attempt to live up to: – to seek to secure:

> the family as an objective social category (a structuring structure) is the basis of the family as a subjective social category (a structured structure), a mental category that is the matrix of countless representations and actions (e.g. marriages), which help to reproduce the objective social category. The circle is that of reproduction of the social order.
>
> (Bourdieu 1996: 21)

Ideas about 'good' or 'better' families continue to be viewed as an active social category and are drawn upon by government, agencies and ourselves (Wasoff and Dey 2000; Rake 2001). Policies, services and discourses promote a notion of the family that is premised upon childbearing and childrearing by heterosexual parents. Further, in post-industrial countries, parents are expected to be engaged in the labour market at levels that ensure the family unit is largely self-sufficient and able to manage or purchase services for care and other needs or desires.

We know that the family life experiences of many people have little or no resemblance to these dominant discourses and prescriptions for the supportive nuclear family with strong inter-generational connections. The principle underpinning the family – namely, cohesion – is evident in the work of integration; that is, nurturing the forces of *fusion* (activities that are generally the responsibility of women) and countering acts of *fission*, such as violent acts in families (usually but not always perpetrated by adults, often adult men) (Bourdieu 1996). Violence is a major cause of fission, challenging others to reflect upon, and potentially work towards, fusion rather than the breakdown of the family.

In/exclusion: being in and belonging to families

Infused with a sense of solidarity, especially in times of crisis, families provide a context to the emotional dimension of life and are still considered the major site for intimacy (Jamieson 1998). Trust in, and respect for, others are associated with being a family member, and when these are questioned or damaged a breakdown in relationships can follow (Misztal 2000; Sennett 2003). Solidarity can be marked by 'sectarianism' or 'tribalism' with families demonstrating hostility to outsiders and strong inward-looking ties to family members (Maffesoli 1996; Misztal 1996). Families are characterized by the strong inclusion of members and the exclusion of those considered to be an outsider, such as a neighbour or work colleague (Crow 2002). Solutions to needs for care, finance, accommodation and intimacy are generally met from within the immediate and wider blood and friendship ties of families in preference to those considered to be 'outsiders' (Finch and Mason 1999).

Shifting attitudes and debates continue to illuminate strands of republicanism and revolution in the evolving nature of family life. Yet the manner in which families interweave the private and the public is an issue that has been evident for quite some time:

> From the Graeco-Roman republics onward, the ideal republican citizen had been seen as a heroic warrior/statesman, a selfless Brutus whose dedication to public duty outweighed his private interests ... In his private domain, however, this freedom-loving patriot was absolute master, wielding inviolable power over his wife, children and servants. In his person, then, political and patriarchal power interlocked to produce an image of masculine authority that, to its adherents, appeared natural, timeless and unassailable. Virility and political potency were one, and womanhood another: no imagined unity was possible.
>
> (Taylor 2003: 211)

More recently, with the growth in commercial activities, and the avoidance of engagement in war for many middle- and upper-class men in most post-industrial societies, ideas on citizenship and family life have adapted further: 'Increasingly the good citizen ... [was] the gentleman of property and propriety who respected his superiors, behaved decently to his inferiors, was kind to women and children, and paid his debts' (Taylor 2003: 211). Notions of civic virtue were illuminated in the chastity and charity of femininity and the gentler but stoic manner of men in business and at home.

It remains the case that members of families come to classify others starts with blood relations, intimate partnerships and relatives, with whom there are particular understandings, intimacies and friendships. Same-sex relationships may not enjoy similar solidarities across family and neighbourhood networks, nor will partners (regardless of their gender) achieve quite the same sense of membership of immediate and extended families as blood relatives. This is very much the case when breakdown occurs in adult partnerships.

Same-sex relationships may be considered 'acceptable' if they fit the mould of a monogamous and stable relationship. However, in contemporary western societies, same-sex relationships continue to be viewed with a level of suspicion, appearing by some to pose a challenge to the institution of marriage and the family. While debates rage on the legalization of same-sex relationships, in the majority of countries these partnerships do not have the same legal rights as heterosexual partnerships (Card 2002; Moran *et al.* 2004). Regardless, notions of families continue to focus upon the intimate adult partnership as the hub around which other relationships revolve. Once breakdown of these partnerships occurs, those who come into a family through remarriage or cohabitation may find their 'membership' diminished. Children, grandparents and wider networks of relatives and friends can also find their connections broken or diminished (Allan and Crow 2001). These bonds of kinship, infusing family life as they do, can offer 'a cover for, if not licence to, the evils of spousal and child abuse' (Card 2002: 140).

There are growing tensions between the solidarity of family members and what is proposed as increasing individualism. The growing range of anxieties that seem to surround everyday life (e.g. job and financial insecurities, breakdown in relationships and threats to safety and security such as terrorism) have become factors in the ways in which individuals and governments anticipate and plan for the future. This analysis has had a discernible impact on mainstream sociological theory but less so on the analysis of families. Wider social changes appear to offer opportunities for choice but constraints are imposed by the contradictions between the realities of a relationship and the requirements of the labour market. In this thesis, family conflicts are inexorably linked to the distortions and interrelationship of societal and familial structures that connect to, and create, inequalities between men and women, parents and children, grandparents and children. Tensions in private relationships can be said to reflect an 'externally induced amplification of conflicts' (Beck 1992: 120).

In societal and familial discourses and practices, life is no longer considered unalterable and fixed but rather moulded around and through autonomy, personhood, choice and identity. Individuals and so-called experts offer the potential for adaptation and possible attainment of idealized notions of lifestyle; for example, life coaching, couple counselling and personal training, all of which offer the possibility of attaining idealized and sculpted careers, relationships and bodies (Eagleton 2003: 110). These trends appear to enhance the opportunities open to some people, creating a greater sense of the autonomous individual who can choose and adapt social and economic opportunities to meet their own needs and aspirations. The phenomenal increase in the search for family trees and biographies, as well as increased involvement in the planning of and participation in family rituals (e.g. birthdays, weddings and anniversaries) is evidence of what has been termed 'moral individualism' (Cheal 1988).

Postmodernism allowed for critiques of rationalism and structuralism and promoted a discursive framework for the analysis of social and gendered practices (Eagleton 2003: 70). Contemporary normative individualization stresses uniqueness and attempts to ignore social and especially gender differences (Beck 1992; Ronkainen 2001). In post-industrial societies the emphasis is on adults engaging in employment or pathways to paid work. Intimate relationships and expectations or needs to care for others mould around economic activities. The dominance of public and social policies emphasizing the 'worker citizen' has created tensions and posed challenges to family solidarities (Lewis 2000; Crow 2002). The irony is that we are all interdependent and in need of care by others at various times of our lives. However, these realities are marginalized in current debates and policies (Watson *et al.* 2004).

Policies and debates seem to slide with relative ease between families and moralities. Discussions on parenting and combining caring and working can easily slide into critiques of parenting in lone-parent families or same-sex families. Debates on families and social change sometimes concentrate on the so-called breakdown in families due to a combination of changing gender and parental roles, and economic fortunes. The prevalence and consequences of violence in families are often put to the periphery in these analyses.

Homeground

Notions of home and hearth are classic ones in many societies. In literature, visual media and everyday commentaries there are images of women and children warm and safe in the home, sitting near to the hearth or in the kitchen enjoying the delights of domestic life. These images are imbued with ideas of interdependency, especially of women and children, and continue to be strongly associated with notions of the dwelling – the home – in which much sustenance and nurturing in parental and adult relationships takes place. The 'home', the 'household', the 'house' are words and concepts that also provoke ambivalent thoughts, values and activities. We return to our home to seek physical and psychological sustenance while attempting to manage the complex interplay and connectedness of the public and private spheres of life (Ribbens McCarthy and Edwards 2002).

In western cultures the home is generally a house or a flat, a secure dwelling associated with family living. This is evidently not the case in many areas of Africa, Asia and the southern Americas where a home might be a shack, pieces of polythene or a space under trees. Given the impact of global poverty and conflict on migration and family life, to have a home at all, any type of home, can be considered a privilege. Nevertheless it is clear that central to human activity is the notion of 'family'. The idea of a space and place on, or in which, to conduct current, past and anticipated part-nerships and inter- and intra-generational relationships is one crucial to a post-industrial sense of what it means to be in a state of fusion with others, and society in general. To capture the notion of the place and the space I use the term 'homeground'. The subsequent arguments on notions of home associated with post-industrial societies draws upon the ideas of a place (some type of construction), a space (the floors, rooms or soil on which people live), the location in which we invest in making plans, the work of 'nurturing' and the promotion of a sense of a group or team: our family.

Through 'dwelling' among things and structures (homes), humans create meaningful things, places and relationships. For most of us, this dwelling, 'our home' is the physical context to families and relationships. These dwellings are constructions (buildings/shelters) in which many of the varied activities of homemaking and home life take place (Heidegger 1971). Construction is defined as the design and activities of making the building and these are the basis to major aspects of our identities. Obser-ving where we live and our involvement, or otherwise, in the building, refurbishment or decoration of that dwelling creates a context to identities and images of the family. The recent upsurge in television programmes and print media on the design and decoration of homes is evidence of an increased sense that identities and relationships are interwoven with the physical entity of the home.

Most of the activities crucial to design and building – construction – are associated with masculinities in so far as these are tasks dominated by men and notions of the physical and resourceful man. Masculine ideas, and men in key professions and jobs, dominate construction industries. This con-tinues despite sustained critiques and attempts to achieve change (Greed 1994). Construction, in whatever form, creates a space in which we live. But this is a process that is time-specific in so far as living in our home creates 'a rupture in the continuity of history' of that dwelling (Young 1997: 153).

By contrast the work of preservation 'entails not only the keeping of physical objects of particular people intact, but renewing their meaning' (Young 1997: 153) in the lives of families:

> The work of preservation also importantly involves teaching children the meaning of things among which one dwells, teaching the children the stories, practices, and celebration that keep the particular mean-ings alive. The preservation of the things among which one dwells

gives people a context for their lives, individuates their histories, gives them items to use in making new projects, and makes them comfortable. When things and works are maintained against destruction, but not in the context of life, they become museum pieces.

(Young 1997: 153)

The labour of preservation is necessary to meet the needs of others and maintain families as everyday entities and social worlds (Young 1997; Arendt 2002). This is labour that is characterized by repetition. Preservation work includes a multitude of tasks, ranging from the mundane, such as the cleaning of kitchens and bathrooms, to the maintenance of family histories and collective memories by keeping photograph albums and organizing events to celebrate birthdays or anniversaries. The raising of children is a form of 'preservation' work and care work and childrearing are elements of preservation work that are 'artisanal rather than industrial' in character (Hagerstrand 1978: 222). In a global sense this labour is typically carried out, organized and/or paid for by women (Ehrenreich and Hochschild 2002).

The labour of housework and homemaking is recorded through oral histories and museums. The histories of 'ordinary' families, as well as the growth in tracing family histories, are examples of an increase in the celebration of family life (Samuel 1999). Much of this celebration of the work of preservation fails to note its gendered and exploitative nature. It also generally fails to acknowledge the violence that may have taken place in the dwelling and the family.

Inviting someone to your homeground is to offer access to a space and place dominated by personal relationships and activities. This is an arena that illuminates social status, material standing and positioning within a family, neighbourhood and community. To exchange hospitality, memories and stories of personal and family life are practical and symbolic ways of achieving cohesion (Misztal 2003: 19). A sense of shared experiences is moulded and shaped through a range of narratives indicative of the current family/relationships context and homeground of the person sharing the memories (Misztal 2003: 51). Individual memories cannot be divorced from the memories of the group, the family. At the same time the decline in the extended family and the increasing mobility of young people and adults of working age appears to create disjuncture in the real, potential and imagined histories of families. Nevertheless, in many families there is one home that takes on the mantle of the 'family home' and adult children, even with children of their own, will speak of 'going home'. This generally means returning to the place and/or relationships of their upbringing. Celebrations of families – weddings, birthdays, anniversaries, religious festivals – are often conducted in and around what is understood to be the 'family home'.

Private, public, privacy

While men may be participating in the activities and discourses of home and parenting, women continue to take on the main burden of family preservation work. Women do this in an era when global cultural pre-scriptions continue to conflate femaleness and home. Given the role of emotion in relationships and parenting, the centrality of emotion work to families and the gendered nature of this, then it can be argued that 'doing' becomes a way of 'being' (Duncombe and Marsden 1995). Identities are formed in, and around, the homeground and these weave with, and draw upon, connections with the spaces, places and organizations outside the homeground. The practices of construction and preservation, in and around the homeground, form a smokescreen to violence. These processes first create a place and space that constitutes boundaries from others through the construction of a dwelling, and second emphasize the everyday and longer-term activities of home life including the con-temporary and longer-term histories of families.

Ideas about caring take on different meanings over time (Jamieson 1998: 9). Over the last century, physical expressions of love and care have changed, and emotional bonds are expressed in different ways to those previously considered acceptable. Alongside the changing nature of care and emotions in families is the impact of diverse social and economic experiences. As a result, the idea that family members, and family groups, pass through life changes in a predictable fashion is untenable. Further, analysts predict and indeed cite changes that may not be borne out by empirical data. One obvious topic for continuous examination is the combination of caring and working. Combining these roles influences the lives and well-being of women to a degree rarely experienced by men. Granted there is a growing number of men involved in care work, and in later life caring for their partner, but often women organize, provide, monitor and pay for care. This combination of work and roles for women is apparent in most societies. These shifts offer a challenge to assumptions surrounding key stages in family life, in particular the bearing and rearing of children. The age at which the first child is born is increasing in many social groups and there is a rise in the number of women choosing not to have children at all (Ferri et al. 2003).

Given the pressures of caring and working, home and family life may actually encourage 'a wrongful escapism' in so far as experiences in families can cloud the exploitative nature of what goes in, and around, households (Young 1997: 156). Analysis must be developed with an appreciation of the complex role the home plays in forming and shifting identities. Indeed, people can relax, even potentially develop a resistance to the oppressions of families, work and life, while being in the home and engaging with other family members.

Government policies, and international appeals on the benefits of sus-tainable communities, draw upon the idea that extended families and family connections need to be promoted and enabled to enhance economic and social regeneration. Families can and do provide a spine of connection running through neighbourhoods. Trends in mobility and economic migration pose a range of challenges to these ideas. However, to achieve a full analysis of 'the home' and 'the family' it is necessary to start from a recognition of the gendered nature of social, economic and familial life. Certainly the low value placed upon the labour of homemaking by many governments, organizations and some researchers does not aid the analysis of violence in families.

The rhetoric of privacy has shielded the violence of families, emphasizing instead the work of preservation. Governments, agencies and religions argue they cannot intervene in families as what takes place in the home is 'private', thus placing violent acts beyond public control and certainly making legal action problematic given the emphasis courts make on the need for witnesses (Schneider and Schneider 1994).

The meanings of 'private', 'public' and 'privacy' shift. For example, the behaviour of pregnant women is increasingly surveyed and scrutinized. This is fuelled by concerns about a range of risks, some self-imposed, others linked to the environment. Some health and legal services contend that pregnant women should actively avoid these risks. Thus pregnancy, and the lifestyle of pregnant women, has become the focus of medical, societal and legal pressures that in the USA have resulted in laws that seek to regulate the behaviour of women (Schneider and Schneider 1994; Young 1997). Here privacy of the person is restricted on the basis that many groups and governments argue that they have the right to impose regulation to limit risks and promote discourses that aim to protect future generations. In this way women are devalued and potentially framed as in need of monitoring and surveillance. Ironically this apparent collective concern often dissipates on birth and at times motherhood becomes a deeply isolating and alienating experience (Card 2002: 164).

The expectation of privacy for adults is problematic and in its current form this is a concept that 'encourages, reinforces, and supports violence' (Schneider and Schneider 1994: 43). Privacy masks inequalities and can act to protect those who perpetrate violence. Achieving a balance is difficult. These tensions might be illustrated by a debate run on the website of the organization Liberty, a UK human rights and civil liberties organization. This debate asked 'why do nearly 1000 different public authorities have the power to keep you under covert surveillance, without proper scrutiny?' (http://www.liberty-human-rights.org.uk/issues/privacy-surveillance.shtml). At the same time the violent death of a partner or children at the hands of a partner or parent leads to a crescendo of calls for enhanced scrutiny of families with intervention to protect the vulnerable.

The world of the homeground is one that many couples and individuals invest in. There is a growing trend in lifestyle consumerism and individualism that fuels investment in the homeground. Privacy is about having control and autonomy over who has access not just to spaces and places but also to personal information, ideas and history: 'a person should have control over access to her living space, her meaningful things, and information about herself' (Young 1997: 163). 'Privacy' should be available to everyone regardless of culture and society and not purely dismissed as western ethnocentrism. To argue for a democratization of privacy would draw attention to the lack of privacy many women and children have as their lives are shaped through the gendered and inequitable practices of societies and families.

Many agencies and professionals are fearful of scrutiny of their practices, especially if these might be considered to promote frequent intervention in family life. Perhaps as a result, services try to operate without recourse to the legal system. For example, when agencies recognize and tackle violence, there is a preference to contain the situation by supporting the person experiencing violence to leave the relationship and home. For some working in relevant services, violence is an everyday reality and supporting those experiencing it to leave is part of what might be considered a 'realist' stance. Few would argue with the need to provide and develop these forms of support and services. Nevertheless, the challenge is to achieve an appreciation of the workings and meanings of private and public as a basis to the development of social and economic policies and practices (Ribbens McCarthy and Edwards 2002: 211). Reclaiming and democratizing the concept of privacy offers the potential to develop positive aspects of home life while, at the same time, admitting to and tackling the inequalities of gender, age and autonomy in family life (Young 1997: 163).

Practices and projects

Family practices invoke a sense of 'flow and fluidity' and interdependence while enabling both description and sociological analysis; for example, the family practices identified with meals and meal times 'could also be defined as consumption practices, gender practices, generational practices and so on' (Morgan 2002: 153). Thus the notion of 'family practices' may be used to describe the set of activities associated with, and undertaken, by family members.

The analysis of families might draw upon the study of professions to explore family processes and practices: 'society ... consists in part of both allowing and expecting some people to do things which other people are not allowed or expected to [do]' (Hughes 1971: 287). Two concepts might be adapted to offer further insights to the study of families, namely *licence* and *mandate* (Hughes 1971). First, licence. This is gained through permission derived from government or licensing bodies. Licence may be technical (e.g. the licence to practise gained by a surgeon and imperative to practice) or may extend to areas of behaviour and thought (e.g. gaining membership of professional bodies or associations by the psychologist or priest). To achieve licence, specific skills and experiences must be demonstrated. Licence can involve legal permission and also sanctions leeway with regards to actual practice and lifestyle; for example, the mannerisms and dress associated with the hospital consultant, the minister or imam. Any licence to practise is subject to ongoing surveillance and processes of control, although these may be fluid.

So what might this concept offer the study of families? A number of models of heterosexual families are supported implicitly through government policies and dominant social and economic discourses. These can be considered to amount to forms of 'permission' for these family forms. In addition, with the continued impact of the sexual contract, that is, the private subordination of women to men (Pateman 1988), there remain gendered roles. Roles are also imbued with ideas on age, culturally appropriate behaviours and responsibilities. The very heterogeniality of family life links the home to nature and the natural. The home and the family become guarantors for identity and intimacies (Lefebvre 1991). In many ways the family and home constitute a licence to intimacy (the private sphere) and support the potential for, and ongoing engagement in, paid employment (the public dimension).

Seeing and knowing what happens in the private world of families where violence takes place does not necessarily lead to intervention. While membership of families may offer the licence to practise certain roles and responsibilities, the licence for organizations and professionals to intervene is keenly debated and under constant review. If those in an occupation have a sense of 'identity and solidarity' they will also claim a mandate: 'They also seek to define and possibly succeed in defining, not merely proper conduct but even modes of thinking and belief for everyone individually and for the body social and politic with respect to some broad area of life which they believe to be in their occupational domain' (Hughes 1971: 287).

The concept of mandate can offer insights into roles that are gained through and around licence; for example, the role of male or female parent, or the allocation of resources and tasks within the household. Many occupations, or familial roles, cannot be carried out without guilty knowledge; that is, knowledge gained when colleagues or clients share information or ideas of an intimate nature (Hughes 1971). Entering into such revelations is generally premised on some sense of trust.

Licence is operated through family titles such as mother, father, sister, brother, etc., and within families: 'Licence attached to the performance of family obligations or duties exists at a less formal level and is subject to day-to-day negotiation, direct or indirect' (Morgan 2002: 156). Guilty knowledge is evident within families and between family members, unlike the one-way flow of knowledge, particularly personal knowledge, between client and professional: 'the question of licence and guilty knowledge within families points to processes of some considerable complexity' (Morgan 2002: 156). At times there might be concealment of certain knowledge (e.g. parents may conceal childhood misdemeanours) although there are times when revelation may be sanctioned (e.g. the parental speech at a wedding).

Physical and psychological violence may be concealed or revealed by victims, perpetrators and other family members. Some people and groups avoid the subject of violence in families. This may be due, in part, to the 'special' meanings afforded to notions of 'the family' coupled with the proximity of the topic to our everyday lives and identities. There are times when the prerogatives of certain professions are questioned; for example, ongoing concerns about the medical profession and consent to use body parts for pathology research (Hughes 1971: 290). The enhanced prominence given to diversities in families and family life evident in social surveys and studies of family life in multicultural societies has led to a questioning of implicit state support for the heterosexual family focused on working parents. Yet the power of a profession, and of 'the family', is to protect its licence and maintain its mandate when under attack. Despite evidence of diversities in families, an increase in solo living and childlessness, there remains much support and nostalgia for the heterosexual family and notions of home.

Nostalgia about homes and homemaking can generate unrealistic and contradictory images and ideas about family life. In previous sections I argued that the meanings attributed to, activities undertaken, and identities created in, and around, homegrounds are complex, gendered and deeply held. Reclaiming, gendering and democratizing the concept of privacy offers potential not just to illuminate inequities in domestic labour and gender but, importantly, to tackle violence in families. 'Doing gender' and 'performing' gendered identities may additionally be conceptualized as 'gender projects' (Butler 1993; Connell 2002: 82). Moving between and across the roles of mother, sister and daughter demonstrates the fluidity and dynamic nature of doing and performing gender in the overarching gender project of being a woman in the context of family life.

Shame and subjugation

The 'feeling worlds' of men and women (emotional differences) reveal the workings of being a man or woman (Bartky 1990: 84). A feeling of particular relevance to violence in families is shame. This may be defined as distress resulting from a state in which someone considers themselves as 'inferior, defective, or in some way diminished' (Bartky 1990: 85). Shame is often verbalized by those unable or reluctant to voice experiences of violence (Fineman and Mykituk 1994; Hearn 1998). Women are typically 'more shame-prone than men' and this is a 'profound mode of disclosure both of self and situation': 'Shame is the distressed apprehension of the self as inadequate or diminished: it requires if not an actual audience before whom my deficiencies are paraded, then an internalised audience with the capacity to judge me . . . shame requires the recognition that I am, in some important sense, as I am seen to be (Bartky 1990: 86).

To sense shame is to acknowledge that we have violated what might be considered appropriate behaviour for our gender, age and social situation. Further, historically most societies have ascribed roles and attributes to men and women which afford men domination over women. While contemporary views may challenge these ascriptions of female roles and obligations, women express feelings of responsibility for others, and these feelings are supported by the attitudes of families, schools, workplaces and churches. Women as mothers and citizens are the hub in the wheel of families without which it is thought domestic tasks and practices cannot operate. In turn, being female and adult in the family presents a woman with a range of roles and responsibilities. To fail at any of these still carries a sense of shame that few men experience. Despite the self-evident capabilities of most women, the subtle and pernicious operation of shame undermines self-worth. The image of the family to those outside the immediate household through, for example, the behaviour of children, perceptions of the adult relationship, or the cleanliness of the home, is a major dimension of life where women can, and do, sense shame if they fail to meet aspects of idealized notion of families and family life.

These emotions of shame become a component of women's identities that perpetuates subjugation (Bartky 1990: 98). Why do women (and children) continue to express shame in the face of experiencing violence perpetrated by others? Is this a mark of powerlessness or personal inadequacy? Men feel shame too but these experiences reflect their positioning in families and society as more powerful. For example, while women experiencing violence may cite shame in an apologetic fashion, expressing concerns that they might be perceived as having failed in their marriage, the perpetrator may express shame in ways that seek to distance him from his actions: 'she nagged me', 'I didn't want to do it but she wouldn't shut up'. Men convicted of violent crimes are subject to social disapproval but they may raise the threshold of what counts as violence. For example, 'they may see violence to known women, "their" woman, as partly legitimate and partly illegitimate' (Hearn 1998: 203) so that they feel able to ignore the disapproval that results from such violence. Expressing shame seems at best ambiguous and at worst disingenuous. Ambiguities that become evident in the retelling of violence can form a defence, a diversion, and an appeal to 'distance himself' from violent acts and relationships. Thus the gendered structuring of feelings and emotions may be illuminated through the telling and explaining of experiences. These are formed in a discursive fashion through the everyday and longer-term workings of families.

Summary

Families are in a constant state of flux and can be irritating places to be but they remain crucial to societal structures and experiences. The attainment of what is considered 'ideal' forms of family life remains an expectation and goal for many, regardless of experiences and evidence. The aim of this chapter has been to establish and examine the meanings and implications of commonly-held presuppositions about families and family life.

In particular I have sought to draw upon the concepts of family practices and gender projects as ways of framing further investigation of violence in families (Morgan 1996; Connell 2002). Nostalgic notions of family life, and families in general, create and reinforce a range of contradictions and ambiguities. All too often, economic factors and the gendering of caring, combined with romantic ideas about families, provide prescriptions about family life that many, especially women, feel obliged to try to live up to. Certainly, the strongly-held notion of families as places of safety and security (fusion) forms an opacity that can act as a smokescreen to abuse (fissions): 'Home and comfort are the cornerstone of a myth of safety. The promotion of home as a location of safety may expose the already vulnerable to further danger' (Moran *et al.* 2004: 172).

Being in, and belonging to, families provides a basis to solidarities as well as meeting a range of needs including physical and emotional care, financial resources, accommodation and intimacy. However, the increased emphasis on individualism results in tensions. Identities are moulded and adapted through family experiences, personal autonomy and choice. Nevertheless, roles in families continue to carry with them public expectations and private responsibilities. The home as a place, and space, is also one in which memories are shared and shaped through narratives and experiences. The work of construction and preservation – as daily and longer-term activities – remains gendered. Thus the social universe of families links to kinship as well as to the range of everyday activities.

Ideas and feelings about families and solidarities are strong in most societies. Families and home life can offer a haven from the pressures of employment and public life. But this 'haven' can create smokescreens to violence in families and promote an averted gaze on the part of family members. A dichotomy exists between 'concern and action' (Cohen 2001: 289). While the public's threshold for tolerating violence in families has lowered, and services and the law have followed or even led this trend, the focus on the victim and the containment of violence does little to challenge the widespread discrimination against women and girls. More often than not, women's and human rights organizations and other agencies working on violence are underfunded and overstretched. No matter how hard they campaign for the elimination of violence in intimate and familial relationships this remains a major threat to the safety and security of women and girls.

I drew upon the notion of shame to explore how violence can be hidden by emotions of self-assessment that belie the realities of the situation (Bartky 1990). The view that the privacy of families endorses the sense of the family as a haven from the pressures of the hectic outer world provides a challenge. Young (1997) proposes we reclaim and reassess the potential for privacy to offer transparency to family life through ensuring that *all* have personal respect and autonomy.

A critical reflection of a number of commonly-held presuppositions about families formed the basis of debate in this chapter. The workings and practices of families are central to self-identification and social and economic organization (Bernardes 1987; Finch and Mason 1999; Carling *et al.* 2002). The solidarities of families (in/exclusion) can depend upon and promote notions of rights and responsibilities. These need not be demarcated along lines of gender and age but generally are (Baxter 2000; Sullivan 2000; Allan and Crow 2001). Trust and respect were noted as premises associated with being in families and when these are challenged or abused a breakdown in relationships and even violence can follow.

The home as a place and space (homeground) is crucial to the well-being and solidarity of families is central to human activities (Heidegger 1971). The construction of the home is followed by the work of preservation that imbues the day-to-day with the longer-term sharing of stories and memories across generations (Young 1997; Misztal 2003). Nostalgia, 'a longing flight from the ambiguities and disappointments of everyday life' pervades our ideas about families, further obscuring the strains of family life and violence in families (Young 1997: 154). This, and the contention, that life in families offers privacy for some at the expense of others can make the revelation of violence all the more difficult and complex (Card 2002). Of relevance here is the adaptation of the concepts of licence (the day-to-day negotiation and permission to perform family obligations and duties) and mandate (negotiation of appropriate conduct) with the potential for families to conceal and share 'guilty' knowledge (Hughes 1971; Morgan 1996).

The gendered nature of feelings and emotions is formed through the discursive workings of family practices and projects. These were considered with regards to the feelings of shame evident around the disclosure and actions on violence in families and how these can be ambiguous between perpetrator and victim (Bartky 1990). Contemporary trends to normative individualization, discourses around familial responsibilities and lifestyles and continuing notions of the home as a place of safety and sanctity interweave to create and reinforce solidarities, tensions and breakdowns (Beck 1992; Rose 2001; Crow 2002). Evidence of fission in families illustrates the dashed hopes and expectations of family life and, for all too many, experiences of violence and violations.

Immediate and wider family and kinship networks form solidarities and support networks that may provide a 'cover for, if not a licence to ... spousal and child abuse' (Card 2002: 140). Such is the generally positive view of family life that it can promote feelings of shame among those experiencing violence (Bartky 1990). The conceptual frame of 'practices' can illuminate processes in the everyday activities of families (Morgan 2002). Practices in families are formed around gender projects (Connell 2002: 82) and these gender projects of construction and preservation take place in and around the home. Nostalgia combined with the necessity of place and space 'fuels a wrongful escapism' when we think of families and homes (Young 1997: 156). A concern is to expose the myth of the safety of the home and the 'safety talk' that continues to concentrate on the public realm of experience rather than the private. Arguing that the concept of privacy be reclaimed and fluidity gained between the private and the public, Young (1997: 163) proposes that we must be afforded opportunities to gain control over our person and personal space. Underlying these theoretical debates is the evidence of fission in families, of levels of violence, of breakdown and of dashed hopes and expectations.

Perhaps a way forward is to explore Young's (1997: 163) call to democratize privacy so that 'a person [can] have control over access to her living space, her meaningful things and information about herself'. The call to privacy as proposed by Young can form an underlying principle to encourage people to change attitudes, activities and responses to violence in families. However, this is a principle that could be difficult to achieve. Privacy in, and around, families has been identified as a causal factor limiting recognition of violence and posing barriers to tackling violent meanings and practices. There are joys and delights in family life but the myths that these relationships are, and should always be, harmonious rest alongside the need for a grouping (a place and space) in which to conduct intimate and inter-generational relationships, warts and all.

PART TWO

Gender, age and violence

4

Embodiment, gender and violence

Introduction

> looked at globally, twenty-first century women can be seen to still
> suffer sex-based discrimination and hardship on a scale that makes
> notions like 'post-feminism' merely fatuous.
>
> (Taylor 2003: 253)

Globally, violence against women is the most pervasive human rights abuse
(Bond and Phillips 2001). Evidence abounds: in South Africa over 50,000
rapes are reported each year and many of these carry the risk of HIV
infection; approximately 130 million girls and women have endured
genital mutilation, and an estimated 250,000 women and girls from central
and eastern Europe and the former Soviet Union are trafficked each year to
western Europe and elsewhere for the sex and domestic labour trades
(Bond and Phillips 2001; Ehrenreich and Hochschild 2002; McKie 2003).
These forms of violence and abuse seem distant from the everyday
experiences of women in post-industrial societies until you consider the
prevalence of domestic violence. Estimates obtained from several statutory
and non-governmental sources in Scotland suggest that between a quarter
and a third of all women aged 16–64 experience domestic abuse at some
point in their lives (Scottish Executive 2002). These forms and patterns of
abuse and violence illustrate the manifestations of wider inequalities
between men and women; inequalities evident in all societies.

This chapter examines the apparent shift from a denial to the
acknowledgement of domestic violence, at both societal and governmental
levels (Cohen 2001: 50). I use the word 'apparent' for this 'acknowledgement' continues to emphasize the agency of and support for those
experiencing violence, rather than the importance of addressing the

problems arising from the gendered social worlds and practices that fail to inhibit or tackle violence. Of course, support for those experiencing violence is imperative, and many aspects of these services continue to be under-resourced, not least woman-centred services and material support for survivors. However, it is my contention that in many ways this 'acknowledgement' has led to action that constitutes a superficial response to violence. This demonstrates an averted gaze from the attitudes and practices in families, culture and socioeconomic spheres that sanction or ignore gendered violence.

The focus of this chapter is domestic violence among heterosexual couples.[1] As discussed earlier the term domestic violence incorporates a range of psychological and physical abuses. Domestic violence can take many forms including verbal abuse, slapping, punches, the use of weapons to injure, restrictions on money and friends, sexual abuse and violence, and murder. This violence can also differ across cultures and countries, and includes forced marriage, rape, honour and dowry abuse, and death. There are no typical characteristics of an abuser. Domestic violence appears in all social and ethnic groups, religions, social classes and age groups (Renzetti *et al.* 2001).

Domestic violence is characterized by the intimacy of current or past relationships and is commonly associated with acts in, and around, the locale of a home. This is the most common form of violence that takes place within families, both during and after the break-up of relationships. Most typically this is violence perpetrated by men on women known to them, through a combination of physical and psychological acts. Often the aim is to control a partner's behaviour. As discussed in Chapter 2, we cannot deny the evidence on the existence of violence *per se* but given the prevalence of domestic violence, it necessitates specific consideration (Weldon 2002).

Violence is all around us, whether in the media, the streets or the home. Much of the media coverage of violence concentrates on war, civil unrest and the experiences and fears of criminal acts in public spaces. Many would argue that this is as it should be. It is not uncommon to hear or read headlines such as 'gun panic sets in' and 'crime rates soar'. Certainly fears about crime, especially crime against the person in public spaces, and what people can do to avoid this, appear to dominate debates on violence: evidence of an emphasis on individualized assessments and management of risks (Beck 1992).

Domestic violence in families can be the subject of media coverage that seems to distort or ignore the evidence. For example, despite evidence to the contrary, recent attention on male victims of domestic violence suggests that women may be just as violent as men. Further, the emphasis

[1] As Kelly (1996: 39) comments there is limited research and reflection on violence in lesbian relationships. The same assertion might also be made about gay relationships. There is a need to examine such violence in the context of intimate relationships but this is not the focus of this chapter (Mason, 2002).

continues to be upon domestic violence in families as a one-off event (e.g. the argument that results in a stabbing) rather than a process of abusive acts over years.

Specific and relevant campaigns can be found, often linked to policy or developments in campaigning and women's groups and government. In February 2003, the BBC ran the 'Hitting Home' week of TV and radio programmes concerned with the theme of domestic violence. This was highly acclaimed and emphasized that help is available for those experiencing abuse. In the autumn of the same year, the *Scottish Sun* newspaper (a daily tabloid) initiated a fundraising campaign supported by the international chain, The Body Shop, and the charity Refuge, which offers a range of support to those experiencing domestic violence. Both of these activities, while welcomed by many women's and family support groups, politicians and policymakers, continued to speak of 'the victim' using emotive language and forms of reporting that individualizes both those experiencing and perpetrating domestic violence.

Consider, for example, the introduction of the campaign in the *Scottish Sun*. This took place at the same time as the Scottish Executive published a national strategy on the prevention of domestic abuse. The strategy developed work on prevention in government departments that commenced two years earlier and as a result the possibilities and plans for prevention received renewed attention in many areas of the media. The front page of the paper had the headline cited below, positioned around photographs of six men (capitals in original quote): 'Once, these men had enough charm to win a woman's heart. But they grew into brutes capable of a sickening crime. They're all ... WIFE-BEATERS ... and we're exposing them today' (*Scottish Sun*, 22 September 2003: 3).

Not all the cases reported involved married couples. The recourse to the term 'wife beaters' is short-hand for abusive male partners and suggestive of ideas about marriage, masculinities, roles and relationships. Over five pages the paper employed terms to describe the perpetrators that included 'nasty vile streak', a 'drunk' and a 'brute', and women were described as 'suffering', 'terrified' and 'brave', with their status as mothers noted. The editorial line of the paper suggested that the women should press charges and leave the relationship. The newspaper finished coverage on that day with a request to readers: 'NOW LET US KNOW WHAT YOU THINK. What do YOU think about the scourge of domestic violence and the women who suffer at the hands of brutes?' To construct the request for reader's views in this way suggests domestic violence may be akin to an affliction and, therefore, could be suffered or treated in a similar manner that an illness might. Using the term 'at the hands of' emphasizes physical forms of violence and the word 'brutes' proposes that perpetrators demonstrate traits in some ways obvious to the eye, that are atypical.

Although published at the same time as the Scottish government's national strategy on prevention of domestic abuse, there is little mention of prevention but rather a focus upon the 'victim' and *her* agency. The reasons why men feel they can abuse and move from one relationship to another, continuing to be violent, are given scant regard. Of course debate on the broader theme of a general desensitization to violence, coupled with contradictory responses to women's rights and roles, might not sell popular newspapers.

Some researchers have asserted that women can be just as violent as men and proposed the notion of 'couple conflict' in which either partner can provoke violence (Stets and Straus 1990; see also Chapter 2). A review of available data on gender and violence led the Department of Health in England to conclude that 'The idea that women are at least as abusive as men is both wrong and dangerous and can lead to the belief that there is no need to provide dedicated services to protect women and their children against domestic violence' (Department of Health 2000: 13).

In the context described above, the aims of this chapter are threefold. First, to compare and contrast debates and policy developments on domestic violence in three countries: Finland, Scotland and Sweden. I approach this as a researcher and academic who lives and works in Scotland and is of Irish origin. Over the last three years I have worked with a range of agencies, as well as academics, to consider and pursue the provision of materials to support the process of disclosing domestic violence in the healthcare context (McKie *et al.* 2003). More recently, research has resulted in comparative work on policies in Finland and Scotland (McKie and Hearn 2004). Colleagues in Finland have noted the manner in which the former imperial power and Nordic neighbour, Sweden, continues to offer ideas and models for policies and services on violence against women that impact upon debates and developments (Nousiainen *et al.* 2001). These various experiences and research activities have caused me to consider the interweaving of history, gender and policy, as a 'relative outsider' in all three countries (McKie and Hearn 2004).[2]

Second, the comparison allows for a consideration of gender and the role of the autonomous woman's movement in these countries, and the relationship, if any, with policy developments. Following the work of Weldon (2002) these are important dimensions in forming the ethos to, and developments in, policies on violence against women. What might the researcher, policymaker or activist conclude from these comparisons? To achieve these aims the relationship between gender, policy and politics, and the historical underpinnings of these in the respective countries, is first considered.

Why these countries? Partially, the selection arose from on-going research work on gender and violence. These are also countries that have similar political structures, post-industrial economic issues and demographic trends. They are stable countries in which women could be said to

---

[2] In the following sections I draw upon collaborative work with Jeff Hearn (McKie and Hearn, 2004) and would like to acknowledge the insights gained from his work on masculinities and violence (Hearn, 1998; Edwards and Hearn, 2005).

have made progress in terms of their engagement with employment, politics and civil rights. Given this, it might be expected that governmental and agency responses to violence against women would be proactive and progressive, demonstrating positive attitudes towards women and the need to tackle evident patterns in men's violence. However, evidence suggests that this is not necessarily the case. Responses, and the (non)-implementation of these, illustrate the tenuous ways in which gender and violence are defined and addressed in policies and discourses. Further, evidence also illustrates the narrow ways in which violence is understood and policies formed; for example, there continues to be an evident and ongoing focus on physical acts manifested in a range of ways. This narrowness allows for a separation of the practices of gender from the practice of violence in so far as causation and the breadth of violence and violations are rarely framed as central to the evolution of policies and services.

Definitions and declarations

The term domestic violence is in common use by international organizations, governments, agencies and groups, the media and the public, and is used to define violence between adults known to each other in familial and intimate relationships. Yet it is a problematic term for several reasons. First, it ignores that this is violence perpetrated by men against known women. The term seems to render these acts of violence ungendered. Dissecting the term, the word 'domestic' implies a location in which violence takes place, namely the home. While violence does take place in the home, it is not always home based. Wherever it occurs, violence shatters trust. Given the association of the word domestic with the home, and in turn the presumed association of families, home and hearth – images of warm and glowing personal relationships – it suggests violence that shatters relationships in a location imbued with great meaning. Lastly, the word violence continues to promote notions of physical rather than psychological acts. It suggests simply physical forms of violence, and by implication excludes a range of violence and violations that includes sexual assault, rape, murder, pornography, sexual harassment, trafficking and emotional, reproductive, social and economic abuses and controls. So what term or words to use?

As discussed in Chapter 1, the Scottish Executive adopted the term 'domestic abuse' to better encompass psychological as well as physical violence. This led to criticisms from some healthcare professionals and the police that the word abuse actually softens the realties of violence, and ironically the impact of physical acts. Other terms such as 'family violence', 'spouse violence' or 'conjugal violence' continue to de-gender violence. 'Wife battering' or 'marital violence' offer notions of gender but in a restricted way that is framed around marriage, excluding cohabiting and same-sex couples. The term wife battering also lends itself to an emphasis on the victim.

Language is situational and expressive of power relations. The situated use of terms illuminates the determination of the problem and policies (Bacchi 1999). Thus debates about terminology, the very discourses about terms to use, reflect how issues overlap across countries but also point to some notable differences that have implications for interpretations and activities. The Swedish term for domestic violence is understood to include both psychological and physical dimensions. In Finnish the word used, *perhevakivalta*, directly translates as family violence and certainly there remains a strong focus in policy and discourses on 'the family'. This also reflects the adherence in Finnish politics and policy to notions of gender neutrality (discussed below) as a supposed mechanism for working towards equality of the sexes. This presumption can and does make debates on gender and terminology difficult to conduct. Further, the Finnish language does not distinguish between male and female in the third person, and this has a neutralizing effect on sensitivity to gender. The term domestic violence translates as *kotivakivalta*, violence at home, and while this might be considered a more apposite term it is not in common use. The World Health Organization report on violence and health adopted the term 'violence by intimate partners' with the aim of capturing violence that is concentrated in personal relationships that are ongoing or have broken down (World Health Organization 2002).

As analysis is concerned with policy responses to all dimensions of psychological and physical abuses, and in this chapter I have adopted the term 'domestic violence'. It continues to be used and understood in most countries and Anglophone contexts, even though there are major shortcomings, most importantly that it does not readily establish the gendered pattern of violence.

Domestic violence is increasingly recognized worldwide as an issue of concern and a problem, particularly for governments keen to promote human rights in their own and other countries (Weldon 2002: 10). The 1993 United Nations *Declaration on the Elimination of Violence Against Women* proved to be a catalyst for a range of international and governmental interventions and activities for which a broad coalition of the women's movement had campaigned for several decades. Over the last 30 years much has been achieved in the European Union in the provision of women-only services, as well as material and social support for women and children. This includes enhanced services such as women's refuges, rape crisis centres, sexual abuse survivors groups provided by governments, voluntary and community sectors, and the women's movement more generally. Laws have been introduced, and refined, which involve a range of service providers and practitioners. The provision of housing and welfare services has been underpinned by greater inter-agency working and media campaigns to raise awareness. The growing recognition of differences among women (race, ethnicity, sexuality, disability) has led to service provision that attempts to meet diverse needs.

In 2002 the Committee of Ministers, the executive body of the Council of Europe, accepted a broad definition of violence against women as a basis for debate and policy in the recommendation *The Protection of Women Against Violence*. This defined violence against women as encompassing domestic abuse, sexual harassment, wartime acts of sexual slavery and hostage-taking, mockery and public insult, invasive looks and exhibitionism. It was further stated that under no circumstances might a country invoke custom, religion or tradition as reasons to ignore violence against women in any community. All measures emanating from the Council of Europe must also take into account an obligation to protect women and children (Council of Europe 2002).

Safety is a prime concern for those experiencing violence, service providers and practitioners. This is offered through a range of services and activities including women–only refuges, legislation that excludes or imprisons perpetrators, and safer housing and personal alarms. Despite enhanced provision, services are always overstretched and under-resourced.

Increasing concern about understanding causation, thereby enabling prevention, has led to increased levels of policy work, legislation and service developmental work with perpetrators. Policies to work with men can lead to the redirection of resources away from services for victims and survivors. The broad coalition of the women's movement remains concerned that governments and agencies may divert funds to work with men at the cost of services for women and children.

Documenting domestic violence

Domestic violence has been of some concern for a number of years but in the last decade national surveys in Finland, Scotland and Sweden have provided details on prevalence and incidence that, coupled with campaigning work by the women's movement and non-governmental organizations, proved to be crucial in provoking government action. Evidence demonstrates that domestic violence is widespread, under-reported, and the level of repeat incidence is high.

In Scotland and across other regions of the UK, a number of trends have been documented (Henderson 1998; Scottish Executive 2000) and it is estimated that up to a third of all women in Scotland experience abuse at some point in their lives (Scottish Executive 2003). According to the report *Faith, Hope and Battering* (Heiskanen and Piispa 1998), 40 per cent of Finnish women reported having experienced male violence (sexual or physical) or threats at some point in their lives. Violence was concentrated in couple relationships that were ongoing or recently dissolved. Where violence was experienced outside of this context, women in two out of three cases knew the assailant. Women rarely sought formal help, with only one in four seeking support and advice from the police, legal services, family centres or crisis lines/women's groups. When help was sought the most common agencies to be approached were healthcare services located in the community, followed by the police and family counselling services. However, most support was gained from friends and other family members (Piispa and Heiskanen 2001). So while legal, health and social services were viewed as potential sources of help they were not readily accessed.

In 2001 the Swedish survey *Slagen Dam* (*Battered Lady*) was published: the first large study of violence against women. It is based on over 7000 responses from women aged between 18 and 64 years of age. The study found that 46 per cent of respondents had been victims of actual or threatened physical or sexual violence, harassment and controlling behaviours since their fifteenth birthday. Approximately 25 per cent had experienced violence during the preceding year, and a third of women who had separated from their partner had been harassed or violated by him after separation. Yet only 15 per cent of the women reported their case to the police. At the same time a review of the legal system and courts found that the overwhelming majority of cases that reached the stage of prosecution were thrown out on the basis of missing evidence: generally due to a lack of witnesses (Pylkkanen 2001). The results of these studies posed a series of challenges to what is often assumed to be Sweden's position as a peaceful country promoting equality and human rights worldwide.

A note of caution should be sounded. It may appear that the prevalence of domestic violence varies between these countries. The definitions employed and questions used in surveys differ, and as a result, so do findings. Nevertheless, these studies provided evidence with which groups and movements could argue for resources, policies and services.

In Finland, the context to debates on violence is framed by trends in homicide and in suicide among men. Finland has some of the highest rates in the EU. Geopolitical tensions about the former Soviet Union have been replaced by concerns about changes to the east of Finland. The trafficking of women and girls has become a social problem that has led to a national programme of policy work on prostitution and the sex industry. A range of initiatives, for example, the position of minors in the sex trade, has followed (Jyrkinen and Karjalainen 2001). Recent media debates about prostitution have also focused concerns on payment for sex (now outlawed in Sweden) and the advertising of sexual services. A number of national newspapers no longer accept such advertisements, as a result of the findings from recent study which concluded that these adverts undermined the rights of women and promoted potentially illegal activities (Laukkanen 2000).

Trends in health in Scotland and Sweden are similar to those in other countries of the EU. Health and socioeconomic inequalities among men and women are generally noteable on the basis of social class. While trends may be similar, actual figures differ. The health status of men and women in Sweden is among the best in the world. In Scotland, certain conditions such as coronary heart disease, stroke and cancer are among the highest in the EU.

Social Movements

In a study of government responses to violence against women it was asserted that: 'the cross-national patterns of government response to violence, which often involves considerable expenditures and substantial legislative change, is quite unlike the patterns scholars discern in relation to women and employment or in the area of family policy' (Weldon 2002: 3). It has been argued that aspects of government responses could 'be meaningfully observed' through an examination of legal reforms on wife battering and sexual assault; the provision of shelters or other forms of emergency housing provision such as crisis centres for victims of sexual assault; government-sponsored programmes to train providers, practitioners, legal and police services, and educate the public; and a central coordinating agency or group for national policies (Weldon 2002: 13). The activities of governments were researched through an overview and ranking of government responses in 36 countries that were defined as 'continuously democratic from 1974–1994'. An assessment was based upon two dimensions: the areas addressed, the more the better (scope) and the point at which a government did so; the earlier the better (timing) (Weldon 2002: 4). In summary, this study concluded that strong, independently organized women's groups and coalitions improve the responsiveness of governments: 'it is women's movement activities who work to get violence against women recognised as a public problem rather than a private affair and thus put it on the public agenda' (Weldon 2002: 195).

Social movements that emerge outside the framework of conventional politics may be described as:

- *defensive*: movements that emphasize romanticized, traditional ways of life perceived to be under threat – for example, organizations that assert family life is breaking down due a decline in the proportion of nuclear families; or,
- *offensive* social movements that assert that society can, and must be, transformed. Offensive social movements aim to tackle repression and generate possibilities for participation and autonomous identities.

Women's Aid might be situated as an offensive social movement as it offers challenges to legislators, professions and services through work on gender, power and domestic violence. At the same time, aspects of the broader women's movement demonstrate tendencies to defensive positions in so far as they retain a concern not to undermine the 'traditional' workings of post-industrial societies. By this I refer to the special claims made for motherhood and the relationship between mothering and working in terms of work-life balance. This has drawn some focus away from caring and interdependency as it tends to emphasize childcare over and above other care needs and care work. This very emphasis upon working mothers reinforces gendered roles and responsibilities. However, a policy with 'low visibility', posing limited challenges to the status quo, can sit alongside prevailing gendered roles and responsibilities and has a greater chance of adoption (Boneparth and Stoper 1988: 42).

Scotland continues to have a strong autonomous women's movement, Sweden less so, and in Finland Church organizations and family groups are more in evidence. As members of the EU these countries have implemented EU directives on equality and they must respond to recommendations such as *The Protection of Women Against Violence* (Council of Europe 2002).

Allies inside government (politicians and policymakers) enable violence against women to be taken up as an issue and placed on policy agendas. While a specific women's policy machinery is not by itself sufficient to produce a governmental response, its existence does strengthen the capacity of autonomous groups and thus governments to respond: 'each factor magnifies the effect of the other and this interaction produced the broadest government responses to violence against women' (Weldon 2002: 196).

Governmental responses

Tackling violence and conflict is crucial to national and global stability and the attainment and maintenance of a civilized society. Yet the greater the tendency in certain societies to manage and control violence, emphasizing the benefits of what Elias (1994) termed the 'civilizing process', the greater the contrast with the challenges posed by violence in intimate relationships. Over the last century the upsurge in international organizations and activities concerned with global and civil conflicts has been remarkable and notable. Concerns about violence in international and public arenas have resulted in a range of initiatives from many governments, keen to establish their credentials as civilized and responsible, as well as to make political and economic gains.

Government in Finland, Scotland and Sweden may be defined as democratic (Freedom House 1997). As democratic countries it might be expected that governments would conduct debates and policy work with a level of transparency. A degree of respect for the rights of citizens might be anticipated, with legislative support for, and public debates, about freedom of speech and association. So, it might also be anticipated that gender and equality would be issues for activity with those concerned about violence represented in the legislature, policy work and government as well as autonomous pressure groups. However, the evidence provided below illustrates that there is no linear relationship between governmental concerns and the content and implementation of policy and service responses.

While these countries may be described as post-industrial, their economic fortunes have varied. Finland, Scotland and Sweden have a number of parallels in geography, and demographic and social trends. These include not dissimilar sizes and dispersal of populations (over 5 million each in Finland and Scotland and 8 million in Sweden); the concentration of around 40 per cent of the population in the south of the country (the localities of Helsinki and Espoo, Edinburgh and Glasgow, and Stockholm and Gothenburg); issues concerning the provision of services in remote and rural hinterlands for sparsely populated areas; and the challenge of social and economic changes at a point when the population is ageing, and solo living, childlessness and family reformation are all on the increase. In these countries women are visible and active in political and public life, although in Scotland this has been greatly enhanced by devolution, which was only achieved in 1997.

Finland achieved independence in 1917, following the Russian Revolution, and remained a largely agrarian society until the 1950s. Fear of possible threats to national security from the former Soviet Union, and more recently from immigration and attendant social problems from the Baltic countries, have left a level of suspicion of countries to the east. There remain historical tensions between Finland and Sweden, with Sweden perceived as more powerful as a result of its stronger international and global relationships. By comparison with Scotland, industrialization in Finland was late, and yet this limited industrial base allowed for flexibility in addressing recent economic shifts. Not so in Scotland, where the successes of early industrialization have left a post-industrial wasteland in a number of localities. The public sector as an employer, and provider of economic incentives, is crucial to economic reconfiguration.

Nordic countries are presumed to have 'woman-friendly' social policies and welfare services. On many indicators of equality between the sexes, these countries are at the top of most league tables and on the whole women appear to do better across the lifecourse than women in, for example, Scotland. Women have gained much from the strong role of the state and the public provision of services (Nousiainen *et al.* 2001). These are countries where centralized, corporatist decision-making structures exist. Given this, it might not be unreasonable to expect that governments and related organizations could coordinate a holistic approach to policies and services. Welfare responses in Scotland and the UK are much less developed. Notable differences are evident between men and women in employment and public life, and there are vocal debates and campaigns on equality. In Finland, where greater equality in public spheres of life is combined with a limited autonomous women's movement, there is limited space in public and political arenas for more passionate debates on gendered social problems such as violence in intimate relationships.

In Finnish social, public and health policies there remains an emphasis on children, and women as 'mothers'. This focus limits debates on, and services for, the diverse experience of women. The model of the worker citizen ensures that governments are grappling with work-life reconciliation and working with employers, professional associations and unions to help parents and carers achieve a balance between caring and employment. Women's labour continues to be undervalued and largely segregated. While pay rates may not differ in Sweden as much as in Scotland, both labour markets demonstrate gender segregation in employment with women over-represented in 'caring' professions and jobs, and under-represented in technology, science and business. Unpaid and paid caring work is still perceived as the domain of women (certainly in terms of the organization and monitoring of care). Informal, unpaid caring work by women is imperative to the continued engagement of adult workers with the labour market and the economy in general (Pylkkanen 2001; McKie *et al.* 2002).

In all three countries there are large rural populations, many of which are struggling to ensure the survival of small communities in remote areas. The recent agrarian past and the high levels of participation of women in education and the labour market following the Second World War have left a heritage of strong, capable Finnish women who fulfil a range of obligations inside and outside the home. Finnish men have been stereotyped as less capable, unhealthy, more likely to be socially isolated and to engage in substance abuse. While women in Scotland are perceived as generally willing to 'multi-task', there is not the same image and notion of the strong female. There are, however, images of the strong drinking, vocal male and these are often linked to notions of masculinities associated with sport. Despite evidence to the contrary, the experience of domestic abuse is commonly associated with excessive consumption of alcohol among working-class males. This leads to the conceptualization of women as victims, and yet, as agents of their own fortunes who should leave an abusive relationship (McKie *et al.* 2002). There are parallels here, as in all three countries the agency of women who survive violence is called into question (Why do they stay? Why can't they leave? If it's so bad no one would stay!). There is limited discussion of the imbalances of power between men and women in intimate relationships. Further, numerous images of violence in culture and the media have reinforced associations between violence and masculinities (Connell 2002).

Liberal notions of equality between men and women emphasize homogeneity (Nousiainen *et al.* 2001). In Finland, the idea of the individual citizen exercising her rights to be free from violence must, however, be framed within concerns about divorce, family breakdown and levels of violence in society *per se* (Carling *et al.* 2002). These latter two factors are of particular concern for all countries but have resulted in specific approaches in Finland, framed around the concept of, and services connected with, the family (Piispa and Heiskanen 2001). Services and policies focus upon the responsibilities of parenthood and family solidarities, promoting reconciliation in an apparently gender-neutral fashion and concentrating on the potential for fusion in families.

Having suggested that there is merit in examining those countries where political structures are broadly similar in terms of the principles of electoral democracy, there are contrasts in approaches to tackling violence against women. In Finland, continued adherence to the concept of gender neutrality in legislation, policies and activities restricts appreciation of gender differences in power and violence. By contrast an acceptance of the gender-based nature of such violence has formed the basis to Scottish activities. In Sweden the adoption of the theoretical frame of the 'normalization of violence' has had a marked impact on attitudes and policies, resulting in the acceptance of the material and discursive nature of gender-based violence. At this point further detail on policies and debates in each of the three countries is offered.

Finland: gender neutrality – disembodying policies

The concept of gender neutrality forms the basis to Finnish legislation and many of its initiatives and services. The meaning and operation of the concept of gender neutrality – genderless gender – (Ronkainen 2001: 45) – is 'characterised by a gender-neutral rhetoric on the one hand and the importance of sexualisation of embodied individuals on the other hand'. Gender neutrality might be a goal for many people concerned with equality and human rights. However, some academics in Finland argue that the rhetoric of gender neutrality, encouraging a normative individualism, leads to a failure to theorize and act upon the gendered nature of violence and power in relationships and families (Nousiainen *et al.* 2001; Ronkainen 2001). As a concept, gender neutrality leaves women and women's groups in a severely restricted space from which to explore and act upon the gendered nature of violence.

The possibility of genderless human rights – of equality in human rights – is an attractive goal for many (Glover 1999). However, there remains 'differentiated citizenship' (Young 1990: 251). There is limited recognition of gender-based inequities and a reluctance to analyse power between genders, across generations and within relationships and families. Finnish legislation and policies are based upon liberal notions of citizenship that include the protection of freedom, family and private life and individuality. The individual right to not be violated, or discriminated against, has not been understood as being equally compelling for legislative activities as other issues addressed by, for example, the European Court of Human Rights, that seek to enshrine access to courts, fair trials and informed consent. With liberal notions of human rights, and the attendant focus on rights in public aspects of life, the private/public dichotomy remains strong. This also promotes a focus upon individual roles and responsibilities, and links to the way in which in Finnish society and policies, women have been framed as strong, and capable of working and caring. Finnish social policies have begun to promote better fatherhood and support for fathers as a solution to a number of problems in families and relationships, including violence.

The publication of the strategy document *From Beijing to Finland: The Plan of Action for the Promotion of Gender Equality of the Government of Finland* (Ministry of Social Affairs 1997) prompted research including:

- *Faith, Hope, Battering: A Survey of Men's Violence Against Women* (Heiskanen and Piispa 1998); and
- *The Price of Violence: The Costs of Men's Violence Against Women in Finland* (Piispa and Heiskanen 2001).

These studies, funded by Statistics Finland and the Council for Equality, provided clear evidence on the prevalence of domestic violence and its economic costs, and identified the need for a systematic approach to support victims and address wider attitudes on violence against women. Many politicians, agencies and groups were shocked by the results of these surveys. After all this is a country and society that prides itself on being at the forefront of promoting women's rights and equality. Across Finnish society there remains a strong adherence to the heterosexual family. With a divorce rate of over 50 per cent, governments have been concerned to promote family mediation and joint custody with limited consideration of men's violence as a factor in the breakdown of relationships (Hearn 2002).

There is no strong tradition of autonomous women's refuges as there is in other Nordic countries such as Sweden, and in Scotland. Women can go to family crisis centres that are open to both sexes but where priority is given to women and children. In centres and services there are evident pressures for those who have experienced violence to participate in family therapy. This is a mechanism that has been criticized for failing to consider power differentials between men and women. Presumptions abound that women will have greater responsibilities for caring and family networks. With few independent women's groups and campaigns, and limited development of feminist or women-only refuges or services, it remains that family mediation can appear to be the main source of support to women experiencing violence.

In 1997, the Minister of Social Affairs and Health launched programmes for the 'Prevention of Prostitution' and 'Violence Against Women'. The National Research and Development Centre (commonly known as STAKES) implemented the content of the programmes with work completed in late 2002. The overall aim of work undertaken in the Programme for the Prevention of Violence Against Women was to raise awareness of violence and of its extent and impact on individuals and society. After much debate and campaigns by Church and women's groups, the basis to the programme of work was that 'when it comes to "family violence" it is pertinent to speak of men's violence against women' (STAKES 1998). Ironically, while basing the programme of work on gender and power, other materials, information and activities employed gender-neutral language. Partly, this reflects accepted practices of gender neutrality but also demonstrates how difficult it is to have a gendered analysis of power and violence activated.

The overall programme of work included projects that involved:

- locally coordinated services;
- service provision that is sensitive to the needs of victims;

- development of programmes and treatment for violent men;
- developing and implementing multi-professional cooperation.

The project involved multi-professional teams, located in 12 regions, which disseminated information, delivered training courses and devised and shared models for practice. Six subcommittees developed and ran work on specialist areas of work including:

- service network development;
- provision of study material and guidebooks;
- development of research;
- development of legislation;
- media and information planning;
- violence against women who have immigrated to Finland.

The Finnish Academy funds an ongoing programme of research on power and violence that is examining gender, social and psychological factors in the practices of violence in Finland. It remains to be seen how far research findings will impact upon policy, legislative and service development.

Scotland: a multi-agency, centralized approach to abuse

In 1999, with the advent of the first Parliament in Scotland for 300 years, a coalition of centre-left political parties in government emerged. This coalition has forged a left of centre route to tackling social problems. The role of an active autonomous women's movement and voluntary sector, combined with the election of sympathetic members of Parliament, coalesced to form a national partnership approach firmly based on gendered notions of violence.

The autonomous women's movement had campaigned for several decades for a concerted, multi-agency plan on violence against women but it was not until 1998 that a consultative document was published on action across government departments (Scottish Office 1998). Again, partly based on the need to meet international obligations, this was revised and formally published in 2001 (Scottish Executive 2001). The year preceding this, the *National Strategy to Address Domestic Abuse in Scotland* (Scottish Executive 2000) was launched, and this offered an overarching strategic approach and action plan to include provision across sectors and organizations, as well as government departments. In all of these documents the premise was clear: namely violence against women is gender based. Fear of violence undermines the position and confidence of women, even if they have not personally experienced violence.

Despite evidence of the gendered nature of much of this violence, an analysis based upon gender and power is not a universally accepted one. Some have criticized this approach arguing that women can be violent too

(Denfeld 1997) and it has been asserted that an ongoing focus upon the violence of men in families can actually encourage further breakdowns in relationships and families. Further, an association between gender and feminism has become problematic for some researchers and policymakers who are reluctant to use the term 'feminism' for fear of being labelled unduly radical and, as a result, they fear, not taken seriously.

The philosophy underpinning the strategic plans are (Scottish Executive 2001: 4):

- *Provision*: to provide adequate services to deal with the consequences of violence against women, and to help women rebuild their lives.
- *Protection*: to protect victims and potential victims from repeat victimization or harassment by perpetrators.
- *Prevention*: to prevent, remove or diminish the risk of violence by various means, ranging from promoting change in social attitudes, to creating physical and other barriers to the commission of violent acts.

The Partnership Strategy (Scottish Executive 2000) required local authorities to establish multi-agency partnerships and develop locality strategies and action plans. This was followed in June 2001 by the establishment of a national group to take a strategic overview of developments and hold an annual review, bringing local and national players together and determining next priorities. The group included the Minister for Social Justice, representatives from the police, health services, education, local government, equalities agency and department, legal and the voluntary sector.

Under the broad heading of provision the Scottish Executive cited:

- Domestic Abuse Service Development Fund, which has had £6 million to allocate to projects, with a requirement for matched funding from local partners and an evaluation of activities. By early 2003 there were 57 projects funded under this scheme. An evaluation of the first round of this funding is currently underway.
- Allocation of £12 million over four years for the further development of the women-only refuge network. Funding provides for additional and improved spaces – for example, self-contained accommodation for women and children with additional support needs. Research on the work of the refuge network is ongoing.
- A free national telephone helpline.
- Funding for children's workers. These posts were developed to meet identified needs and to offer specific support and services for children.
- Strategy on training for professionals and workers.

Work on protection has concentrated on the review of legislation. The Protection from Abuse(s) Act came into force in 2001, and enhanced protection for women while clarifying and strengthening the work of the criminal justice system. The Criminal Justice Bill and the Sexual Offences

(Procedures and Evidence) (Scotland) Act 2002 reinforced aspects of the protection legislation on a range of offences, most notably sexual offences.

Lastly, the publication of a national strategy on prevention (Scottish Executive 2003) heralded a programme of work that seeks to:

- Stop abuse before it happens by changing attitudes which excuse or condone it. This work targets the whole population but with an emphasis on children and young people and is termed 'primary prevention'.
- Work that seeks to reduce the incidence and effects of domestic abuse. The focus is on women and children who have experienced violence and the men who use violence. This work is known as 'secondary prevention'.

This definition of primary prevention offers the possibility of addressing the social practices that pose barriers to tackling and challenging domestic violence, within an ethos characterized by respect for human rights and the development of capacity to make ethical and moral decisions. In particular the strategy calls for multi-agency programmes to 'challenge myths, cultural beliefs and stereotypes which help to sustain a toleration of violence' and 'challenge abusing men to accept responsibility for their behaviour' (Scottish Executive 2003: 6). These should be critical dimensions of any strategy. Advice is offered on materials to adopt and adapt, and on the potential role of local authorities, education and other departments, and relevant organizations.

Yet there is little discussion of wider cultural and social dimensions and individual responsibilities, with secondary prevention concentrating on acts of domestic violence and the implications of these. Few resources are available. This strategy is a useful and necessary, but sadly limited, start to prevention work.

A national network of domestic abuse coordinators and multi-agency domestic abuse forums underpins and links the autonomous women's movement and statutory sector. Through these mechanisms communication, campaigning and service provision are regularly reviewed and government-led strategies are adopted and adapted to local needs. While there is no programme of research akin to that of the work funded by the Finnish Academy, many academics have been involved in research work to underpin debates and policy developments (e.g. Scott *et al.* 2004). The gendered based definition of domestic abuse in Scotland forms the spine to debates and work.

Sweden: challenging the normalization of violence

Contemporary Swedish policies and service developments on violence against women illuminate the emphasis upon achieving greater equality through social welfare. From the 1920s the aim of social democratic governments has been the social welfare of the population in the 'people's home' (*Folkhemmet*) based upon a just distribution of goods and services. The place of the 'home' is strong in Swedish culture and social and employment policies promote a corporatist approach to welfare. Until the 1990s the idea of the 'good state' formed the context to support for women and children. Subsequently, an analysis of continuing levels of inequalities between men and women and across social classes caused a shift to individual rights as a mechanism for tackling differentials in power and resources. This was further supported by EU legislation and general trends in international organizations and UN conventions on violence and women: for example, the Beijing Platform of Action which also emphasized individual rights.

Partly through addressing the recommendations of studies demonstrating inequalities, and through the need to fulfil obligations in international law, Sweden introduced a major programme of legislation, service and educational developments. Underpinning this range of initiatives was the remodelling of understandings of gendered violence (Pylkkanen 2001) established in what has become known as Women's Peace Reform (*kvinnofrid*) (Nordborg and Niemi-Kiesilainen 2001). This remodelling was based upon research in the field of women's studies and the theory of the 'normalization process of violence'. According to this theory, violence is viewed as a continuum in which severe and less severe forms of violence and intimidation fluctuate. Violence – the experience and the avoidance of it – frames the lives of women and girls (Pylkkanen 2001). Women position themselves according to 'rules' of avoiding or managing violence. This theory had a major impact on Swedish policy and legislation because, by recognizing the social construction of gender and power relations, the language of the law has moved from gender-neutral to gender-specific – a major change in policy and political circles.

This focus on women's everyday experiences challenged previous research that quantified acts of violence as largely physical in nature, but failed to document or explore the gendered dimensions of ongoing patterns of abuse (Lundgren *et al.* 2002: 11). A new understanding of the issues has been generated in the last two decades. In the 1980s, laws relating to sexual offences were changed and visiting bans were introduced to protect those experiencing harassment. A Commission on Violence to Women was established in 1993 and the Commission overhauled the relevant penal code, introducing a bill, the Protection of Women's Integrity, in 1997. The effect of this Act was to raise the penalty value of acts which, 'viewed separately, are relatively minor but when repeated may lead to substantial violation of the victim's integrity' (Lundgren *et al.* 2002: 13).

Governments in Sweden have worked for many years to promote peace and human rights across the globe, working with a range of international and non-governmental organizations. Human rights only came to prominence in domestic discourses, policies and politics in the mid-1990s. The interpretation of human rights is less concerned with the protection of the integrity of the individual, and more with the portrayal of violence against women as a violation of the welfare state and democracy of the country. This, combined with a greater acceptance of intervention in private homes, has greatly enhanced the development and delivery of legislation and policies that are premised upon structural interpretations of gender and violence against women.

The Minister for Equality Affairs coordinates measures that arise from the Violence Against Women Act. Legal reforms have included:

- nationwide training for professionals;
- improved professional education with a call that questions of gender equality and violence against women should be emphasized in education;
- increased financial support for women's shelters and the national centre for battered and raped women;
- a crisis telephone line for women.

Protection for women and girls is enhanced through:

- criminalizing the ongoing nature of violence and the aggravating nature if repeated, now known as 'gross violation of integrity';
- prohibition on the purchase of sexual services;
- widening the definition of rape and an ongoing review of sexual offences;
- specific regulations on genital mutilation;
- social welfare legislation to ensure that local service responsibilities are made clear and that local plans and guidelines are drawn up and implemented by the National Board of Health and Welfare.

Preventive and planning measures include.

- public sector and related agencies drawing up action plans with the overarching aim of increasing efforts to prevent violence;
- improved statistics and research work on the scope and meaning of violence against women;
- introducing and ensuring a gender perspective in criminological research;
- an audit of police work on violence against women;
- a survey and evaluation of treatment methods for men, and a study of electronic monitoring of men who breach a restraining order;
- development of work concerning violence against women and prostitutes that will seek to 'expand competence and improvement of methods within social and health services' (Swedish Government 1999: 5);
- a range of measures and investigations on the trafficking of women;
- information for those seeking residence permits;
- support for voluntary organizations including youth, immigrant and disabled women and men against violence;

- increased funds to the UN to support ongoing human rights work.

The National Council for the Protection of Women Against Violence acts as an advisory and exchange body offering support for various aspects of policy, practice and planning work. A basis to these activities was the exploration of how the theory of the normalization of violence was understood and could be adopted in policies and practices. A review highlighted the need for ongoing monitoring of the implementation and the everyday interpretations of legislation, often the point at which the spirit of the law is dissipated. Issues to emerge included the need for concerted and detailed local planning to enhance information collation and exchange, and for further access to services. In addition, the introduction of relevant subjects to the education and training of health, social, legal, police and theological professionals has led to changes in university and professional assessment and examination systems.

Summary

Surveys in each of these countries revealed high and increasing levels of domestic violence. These results were greeted with some surprise, if not a little suspicion, in all three countries. How could there be so much domestic violence in peaceful, civilized societies whose governments are actively engaged in managing global conflicts and promoting human rights? Examining the amount, nature and trends of the violence also established the overwhelming gendered nature of domestic violence; of men's violence to known women.

To summarize the basis to the three countries' approaches to violence:

- The concept of gender neutrality in Finland is premised upon gendered assumptions about roles and responsibilities, largely negating the very idea of neutrality.
- In Scotland, the women's movement and the government have promoted a broader definition of violence through the use of the term 'domestic abuse', emphasizing psychological and physical dimensions, and through campaigns drawing attention to the gendered and classless nature of abuse.
- Acceptance of the theory of the normalization of violence in government and policy circles heralded a dramatic change in the range of legislation and services in Sweden.

With regards to domestic violence, the pace of response rose rapidly in the 1990s and this would appear to be linked to national and international calls for action often, but not always, initiated by campaigns from broad coalitions of the women's and human rights movements. Parallels are evident as governments in each of these countries have emphasized the need for local planning and coordination, appropriate guidance, education and training for service planners and providers, with these activities underpinned by media campaigns seeking to raise awareness of violence in relationships.

Across the case study countries contrasts are evident in the theorization of gender, violence and families. In Scotland and Sweden, academic research, the women-only refuge movement, and related autonomous women's groups, have been successful in securing the adoption of a gender-based definition of domestic violence and additional resources for refuge provision. This is not to say that gender-based domestic violence will remain centre stage without continued agitation and research. There remains uneasiness among, for example, healthcare professionals, many of whom question their skills and abilities in identifying domestic abuse. Further, in Finland, continued adherence to the concept of gender neutrality, coupled with a recent focus on fatherhood, has made it problematic to consider domestic violence as both a material and discursive practice imbued with differentials in power and gender. This is further complicated by the images of women in Finland, especially mothers, as strong, stoic and selfless.

As democracies these countries are linked through legislation and directives of the EU and adhere to the obligations and spirit of UN declarations on the elimination of violence. While recognition of the topic has grown, the basis of initiatives varies somewhat, reflecting differing conceptualizations of gender and power. At a superficial level the concept of gender neutrality might seem to offer great potential for equality in all aspects of public and private life. An unwillingness to recognize that gender neutrality (and related services such as family therapy) are premised upon gendered assumptions about roles, results in inadequate and narrowly-framed policies and activities. The limited nature of the autonomous women's movement and women-only services in Finland must also have a bearing on discourses and policies. Much has been achieved in terms of equality for the individual but in terms of gender equality the gaze remains firmly outside the family. In short, there is extremely limited appreciation of the notion of 'family practices' and how these reflect the multi-dimensional workings of those forging relationships in families.

By contrast, in Sweden, the acceptance of the theory of the normalization of violence has allowed for a stronger material and discursive basis to the analysis of domestic violence. There is also greater tolerance for state intervention in the family and family practices. The support those social policies offer to many women has also been a key element in campaigns for the retention of a close relationship between the state, individuals and families. Yet the relationship between women and the state has resulted in a highly segregated labour market. Many women prefer the flexibility and security offered by employment in the public sector, thus reinforcing the relationship between the female worker citizen and the female carer citizen. The study of the legal support for individual human rights is less well developed (Svensson 2001: 72).

Violence against women is a social problem that gave the new Scottish Parliament the opportunity to achieve cross-party and multi-agency working at a time of increased public and international concern about violence in general. Nonetheless, responses in Scotland illuminate the classic British dichotomy of private and public spheres of activity. While there is an analysis based upon the gendered nature of violence in families, this can be difficult to realize as welfare policies and services are disjointed and each works with differing statutory responsibilities. For example, social work has statutory responsibilities for the protection of children and the police service has responsibilities to detect and, if possible, charge the perpetrators of violent acts. Nevertheless, local domestic violence fora are a welcome and extremely useful development as they bring together the multiple agencies in health and social care, and police and legal services, that can provide support for women experiencing violence.

Responses, and the basis and content of these, illustrate both overlapping and diverging ideas on the practices of families, gender and violence. The emphasis upon the responsibilities and obligations of the individual in Finland leaves little room for an analysis premised on the concept of family practices (Morgan 1996). And while most governments may be working towards an explanatory critique in so far as knowledge of violence in general and violence in families in particular is now framed as a challenge to human rights, few actively address the gendered basis to the workings of power and privacy in families. The Women's Peace Reform in Sweden is notable as an overarching conceptual framework that accepts and works with the lifetime experiences women have of violence. In summary, this frames violence in families, public spaces and cultural images as gendered. The impact is both spatial and temporal as women anticipate and attempt to avoid or manage experiences of violence and violations (Pylkkanen 2001).

International obligations as proffered by the UN and EU have brought violence against women to the attention of many governments, necessitating action. Global relations and shifting boundaries have also placed issues of immigration and asylum seekers on national and international agendas on violence against women. Thus the relative isolation and homogeneity of both Finland and Scotland (in comparison to Sweden) is gradually being changed. Nevertheless, the intersection of class, gender and race continues to be premised upon historical constructions of masculinities and femininities, making change in attitudes and service provision a longer-term process than many would wish (Hearn 2002).

Domestic violence constitutes and reinforces 'a form of social division and social inequality' (Hearn 1998: 207). Violence against women is central to the subordination of women. Domestic violence is particularly pernicious as it challenges self-identification with, and the safety and security of, family, home and intimate relationships (Elman 1996; Kelly 1999; Nousiainen *et al.* 2001). Until the role of violence in the (re)creation of patriarchy is challenged then the achievement of full citizenship and human rights for women will remain elusive (United Nations 1995; Elman 1996; Lister 1997; Ronkainen 2001; Hearn 2002; World Health Organization 2002).

The women's movement and human rights organizations remain vigilant as violence against women is the most pervasive violation in the world. To provide relevant and additional services for women and children is important, but this addresses the *consequences* of violence in families and only when that violence becomes visible. Domestic violence can be obscured in the construction of politics and policy in an almost taken for granted manner in so far as the gendered structuring of knowledge and policy can focus upon the victims and survivors. Limited resources, historical and cultural constructions and the failure to link meanings and actions to social and gender practices in families can lead to a deconstruction of violence, reinforcing the idea that it is perpetrated by the rogue individual.

5

The ambiguities of elder abuse: older women and domestic violence

Introduction

> Elder abuse and neglect is the latest discovery in the field of familial violence.
>
> (Bennett and Kingston 1993: 1)

This assertion was offered in 1993. In the intervening years a number of researchers, practitioners and policymakers have set about tackling this 'discovery', and addressing the implications for services and for society more generally. More than a decade on, however, there remains limited reflection upon, and attention given to, the abuse of older people. When that abuse is gendered and originates in intimate relationships it is further marginalized from debates and activities. In recent years there has been a notable growth in research and policy work on the experiences and implications of ageing. Less attention has been paid to violence among intimates who are older.

In many post-industrial countries there has been a tendency to emphasize issues and services for children and to encourage social research that will provide the evidence to underpin public policies. In many societies there remains the thesis that children are our future and thus require particular and specific attention. When rationing of resources and services occurs, the needs of children are generally placed above those of other groups in the population. Children are vulnerable, and do need nurturing, care and guidance. But this focus can, and does, promote the idea that older people should expect less, and should put the needs of those younger than themselves above their own. Demographic trends suggest that the needs of older people will become paramount in the next decade, and increasingly prominence is given to these issues.

Like much violence experienced by those who are economically, physically or socially dependent on others, it is those who are in positions of trust and intimate relationships who are most likely to perpetrate violence – namely partners, relatives, parents and friends. In response to evidence on sources of violence there has been a debate on the rights of children and the need for specific services to protect children. While much needed, the debate and resultant laws and policies have created some contradictions in perception and experience. Attention to the safety of children is surrounded by moral panics concerned with 'stranger danger', and these are actively promoted in many quarters of the media with the implication that strangers are the main perpetrators of child sex abuse and murders. Stranger danger for older people is linked to con artists and burglars, with attendant fears of violence. Particular fears are reserved for the threat of violent beatings, perpetrated by strangers trying to steal money or items of property. These crimes do take place but remain unusual.

In an analysis of 2400 complaints to the UK charity Action on Elder Abuse (2002) (www.elderabuse.org.uk), almost half of the reported abuse was perpetrated by relatives, 11 per cent by a friend, and 28 per cent by a paid worker. In two thirds of these cases abuse took place in the person's home, with just over 20 per cent in either a nursing home or residential setting. These findings challenge myths that the abuse of older people is more likely to be perpetrated in residential settings by those paid to care. By implication, this promotes the idea that unpaid care provided by relatives is less likely to result in violence and abuse. Key elements of this myth, namely the location for care (outside the home) and the relationship (between paid carer and the cared for) emphasize a distance from families, homes and familial networks. The home as a location for violence and family members as possible perpetrators can seem distant when abuse in residential settings is presumed.

This chapter explores the contingencies and ambiguities of growing older as they manifest themselves in the experience, reporting and analysis of abuse. The chapter opens with a discussion of definitions and the exploration of some fundamental questions. How might we refer to older people? What terms might be used to cite the many dimensions of physical, psychological and socioeconomic violences perpetrated against older people? Why has it taken so long for what is commonly termed elder abuse to come onto the agenda for policy and research? And what of domestic violence and older women? Subsequently, the family and community context to growing older is analysed through a consideration of boundaries, solidarities and assumptions.

Despite the acknowledgement of elder abuse as a problem, there remains limited reflection, theorization and action. Inevitable and growing dependency, in societies dominated by market economies, leads many people to feel uneasy about, even fear, old age. With increasing pressures on the public sector provision of services, families are often expected to provide support either through a combination of unpaid caring work or the sourcing and resourcing of formal care services (Wilson 2000). Familial provision of care emphasizes economic reliance across generations and yet can form a shield to the prejudice and exploitation of older people in families, and more generally.

Definitions and debates

It is a truism that the manner in which we examine social problems is shaped by the definitions employed and the theories adopted. Responses are in turn dictated by contemporary policy priorities and resource allocations (Estes *et al.* 2003). The contested nature of definitions of families, violence and social change was considered in Part 1. In earlier chapters it was noted that debates on the term 'domestic violence' have profound implications for the identification, recording and analysis of abuse. Likewise, the abuse of older women is dogged by debates on how to consider age, gender and violence.

First, age and ageism. At what age is someone considered 'elderly' or 'old'? For most governments old age is linked to the end of active involvement in paid employment and marks the point of access to pensions. A retirement age of 65 for men was introduced in Britain under the 1908 Pensions Act, when average life expectancy at birth was, allowing for socioeconomic inequities, about 50. By 2000 life expectancy in the UK for men had risen to 75 and to 80 for women. A baby girl born in the early twenty-first century in France or Japan, the two countries with the highest life expectancy, has a 50/50 chance of living until 100.

We may be living longer but in market economies do we work for more years? Britain has one of the lowest participation rates of older people in the labour market in the post-industrial world. Only 5.2 per cent of over-65s are in paid employment, compared with 12.4 per cent in the USA, 10.2 per cent in Sweden and 22.1 per cent in Japan. It should be noted that these figures conceal marked social class and geographical inequities in longevity and participation. Labour market participation in later years is often skewed in favour of those in professional and managerial jobs. Inequalities among older people reflect opportunities and constraints experienced across the lifecourse. Added to that is ageism and assumptions about the abilities and capacities of older people. These lead to discrimination on the basis of age. For older women there is the double jeopardy of the intersection of age and gender.

Pressure groups – for example, Help the Aged and Age Concern – and companies that provide specific services for older people, challenge negative assumptions and emphasize the potential for independence. One of the more pernicious assumptions is that being old brings with it increased costs for governments and families. The main governmental and personal costs associated with social and healthcare are concentrated among those aged 80 and over. The age at which increased costs become worthy of note continues to rise.

Despite these debates and activities there is still no term that describes later life in a manner that is without negative connotations (Bytheway 1994). The term 'older people' distinguishes on the basis of age. It does so in a manner that suggests a homogenous group with similar experiences and potential futures. It also blurs the thorny boundary of economic activity and retirement. 'Elders' has been used interchangeably with 'older' on the basis that 'elder' could promote respect for the experiences and knowledge of previous years. Contemporary foci on youthful images, negative discourses of ageing and the promotion of services and lifestyles to lessen the progress of ageing, render the term 'elder' problematic. No matter which term is used, there continues to be a view of older people as a 'bloc of the population' (Biggs *et al.* 1995: 2). This is dangerous for there are gender, social class and ethnic differences in the experiences of ageing, and of abuse. Over recent decades, researchers and theorists have spoken of 'elder abuse', and while noting concerns with this term it will be used in this chapter.

The second major debate concerns violence in later life. The violence experienced by older people can range from the physical to the psychological. As some older people become vulnerable and dependent on bodily, emotional and economic support from relatives and friends, violence can include the wilful neglect of basic care needs. The potential for other generations to inherit property or income from older relatives can result in the control and manipulation of economic and social support, a further form of abuse.

Families are encouraged to provide support for vulnerable relatives, whether they reside nearby or at a distance. Friends and neighbours can offer support but with age comes diminishing social and friendship networks. Often families are creating a patchwork quilt of care and emotional support (Wilson 2000). Presumptions about trust and intimacy in family life may form a screen, and as a result it may be asserted that some abuses are sanctioned by social policies and wider societal presumptions. As with other forms of violence in families, the physical abuses of older people are easier to identify than those of a psychological or economic nature. In addition, older people may experience active neglect – withdrawal of care – and passive neglect – the failure to fulfil all or part of caring obligations. Care in the community is proposed as a means of addressing vulnerabilities that families and the private sector cannot manage, but this mixed economy of sources of care can be difficult to organize and resource, leaving many psychologically and physically vulnerable (Goodin and Gibson 2002: 246).

So is violence perpetrated by intimate partners elder abuse or domestic abuse? The abuse of older people is a complex phenomenon (Biggs *et al.* 1995: 35). Elder abuse can also be described as 'granny battering' or 'elder mistreatment' (Baker 1975). However, it is the term 'elder abuse' that has achieved acceptance by government, pressure groups and providers of elder care (Biggs *et al.* 1995). Contact with health and social care services is often the point at which identification of elder abuse occurs. Subsequent interventions are generally based upon securing the safety of the person experiencing abuse; necessary, but a further example of containment in so far as the vulnerable person becomes the focus for action. However, health and social care services are charged with statutory duties that reflect governmental policies and societal concerns, and currently these emphasize securing the safety of the patient or client. The need for a multi-agency and broader approach is promoted by the work of, for example, local domestic violence fora and similar frameworks but these are not in existence in all regions and countries.

Reviewing literature, policies and services, it could appear that domestic violence is only experienced by women under 50. Literature on older women and domestic violence is largely found in the area of elder abuse. This violence is considered as a subset of elder abuse in which the woman is framed as vulnerable, requiring protection and care from others. By contrast, the major analyses of domestic violence consider the gendered abuse of power. In elder abuse the concepts of gender and power, and the relevance of these for analysis and future work can be lost. Access to health and social care services, with a focus upon health and well-being, can promote an agenda of risk management, emphasizing the attainment of safety, over and above any reflections upon relationships, gender and age (Sedger 2001; Scott et al. 2004: 12).

The recording of all forms of violence in families and relationships is limited. Often definitions and identification are organized to meet the needs of specific services rather than national or international recording. As with domestic violence, few services that may detect elder abuse 'look at the characteristics of those abused older people and their family situations as they are known to the social and health care services' (Bennett and Kingston 1993: 153). Noting that abuse and neglect is evident among differing ethnic and socioeconomic groups, as with domestic violence, many commentators and researchers have called for documentation and consideration of social and familial circumstances (Bennett and Kingston 1993). These calls herald a growing acceptance in policy and research circles of the need for a critical analysis of families and violence, and the boundaries between care, gender, violence and intimate relationships (Biggs et al. 1995: 75; Scott et al. 2004).

Families, gender and prevalence

As with domestic violence it is difficult to determine prevalence, as there are limited studies to draw upon. Studies have excluded, or under-represented, the experiences of the very frail and psychologically confused, those residing in deprived localities and ethnic groups. These are the very groups in which it might be anticipated that abuse is less likely to be reported or detected. From what limited research there is, there are unique experiences and patterns of abuse and neglect among some of these groups (Wilson 2000).

A review of available studies illuminates the range of definitions and the research methods employed. In an interview study of elder abuse undertaken in Boston (Pillemer and Finkelhor 1988), it was concluded that 58 per cent of cases were of spouse abuse and 24 per cent of abuse by adult children. Physical mistreatment was the most common form of abuse. There were about the same number of male and female victims and no apparent relationship between age or economic status and the risk of abuse. If a national survey were to produce similar results then around 1 million people in the USA would have experienced some form of elder abuse. By contrast, a study in Canada (Podnicks 1992) found material and chronic verbal abuse were most widespread. A survey in Britain comprised structured interviews with 600 people aged 65 and over, and 1366 adults in households in regular contact with an older person. One in 20 reported some type of abuse but only 1 in 50 reported physical abuse (Ogg and Bennett 1992).

The component of this latter study in which adult members of households are asked about their involvement in and attitudes to abuse, has been criticized. For most, it would be socially unacceptable to admit to perpetrating any form of abuse, especially physical abuse. Likewise, those experiencing abuse may not report it due to social taboos, fears of further abuse and concerns about who else may care for them. It would not be unreasonable to presume, as with domestic abuse, that studies underreport elder abuse and the experience of domestic violence among older women.

Women dominate older age groups and so a gender perspective is imperative. They are over-represented in global statistics on poverty in old age. In some cultures women are perceived as a drain, even an embarrassment, in widowhood. Older women can suffer a unique range of social and economic sanctions and problems. The emphasis upon youthfulness, and coupledom, further marginalizes older women and older women who are single. Older women, as a group, experience the double jeopardy of negative images of gender and ageing, and, for many a limited income. The relationship between policy and gender might be summarized as follows: 'Just as few feminists would now rely wholly on a universal approach to citizenship rights, with no distinction between men and women, so elders and their pressure groups need reforms targeted at older men and women as well as universal reforms aimed at equality for all'. (Wilson 2000: 6).

As with other forms of violence in families, there remains a reluctance to involve statutory services and take legal proceedings. Little use is made of legal sanctions in the identification or management of elder abuse. This is due in part to limited legal statutes and legislation and inadequate knowledge and use of these. Violence against older women may be domestic violence and refuges offer them available places regardless of personal circumstances. However, the presence of children does ease access to services for women experiencing violence. Those without children may feel that women with dependants should be prioritized and offered support first (Scott *et al.* 2004).

Moving on from violent relationships is particularly complicated and exhausting for older people. A move may fracture networks, constructed over time, that provide social and emotional support. Generally, moving on will necessitate leaving a home built up over many years. Further, the financial and housing considerations, combined with limited employment opportunities for older women, can pose a complex array of economic and social barriers to 'starting again'. The contradictions are evident. Reverence for older people, demonstrated in many social practices in public and private spaces, exists alongside an averted gaze to potential abuses within the family, and to women who may be vulnerable and frail (Wilson 2000: 144). I would argue, indeed, that older women who experience domestic violence grapple with a triple jeopardy of assumptions premised upon gender, age and intimate relationships:

> Consideration must be given to the consequences of defining the type of abuse by age as the only criterion. The literature points to the deferential need for assessment of violence directed towards older women, in particular assessing for past history of violence in the relationship, differentiating between age related dependency and fragility and helplessness resulting from issues to do with life stages (less employment opportunities) and the impact of domestic violence on women's capacity to take charge of their lives.
> (Morgan Disney and Associates 2000)

Older women are often dependent on others. Dimensions of dependency can include income gained through a partner's pension; to access and ownership of housing; the receipt or provision of care; and emotional and social esteem that, as a result of prolonged trauma, may be low. Women with an impairment, whether physical or psychological, are especially vulnerable to prolonged abuse and may consider themselves to be so dependent upon their abuser that any thought of disclosure becomes too traumatic to consider. Further, the impact of sexual violence is rarely considered, and older women are often presumed to have limited engagement in sexual activity. Same-sex relationships among older women remain a taboo topic. However, evidence demonstrates that sexual violence takes place and older women are vulnerable to sexual taunts and abuse. In sexual violence the triple jeopardy and intersection of age, gender and relationships can become especially pronounced.

The barriers to disclosure are similar for all women, regardless of age. In addition, however, older women may be reluctant to disclose violence as they feel too ashamed or are fearful of being offered or cajollged into institutional care. Shame, as noted in Chapter 3, is an emotion that women experience in a profound and gendered manner and such feelings maybe pronounced for older women.

Boundaries, solidarities and assumptions

The growing number of professional and support groups, and companies concerned with the care of older people outside residential settings, coupled with the scrutiny of violence in families, has enhanced the potential to identify elder abuse (Bennett and Kingston 1993). While in recent years the topic of domestic violence and older women has received increased attention, it remains a marginal one in both the general study of violence in families and in gender and women's studies. This partly reflects the complex characteristics of this problem and the range of people and services that might be involved in its identification and management. For example, the development of policies on care in the community – namely, the ethos that care is best provided in familial, social and economic networks in and around the home – can present tensions and challenges for families. Should families feel obligated to provide support in the community? Are such policies conceived in terms of idealized notions of strong supportive families? What happens when a partner is a carer *and* the abuser?

With regards to families, communities and care services are situated in a variety of ways. Violent behaviour is treated differently if it emerges in public or quasi-public settings (e.g. residential care), as opposed to the private spaces of home and families. These boundaries, while permeable, continue to draw upon familial solidarities in so far as families, 'the private sphere', are perceived as locations in which safety should be offered and therefore limited surveillance is required. Interdependency between communities, families and services might be presumed but is not always evident. Indeed, the very interplay between these groups and individuals can pose barriers to the reporting of, and challenges to, violence.

Concerns about the costs and practicalities of providing adequate care for older people are ever more vocal. What may be termed the 'welfare contract' (that is, the relationship between the state and citizen in which welfare systems provide a minimum level of income and services, combined with support from families and friends) is under threat in so far as policies and families can no longer be relied upon to provide adequate care and support. In response to the limited availability of resources, governmental responses have promoted a 'mixed economy' of care and interdependency. Families, communities, and public and private sector services (with associated costs) are encouraged to interweave to ensure an older person is integrated and not destitute or isolated. Generally, families are the hub in the wheel of care provision and social integration.

Feminist perspectives on care and violence propose that presumptions on femininities and gender should form the basis to familial, societal and governmental discourses and policies on care for older people. Caring, as a combination of feelings with tasks, has been conceptualized in two ways: as 'caring about' – the feeling part of caring – and 'caring for' – the practical work of tending for others (Parker 1981; Ungerson 1983; Sevenhuijsen 1998). Social change, in particular the engagement of adult children in paid employment, has resulted in notions of 'caring about' (the organization of care and care delivered through support and emotion) taking centre stage. Few adult children, even female children, can afford the time or resources to 'care for' despite continuing images and notions of the caring, sharing family. In feminist work there has been a tendency to emphasize the need to free up women from assumptions about caring. However, aspects of feminist work have been criticized for placing undue focus upon carers, at the peril of not addressing the needs of the cared for (Watson *et al.* 2004). It should also be noted that there are significant numbers of male carers, especially among spouses aged over 75.

Social aspects of ageing

The large body of work in social gerontology, the study of the social aspects of ageing and old age, has tended to concentrate on physiological experiences and engagement with health and social services. More often than not, this focus has presumed and reproduced negative images and experiences of ageing (Bury 1995). The emphasis is upon the biological and the processes of decline coupled with increasing dependency. For many social researchers the experience of later life was understood principally through concerns for social and health service provision (Blaikie 1999) and certainly social research has been at the forefront of identifying and exploring explanations of elder abuse. Limited attention has been given to elder abuse in sociological theory. Social theory has tended to marginalize old age in sociology (Tulle–Winton 2000: 65). Sociological inquiry has become increasingly critical of the sometimes 'normative role of sociological theorizing' and the problematization of an ageing population epitomized in debates on pensions and health and social care (Tulle–Winton 2000: 68). Yet there is a body of theoretical work in the broad area of growing older and ageing, and aspects of this should underpin any analysis of elder abuse.

Diversity, continuity and change in growing older are considered in a number of studies and theoretical expositions (Featherstone and Wernick 1995; Gullette 1997; Blaikie 1999). The focus of much of this work is on individual adaptation to malfunction and underpinning this is the medicalization of old age (Katz 1996). Older people are caught up in what has been termed the 'narrative of decline' (Gullette 1997). As a counterpoint to this discourse of decline there are alternative prescriptions for managing later life. These range from, for example, the extension of mid-life, successful and positive ageing, the postmodern lifecourse and the adaptation and maintenance of identity and self (Featherstone and Hepworth 1991;

Thompson 1992; Hepworth 1995; Tulle-Winton 2000). Contemporary discourses promote attempts to postpone ageing, often by techniques which are ambiguous in that they can alienate people from their ageing and thus further denigrate growing older (Biggs 1999).

Situational exchanges

Changing levels of dependency and the relationship between carer and cared for elder have led to analytical assertions that may be broadly termed 'situational'. In this body of work a number of issues and factors come into play. These range from physical and emotional dependency, emotional strain and social isolation, to exhaustion with caring. In policy and practice analysis the focus tends to be upon the 'stressed carer' but not all carers experiencing stress become abusive. For many carers there are the everyday dynamics of caring that shift back and forth between feelings of delight and drudgery. This can pose a barrier to seeking help with an attendant emphasis upon physical violence as an expression of frustration and exhaustion (Wilson 2000).

Then there are theories that consider the processes of exchange – rewards and punishments – and the ways in which care may continue or cease on the basis of these ideas (Gouldner 1960). It has been argued that conflict and abuse can result from a breakdown in what the carer and cared for consider to be a 'balanced' exchange. Where carers consider there is not enough reward (this can incorporate emotional, social and financial dimensions), they may attempt to gain reward and restore control through abuse. Those being cared for may appeal to notions of reciprocity and solidarity that carers feel place undue pressures upon them. These tensions may be especially heightened in terms of the provision of informal care for older people as this offers limited structural rewards (Jack 1994). Family relationships and solidarities may also be implicated. Previous research has proposed that the more intimate and positive the relationship prior to dependency and caring the more likely notions of fairness and extrinsic rewards are to be evident (George 1986).

Wider social factors also come into play. In Chapter 3 it was asserted that 'society ... consists in part of both allowing and expecting some people to do things which other people are not allowed or expected to' (Hughes 1971: 287). The concepts of mandate and licence in terms of the sanctioning and working of roles through recognition from others, may be utilized to reflect on the prerogatives of some to act as carers, and others to be cared for. However, in much of the work on exchange theory, the concept of dependency remains under-theorized and inadequately considered.

In pre-industrial times, dependency was the norm and was described as a 'social relation as opposed to an individual trait' (Fraser and Gordon 1994: 7). In industrial times, dependency was deemed antithetical to citizenship because some people were excluded from wage labour. This was a period of the rise of the ideal of the family wage, where working men were deemed, albeit fallaciously, to be independent. There is a legacy of a welfare ideology that presupposes, and makes plausible, claims and statements about *particular* needs and dependencies. It is important to reflect on the histories of (in)dependency and engage with these, as well as contemporary material and ideas (Fraser and Gordon 1994: 5). A language of (in)dependency also reveals the ways in which the mainstream characteristics of welfare regimes betray underlying assumptions and endorsements of gender and gendered patterns of caring. Policy discourses can easily become a medium through which political hegemony is reproduced.

Actors, structures and meanings

Underlying assumptions and endorsements about ageing can be explored through the analysis of actions based upon perceived images of the self and others; through symbolic interactionist approaches. In contrast to theories that emphasize notions of rewards and punishments, social interactionism maintains social actors' work towards goals they assume to be valid while also reflecting on the motivations of others. These reflections may or may not be what the other person intends or takes for granted. Thus, through this perspective, ageing might be explored through the expectations that older people have and the level of agreement (or otherwise) between their views and those of others. Interactionism is premised on process and experience (Benton and Craib 2001: 87).

As our knowledge of ageing increases so we develop more complex and nuanced ideas about growing older. With increasing knowledge of the social world and ageing we develop ever-shifting meanings and ideas that we share with others. In this perspective elder abuse might be understood as a consequence of the social, physiological and economic meanings of, and interactions between, various systems, including families, friends and institutions. As people age, changes in role and role expectations might cause disruption to presumed identities and familial roles. For example, other family members could construe a grandfather who is no longer willing to be an active participant in caring for grandchildren as 'difficult'. It may require shifts in roles and expectations that, for some people, may not correspond to their assumptions about grandparenting. Stereotypes form the basis to many of these assumptions (in this case that grandparents should provide care) and the process of recognizing and managing change suggests a complex world where interactions may become disrupted.

In the course of our actions and interactions we negotiate the meanings of objects in our world. The social construction of older age addresses the ways in which meanings are sustained between people and draw upon the historical and social construction of issues and social problems. Meanings are (re)created through our engagement with social institutions, one of which is 'the family'. Beliefs are conceived as being comprised of subjective interactions and having qualities that are objective and external to the social actor. Patterns of assumptions and behaviours construct notions of a 'common sense' reality that may be taken for granted. Disruption to this 'reality' through shifting roles and responsibilities arising from growing older can lead to uneasiness. The person perceived to be the cause of the disruption can be marginalized.

Prejudice about older people, drawn from notions of dependency and economic inactivity post-retirement, is indicative of the vast array of inequalities premised on age and ageing. In this analysis, elder abuse may arise from the way in which older people are marginalized from what have become highly valued arenas of society, namely economic activities and consumerism. Economic and social dependency is a reality for many older people, and the attendant fears give rise to tensions across generations. These notions of dependency may also form a smokescreen to abuses. Health and social care institutions may not wish to unravel familial/care relationships for fear of not being able to provide adequate services or of unsettling existing care relationships. Thus services can reinforce the very dependencies created through the workings of wider social and economic structures and practices.

Drawing upon the concepts of family practices and gender projects enhances the potential for a critical analysis of relationships, gender and violence (Morgan 1996; Connell 2002). Notions of families as places of safety and security (fusion), constitutes opacity to abuses (fission). Being in, and belonging to, families provides a basis to solidarities as well as meeting a range of physical and emotional needs. Identities are moulded and adapted through family experiences, and personal autonomy and choice. Further, as we grow older, and the context of experiences and images of ageing shifts, we interchange and process memories, anticipations and contradictions that shape the social universe of families.

The tenets of an explanatory model on elder abuse might be drawn across the following considerations (Biggs et al. 1995: 29):

- How elder abuse is socially constructed – that is, the social and historical context. Here Biggs et al. draw upon the shifting basis to definitions and responses to elder abuse and in particular assumptions about vulnerability and the provision of care across families, public, voluntary and private sector providers of care.
- How social actors interact within the space in which violence takes place. The roles and responsibilities of families within the social and physically constructed space of the home are of relevance, as are the processes of negotiating different roles.
- The way in which issues are perceived and conceived by those involved. How do they perceive themselves and explain the circumstances and events? Do the stresses of caring come into play? How do those involved engage with or avoid other family members, friends, neighbours and professionals?

These provide a framework for analysis and can be further developed through a critical engagement with the formation of familial and social practices.

Older women and domestic violence

A common formulation of elder abuse is that of the stressed carer who may be a relative, a paid carer or a professional. The explanations offered by situational or exchange theories come to the fore in these formulations. Imbalances in power, assumptions about roles, obligations and rights, are all dimensions of family life that may be of relevance to understanding incidents of abuse. Images and ideas of older people as burdensome, decrepit and in decline constitute a unique framing to elder abuse. Notions of societal support and care for the vulnerable, and in the case of older people, of reverence for ageing citizens, rest uneasily alongside negative ideas on ageing in societies obsessed by youth and youthfulness.

The 'stressed carer' may well be a factor in many forms of abuse but it is an explanation that tends to emphasize the immediate context and current events. It could be argued that it encourages limited engagement with 'retroduction', namely, the separation of the meaning of an act and its intention. The concept of retroduction suggests that social scientists reflect upon the interplay of the conscious and unconscious production of society through their engagement with the material and structural dimensions of 'the ever-present condition' as a 'continually reproduced outcome of human agency' (Bhaskar 1979: 15).

Reflecting upon the wider social and economic practices evident in elder abuse, it can be argued that differing intellectual and organizational contexts are in operation. Social work and health services have tended to emphasize situational and exchange explanations, often seeking to relieve immediate dangers and pressures. Others, notably those in non-governmental and women's organizations, and campaigners, challenge this focus, arguing that immediate relief from the dangers of abuse, while an imperative, fails to address the underlying processes in operation.

In the conclusion to the book *Old Age*, de Beauvoir (1970: 517) comments:

> The old person remains on the alert even when his security is guaranteed because he does not trust the middle-aged: this distrust is the figurative expression of the dependence in which he lives. He knows that the children, friends and nephews who help him live, either by giving money or by looking after him or by housing him, may refuse their assistance or diminish it; they can abandon him or dispose of him against his will ... He is acquainted with the double-dealing of the adult world.

A recognition and conceptualization of gender is crucial to a compre-hensive understanding of 'double-dealing' across generations in societies that 'care about the individual only in so far as he is profitable' (de Beauvoir 1970: 604). Women may live longer but wider speculation about old age is 'considered primarily in terms of men', in terms of the 'masculine state' (De Beauvoir 1970: 101). This 'primary' focus is evidenced through concerns upon retirement from employment and access to an occupational pension or other forms of income related to lifetime income from paid work. Women are less likely to have access to these resources at the same level as male partners, relatives or colleagues. Older men do not experience the level of pressure to conform to an image of youthfulness and social engagement with families, and, for example, grandchildren. Thus older women's lives are seemingly more ingrained with that of the immediate family. This can offer benefits in social and economic terms (to all con-cerned) but can also result in an opacity to the everyday experiences of being older and female. As a consequence, older women's experience of domestic violence is a subject lost to most sociological, political and policy analyses.

Elder abuse is understood to involve those over retirement age, espe-cially those who are frail and confused. A spouse may be a perpetrator, but commonly-held notions of the abuser are of an adult child or relative who has become stressed or is seeking economic gain. Given the greater longevity of women, coupled with a lifetime of inequities, they are more likely to be vulnerable in health, social and economic terms. Figures for elder abuse conclude that women are more likely to experience violence than men, and that men known to those women are more likely to be perpetrators. However, some argue that this might be explained by demographic patterns (Garrod 1993). Whatever the explanation, it is the case that women dominate in the most vulnerable groups. They may have limited access to the resources that could facilitate reporting violence and the attainment of a safe and secure environment.

In summary, there are major and, sometimes, problematic differences in the theoretical frames of domestic and elder abuse. Older women appear to fall between policies and services aimed at, in the case of elder abuse, violence that might be explained through situational or exchange theories, and in the case of domestic abuse explained in terms of gender and power. Framing this dichotomy are cultural discourses and images in which ageing is perceived in largely negative terms. Ageing is a narrative of decline to be fought against and, for many, later life is comprehended through the issues of health and social care and the management of vulnerabilities and dependences (Blaikie 1999). With the major emphasis in contemporary societies on youthfulness and active engagement in employment, growing older marks a progression of time that, in physiological terms, transcends dominant social and economic discourses.

All too often, domestic violence is considered a problem that affects younger women, and in particular women with children (Scott *et al.* 2004: 1).

A focus on those aged 15 to 50 means that about half the female population are not adequately considered. Research illustrates that any statistics provide only a partial representation of the incidence of domestic violence. Sources of information include civil judicial statistics which demonstrate that many more women than men file for divorce on the basis of unreasonable behaviour, although it is not known how many of these cases include domestic violence. Social work services collect data in case records but these are not collated centrally. In the year ending March 2002, Scottish Women's Aid received enquiries from 65,300 women with 5783 requests for refuge accommodation (of which they were only able to meet a quarter). These figures are not broken down by age but do illuminate the pressures upon services. The 2001 (self-completion) *Scottish Crime Survey* found that 66 per cent of violent incidents experienced by women, and 6 per cent by men, were domestic in nature. While violent crime is not frequent, and statistics are not presented by age, they do indicate the gendered patterns in the experiences of violence. Data collected by the police are based on incidents reported to them. These are broken down by age of the victim and between a fifth and a quarter of all reported incidents are perpetrated against women over the age of 40. In 2001, 32,509 incidents were reported to the police of which just under 23 per cent (n = 7393) involved women aged 41 or over, with 16 per cent (n = 5270) reported by women aged 41–50.

The policy and legal context

There is a lack of specific visibility for older women in policies, services and the law. The experiences and views of older women are rarely sought, listened to, or have the potential to inform policy and service developments and evaluations. Issues relevant to older women are absent from most policy documents although there have been some notable shifts in recent years, as described below.

In earlier chapters, the progress in Scotland, and the significance of partnership working on domestic abuse, was noted. Since the late 1990s domestic abuse has had what many have termed an unprecedented prominence in public policy in Scotland. The inception of the multi-agency partnership group in 1998, followed two years later by the *National Strategy*, and in 2001 a document on action across the Scottish government to prevent violence against women marked substantial growth in policy work. The acceleration of government activity resulted in additional generic provision of services for all women and, as a consequence, older women have benefited.

The *National Strategy* (Scottish Executive 2000) in Scotland provides a consensus on policy and proposes how provision could best be developed. While reference is made to the particular needs of disabled or ethnic minority women, older women without dependent children are absent, suggesting a general approach that lacks awareness of the heterogeneity of the female population (Scott *et al.* 2004: 42).

By contrast the document on the prevention of violence against women does note that there are particular issues for older women (especially fear of crime), with implications for responses from health and social professionals and the police. Later in this document the abuse of the elderly is considered as follows: 'Abuse of the elderly can include: physical, emotional, financial, or sexual abuse and neglect. While it is not gender specific, there is a gender dimension in that there are many more women than men in the age groups over 75' (Scottish Executive 2001: Section 3.7). The gender dimension is considered but in terms of demography; there are more women than men aged 75 and over and therefore it is likely that elder abuse will involve older women. Yet earlier in this document, and in other Scottish Executive documents on the topics of violence and domestic abuse, gender and power inequities are referred to. One example is the definition of domestic abuse: 'An imbalance of power between men and women and also more general gender inequalities. Such abuse cannot be eradicated until there is an equal balance between men and women in society and relationships' (Scottish Executive 2001: 3). Such apparent contradictions are born of framing women as older people rather than older women who experience a range of inequalities.

The law, legal and other services take a generic approach to domestic abuse in so far as they rarely differentiate among women regardless of differences in experiences and needs. From 1981, women in Scotland have had the right of occupancy in the matrimonial home, without being the tenant or owner of the home. Available alongside these occupancy rights are exclusion orders in which the courts have the right to suspend a spouse from occupancy of the martial home. It can be difficult to secure such orders as conditions are stringent and cases must be brought by legal services. Access to exclusion orders has been a cause of some concern and debate. The ability of a violent spouse to have contact with a survivor of abuse can also be controlled through a civil action known as an interdict. While the legal test is weaker, women can incur some expense in securing these. However, about two thirds of civil legal aid in Scotland is for matrimonial cases and this is available to many low-income litigants. Nevertheless, the courts may ask for some costs to be met although this clawback is under review. Recent changes allow for a power of arrest to accompany an interdict but this form of protection requires the police to be willing to act. Cohabitees have limited rights but can apply for an occupancy right to cover a limited period of time and to apply for a matrimonial interdict. These are important as they allow women experiencing domestic abuse to remain in their own home while removing the perpetrator. Recognizing that violence may take place over extended periods of time and in other locations, the vicinity of interdicts has been extended to the place of work or area around a child's school and they can last for up to three years even if a divorce has been granted.

Reports and strategies have promoted, and resourced, a range of activities in awareness-raising and service developments. Over the last decade police services have set up dedicated units on domestic violence, improved police training and supported calls for a review of criminal law in relation to domestic abuse, arguing for a single piece of legislation. Guidelines on abuse and supporting the process of disclosure have been produced and circulated to all community doctors and nurses as well as a range of related health and social care workers. In housing services, recent changes in legislation will place people deemed vulnerable by virtue of age and domestic abuse in priority groups. However, many areas of social and health policies prioritize the needs of children and parents, and women who are childless or older still lack visibility in a range of policies and services.

'For years I got on with it'

Older women experiencing violence and abuse can find themselves trapped by the narrow theoretical models that inform policies and services. Disclosure of elder abuse initiates action from health and social care services whose main concerns are safety and risk management. Acknowledgement of domestic violence is likely to bring a woman into contact with voluntary sector groups and social movements such as Women's Aid that treat domestic violence as a gendered abuse of power. Very different responses and reactions may follow depending upon an assessment of violence as elder abuse or domestic violence. The interaction of services with carers who may be abusers, combined with presumptions that after many years in a relationship all must be bearable, creates additional barriers and taboos to the disclosure of violence.

In a recent review of the limited number of studies available on older women and domestic violence in Scotland (Scott et al. 2004), work was sourced from the UK, North America, Canada, Australia, Sweden and Finland. Primary data was also collected in a telephone survey of service providers (24 interviews with Women's Aid projects) and interviews with survivors (n = 5) and those organizing services and implementing policies (n = 5) in Scotland.

Previous research studies suggested that data on prevalence were more often collated from research studies than from statutory sources. Violence tends to be extreme by the time it is reported to the police or other services and this would appear to be particularly so in the case of older women. In a US-based comparative study of rape and physical violence in cohorts of older women (aged 55 to 89), and younger women (aged 18 to 35), lower prevalence rates were found among older women (Acierno et al. 2001). There were no other significant differences in the characteristics of assaults across the age groups. The research team speculated that these results may be expressive of lower reporting rates rather than lower levels of violence:

It may be the case that older adults simply do not report some violent events, either due to memory bias, fear of negative consequences to victims who report, or to generation-specific prohibitions against such disclosure ... There is some indirect evidence that older adults are more reticent to report instances of criminal victimization.

(Acierno *et al.* 2001: 692)

Other studies in the USA (Harris 1996; Seaver 1996) found similar parallels between younger and older women: 'There is no common profile of older women suffering abuse just as there is none of younger women. What they have in common is living with an abusive mate or relative' (Seaver 1996: 15).

While in many ways the barriers to reporting are similar for women of all ages, older women may have heightened fears of violence and victimization on leaving a relationship and home. They may also be concerned about the possibilities of institutionalization and the resources required to establish a new home. Women may also be in the position of receiving care from an abuser or being the main carer for the perpetrator, or other family members. Any or all of these factors can combine to pose particular barriers for an older woman leaving an abusive relationship.

The telephone survey conducted in the study by Scott *et al.* (2004) posed a range of questions including:

- Does your agency track the numbers of women served by their age? If so, how many were aged over 45 last year?
- In your experience do older women access services differently from younger women?
- Do you think older women need different services from younger women?
- Does your organization provide specialized services for older women? (If yes, how do they work and why have you designed them this way? If no, would you like to?)
- What are the barriers to serving older women?

Interviews were also undertaken with relevant projects or organizations; for example, a project leader from Age Concern (a non-governmental organization concerned with issues for older people); the author of a report for the Church of Scotland; three staff from Women's Aid involved in specialized services for Asian, black and ethnic minority women in the Glasgow area; a project which recently made special efforts to provide individualized services for older women; and a project which has provided specialized services for older women for some time, including a support group and a refuge.

Overall, these interviews revealed limited appreciation of, and attention to, the needs of older women experiencing domestic violence. Providers stated that older women were invisible and they did appreciate that they could find it difficult to access services. Most suggested that older women may not require specific services but they may need opportunities to engage with services in ways that recognize their situation and attendant social expectations about age and gender. This element of the research 'underscored the need to offer appropriate *choices* to *all* women' (Scott *et al*. 2004: 40). Identifying abuse as domestic violence was said to evoke a 'deep sense of shame' among older women. The experience of violence was all the more problematic for some women who berated themselves for not having 'fixed' the relationship and putting up with abuse over many years.

As discussed in Chapter 1, it is difficult to estimate the prevalence of domestic violence, and this is especially so among those over 40. Women in this age group tend to have less contact with statutory services where they might disclose violence than, say, childbearing women and mothers. Those interviewed estimated that between 10 and 30 per cent of their clients were aged 45 or over. In response to an analysis of users that found 20 per cent were aged 50 or over, one Women's Aid project set up specific services, including a refuge. This has operated at over 90 per cent capacity from opening in August 2000, with women aged from their late forties to their eighties having found safety there.

Scott undertook interviews with five older women who had experienced domestic violence and had left these relationships (Scott *et al*. 2004: 28). Between them these women had experienced over 200 years of violence. Generally they had hoped that over time the violence might dissipate. Meantime they hoped that service providers might ask if something was wrong, and do so in a context where disclosure would not be threatening. Some asked for assistance but did not receive a supportive or constructive response. These findings are strikingly similar to that of earlier studies involving younger women. Over a decade earlier, a study conducted in Northern Ireland reported that women regarded it as useful if professionals initiated discussion about domestic violence by asking questions in a 'sympathetic' and 'non-judgemental' manner (McWilliams and McKiernan 1993).

Of the women interviewed the ages ranged from 52 to 77. The issues raised by these women were similar to those raised in the review of previous studies. The dawning realization that they were growing older and violence was continuing left many feeling they had to leave:

> I was married at sixteen but I met him at fifteen. And from the beginning really – but you don't see it when you're in it. From the beginning, the violence and the power – you're just ruled by fear. Or I was, just by fear. And what he would do to you if you ever left. And I always believed that and you do believe that ... three children before I were twenty and then I had a daughter. So three sons quick and then a daughter. But all the way through you ask for help but you don't actually stand there and say will you help me, my husband beats me up. For many years I'd looked for help through the doctors, the Health Board, various numbers that were there to ring. But when you

rang they wouldn't be there or they would say ring back later. And um, there wasn't the help in them days, you just got on with it. And for 39 years I got on with it.

(Scott et al. 2004: 28)

As one woman put it, 'you couldn't see yourself growing old with that still happenin' (Scott *et al.* 2004: 28). Adult daughters and other relatives provided information and support. There were varying responses from the police and women expressed little confidence in receiving support from this source. Women did not conform to common images in elder abuse of the frail, vulnerable older person and perpetrators could potentially gain from ageism in so far as they were less likely to be viewed as dangerous as they grew older. Thus many years of fear and violence, coupled with stigma and a series of practical problems, presented enormous barriers to leaving. The focus was often on the women: their behaviour that might provoke violence and their ability to leave. One woman commented, 'I told mysel' in the end, ye jus hae t' dae it yersel' (Scott *et al.* 2004: 34).

Summary

It has been said of elder abuse that 'its importance as one of the major sociological issues of the 1990s will become quickly and uniquely apparent, as did the social problems of child abuse and spouse abuse in the preceding two decades' (Bennett and Kingston 1993: 1). There has been a flurry of research, analysis and concern from non-governmental organizations and public sector agencies. However, an acknowledgement of elder abuse has not led to similar concerns about older women and domestic violence. Why is this? Slater (1999: 39) comments that 'the age focus can unwittingly reinforce the uncritical, and fundamentally ageist, terminological segregation of "elders" '.

The topic of older women and domestic violence illuminates ongoing presumptions about familial solidarities and ageing. Presumptions about the 'health' of relationships can often appear to be based upon the number of years a couple have been together rather than any consideration of the everyday experience. Women also continue to grapple with gendered and economic inequities. Adult children can offer support, or place pressures on mothers to stay with their partner and remain in the family home. Fear of wider family breakdown, and the additional costs and social taboos of leaving, can influence decisions to stay or go.

The increased recognition of the need to critically review definitions and experiences of violence, gender and age, enhances analysis of social roles and interactions. The manner in which families and individuals, legislators, policymakers, services and non-governmental organizations conceive of the intersections of age, gender and violence has wide and long-term implications for sociological analysis. Both elder abuse and domestic violence are socially constructed paradigms. The former emphasizes risk management and is associated with institutional forms of support and care. The latter seeks a gendered analysis of power in relationships and seeks to provide support while women become independent. These can be competing paradigms with older women caught in between expectations and service provision. The complex and ambiguous interweaving of the contingencies of growing older and being female cannot be adequately explained or addressed through the paradigm of elder abuse.

PART THREE

Towards a critical theory

6

Unpalatable truths: recognizing and challenging myths

Introduction

Almost 50 years after its creation, the UN recognized violence against women as a human rights abuse in 1993 (Bond and Philips 2001). Two years prior to that the *United Nations Principles for Older People* were published (United Nations 1991). These elaborated rights in the areas of independence, participation, care, self-fulfilment and dignity for older people. These declarations and principles, combined with the work of the World Health Organization (2002), and allied international organizations, such as the Pan American Health Organization (2000), is providing parameters for global strategies to respond to domestic and elder abuse.

Progress has been slow. Often policy and service developments have been concentrated in health, social care services and legal systems. Non-governmental organizations, women's and related movements continue to act as catalysts for debate and change through long-term campaigns and agitation (Weldon 2002).

The intimacy associated with living in a location (the home) promotes a close physical and psychological proximity. The search for safety and security from the pressures of everyday life encourages most of us to form families and relationships within the locale of the home. Despite changes in legislation and legal services that allow for the removal of the perpetrator of violence from the family home, it continues to be those experiencing violence who are expected to take action, including leaving the household.

Much of the attention upon those purveying violence originates from legal services and the courts. The concept of the 'victim' evokes a range of activities, concentrating upon *their* agency. While there is legislation in many countries to remove the perpetrator in the workings of policies and services there remains a focus upon the experiences and agency of those who are vulnerable, exhausted and economically weak; those who experience violence. Thus it can be argued that governments, services, communities and individuals have an averted gaze from key aspects of violence in families.

While not denying the relevance and importance of work to secure the safety of those experiencing violence, I wish to argue that we also need to tackle social, political and family practices that continue to render acts of violence in families marginal, despite evidence on prevalence. In this penultimate chapter I seek to provoke a dialogue on the way we define, perceive and debate violence in families, drawing upon issues and evidence from previous chapters. To summarize, while there is recognition among services, agencies and many groups that violence can take place within the context of families and intimate relationships, there remains ambivalence about tackling the causes. Concentrating upon developing policy and practice work with those experiencing violence is necessary. However, this reinforces tendencies to marginalize any analysis of the gendered social practices and relations that underpin discourses and practices of violence in families and relationships.

Crucial to addressing violence in families is recognition of the ambiguities and ambivalence that are a feature of the actual acts of violence, and debates and policies, on this topic. Ambiguities surround definitions, policies and services. Ambivalence is experienced as uncertainty, confusion and discomfort, carrying 'a sense of danger' (Bauman 1991: 56). This sense of danger is for many governments, agencies and individuals illuminated in the shifting boundaries around the private (the family) and the public (legislation and interventions in families). For many politicians and individuals there remains a concern to have freedom from state interventions and so-called 'prying' on the part of neighbours or relatives. The freedom to live without fear of violence in intimate and family relationships is discussed, debated and addressed in laws and policies but in ways that continue to place emphasis upon the sanctity of families and homes.

This chapter opens with a synthesis of empirical and theoretical work on the key concepts of families and gender. A definition of 'myths' provides a broader conceptual frame for the analysis of the images and ideas that surround and imbue families and family life (Midgley 2003). The romantic images of love and families in fiction are contrasted with work on violence where romantic images of life and love are identified as screens behind which the everyday realities of violence can be placed. Across subsequent sections, evidence from previous chapters is reviewed and extended through an exploration of the workings of reactions to violence. Women find themselves in the midst of contradictions in terms of families, gender and culture. Their loyalty and behaviour can become a focus for fundamentalist religious and social movements. Family values are so basic to some religions and communities that any change, or sense of, change may provoke fears of undermining their foundations. For women, social change can pose threats, especially economic ones, alongside potential to develop many aspects of their lives. Women, and female sexuality, can quite literally become the battlefield in periods of rapid social change and challenges. In the closing sections the potential for women to be heard and inform developments is examined. Avoiding atomistic approaches to analysis and explanation reaffirms the need for theoretical pluralism (Eagleton 2003).

Romantic myths and hard realities

Many aspects of family life are imbued with myths: 'Myths are not lies. Nor are they detached stories. They are imaginative patterns, networks of powerful symbols that suggest particular ways of interpreting the world. They shape its meaning' (Midgley 2003: 1). Myths about families draw upon historical as well as everyday experiences and interpretations of family life and relationships. They are powerful, as they suggest a shared experience of families that individuals, groups and organizations expect to be a positive and supportive one. A range of service industries and aspects of the media emphasize the home as a space which families or couples should own and design to suit their preferred image. These are among the many ways in which homes become sites for forms of consumerism. The promotion of the happy home, which we also physically create through 'do-it-yourself' and decoration work is an extremely strong image in many societies. Yet the idea that families and relationships form a wholly positive and nurturing contrast to the worlds of work and public engagement is a far too simple one.

It would seem that the experience of, and analysis and discourses about, families are everywhere: 'It might be argued that all literature is ultimately about family, the creation of structures – drama, poetry, fiction – that reflect our immediate and randomly assigned circle of others, what families do to us and how they can be reimagined or transcended' (Shields 2001: 8). This quote is from a biography of Jane Austen written by the late Carol Shields. Austen is an author renowned for her novels on love, families and relationships. With reference to the work of Austen, Eagleton (2003: 96) commented that 'Jane Austen is about love, marriage and moral values; only those deaf to the claims of the heart see all this as inseparable in her novels from property and social class'. At the time of her writing, in the early eighteenth century, there was general acceptance of arranged marriages as the appropriate form of union among the middle and upper classes. Austen suggested that the best foundation to family life was most likely to be a love match, a heterosexual relationship, formed among socially and economically suitable young men and women. Through the promotion of the idea of love and love-based unions, Austen's work provided a challenge to commonly-held ideas of that era on marriage as the acquisition and maintenance of economic and social position. Middle-class women entered into the social circles through which marriage might be secured and for Austen's characters this process combined the attainment of love with the acquisition of social standing. Economic benefits were downplayed in the face of achieving a love match. While Austen's work addresses economic and social abuses in families, it pays limited attention to physical and psychological violence in families and relationships. Two hundred years on from the main body of her writing, her work and ideas from literature more generally continue to infuse nostalgic notions of families and relationships. It would seem that the attainment of love, and a home and hearth, resonates with aspects of contemporary expectations for relationships and family life.

If some aspects of literature can promote a largely romantic view of relationships and marriage, Roddy Doyle's (1998) contemporary work *The Woman Who Walked into Doors* charts the decline of a relationship into one of chronic abuse. Doyle provides a detailed and sharp description of the life of a woman, Paula, whose dreams continue despite experiences of violence, poverty and the daily grind of work and mothering. Her love for her husband is called upon, by her and him, during and after acts of violence: 'He demolished me. He destroyed me. And I never stopped loving him' (1998: 177).

While recognizing that her dreams of the perfect relationship, and love for her violent husband, shield her from the realities of being trapped in a mêlée of violence, Paula tries to create a happy home for her children. The escapism offered by her dreams is captured when she comments, 'when I think of *happy* and *home* together I see the curtain blowing and the sun on the wall and being snug and ready for the day, before I start thinking about it like an adult' (Doyle 1998: 7, original emphasis). The imagery suggests hope, warmth and security. It also proposes that thinking like an adult brings with it unpleasant realities.

For many years of married life Paula blamed herself for her husband's violence, lost herself in dreams, lost her sense of self and began drinking heavily. Family, friends, doctors and nurses noticed her drinking and the bruises. She was asked about her drinking time and time again. Nobody asked why she drank or explored the obvious physical injuries, never mind the manifestations of psychological trauma. It was easier for all concerned, including Paula, to believe that her bruised face did result from walking into doors.

In the following excerpt from the book Paula reflects on one of many visits to the hospital:

> No questions asked. What about the burn on my hand? The missing hair? The teeth? I waited to be asked. Ask me. Ask me. Ask me. I'd tell everything. Look at the burn. Ask me about it. Ask.
> No.
> She [the nurse] was nice, though. She was young. It was Friday night. Her boyfriend was waiting. The doctor never looked at me. He studied parts of me but he never saw all of me. He never looked at my

eyes. Drink, he said to himself. I could see his nose moving, taking in the smell, deciding.

(Doyle 1998: 164)

Paula stayed in the marriage for nearly 20 years. She believed if she worked harder and kept her love for her husband alive, then their lives would change for the better. She accepted responsibility to make things better believing that she was in some way to blame. Fear of the shame that came with being open about violence in a family also kept her from speaking out. It was only when her husband began to intimidate their teenage daughter that she realized change was highly unlikely and she threw him out.

The perpetrator exerted power. He was shielded by her embarrassment and shame and the response of others to Paula. He paced up and down outside the screens around her hospital bed, his shadow evident, and yet he was invisible to the professionals and those who might have helped. This is a work of literature that resonates with, and draws upon, the experiences of many women recounted in numerous studies (Hester *et al.* 1997; Hague *et al.* 2003). The stigma and 'spoiling of identity' for women has the effect of cutting them off from others as they become discredited. More often than not the process of discrediting women is promoted through a prevalent idea among professionals that if women stay then it cannot be that bad, and, perhaps, they are in some way to blame.

Literature and other forms of media are littered with examples of the romantic versions of relationships. The violent relationship receives much less attention in cultural and sociological work. Not surprisingly, many wish to emphasize and explore the positive: the search for the 'perfect' love match that can form the basis to longer-term living and familial arrangements. In Part 1 a number of contemporary presuppositions about families were considered, including (Bourdieu 1996):

- families are viewed as *transcending their immediate members*;
- families are seen as having a *separate social universe*;
- the very *privacy* of families has evolved as the notion of a haven from the troubled, hectic outer world and yet forms the *backstage* to life;
- the *'home' as an idea of a place and space* that is permanent and endurable;
- the language family members use about their family proposes *a unit capable of agency and endowed with feeling and actions*;
- *exchanges in families are paramount* and these are infused with notions of trust, reciprocity, giving, intimacy and feelings.

Presuppositions can be, and are, implicated in a symbolism that becomes 'an integral part of our thought-structure' (Midgley 2003: 2) and creates a 'matrix of thought, and background' (Midgley 2003: 4): 'The way in which we imagine the world determines what we think important in it, what we select for our attention among the welter of facts that constantly flood in upon us. Only after we have made that selection can we start to form our official, literal, thoughts and descriptions' (Midgley 2003: 2). Families are networks that pattern relationships. They are sites in which identities are formed but also locales in which ambiguities about safety, security and intimacy may be evident.

'Patterns of thought that are really useful in one age can make serious trouble in the next one' (Midgley 2003: 4). How do we tackle the myths of 'home and hearth', and those that propose strong associations between femininities, mothering, home and masculinities, employment and the potential use of violence? Families and relationships are dynamic and adapting to demographic and economic changes, and yet images and expectations of family life continue to evoke images and myths that bear little relevance to the experiences of many of us. Perhaps we might 'do better to talk organically of our thought as an ecosystem trying painfully to adapt itself to changes in the world around it' (Midgley 2003: 5).

Families tend to be viewed as a separate social universe with their very privacy offering a backstage to the hectic outer world. Wider family networks transcend immediate members and endow those included with commonalities, ideas, experiences and plans. However, growing tensions between the solidarity of family members and increasing individualism leads to tensions in private relationships that reflect the 'externally induced amplification of conflicts' (Beck 1992: 120). Social change offers opportunities, constraints and tensions that add to the discursive workings of families.

Homeground revisited

The concept of the 'lifeworld' provides a context through which the shared ideas and values that form cultures and relationships therein may be explored (Habermas 1987). The private lifeworld of families is (re)created through economic necessity and governmental policies, as well as the search for physical and emotional sustenance. The idea of 'family practices', that is, the practices that may be used to describe activities associated with and undertaken by family members, may be further refined through the concepts of licence and mandate (Hughes 1971; Morgan 2002). If licence is gained through social permission, for example, the role of parent, grandparent, husband or wife, and mandate refers to appropriate conduct in relation to particular work for themselves or others, then family practices may offer protection to perpetrators of violence (Card 2002: 146). This is certainly the case when families retain 'guilty knowledge' and the sense of securing the future of the family is felt to outweigh the disclosure of violence (Morgan 2002: 158).

The idea and experience of 'home' is worthy of close scrutiny. There is a duality of processes in achieving a dwelling or home – namely, construction and preservation (Heidegger 1971). Construction is defined as the design and activities of making the building and by contrast preservation 'entails not only the keeping of physical objects of particular people intact, but renewing their meaning in their lives' (Young 1997: 153). The process of constructing and maintaining a dwelling – a home – forms obvious and increasingly popular barriers to the world outside the immediate members of the household or family. Preservation work includes the development and exchange of family histories, ideas and forms of interaction. The work of preservation is a critical dimension to creating unique forms of familial relationships (Young 1997).

In order to capture the dynamics of the places and spaces in which we conduct familial and intimate relationships, the concept of 'homeground' was offered in Chapter 3. In summary, this concept seeks to capture the combination and interaction of a place (some type of construction) and a space (the floors, rooms or soil on which people live), forming the location in which we invest in plans, nurturing work, and the promotion of a sense of our family grouping (preservation).

It is the failure to critically explore the potential for control and autonomy over all aspects of one's life – to create and implement a radical and gendered version of privacy – that is the core issue (Young 1997). The selective application of the law and cultural practices premised upon notions of nurture and privacy in the sphere of the home and family, can appear to place violence in families beyond societal concern and control. It is ironic that while bodies are increasingly surveyed and we are entreated to have control over diet, exercise and lifestyle, bodies that are abused can be readily ignored. Our averted gaze becomes, quite literally, and para-doxically, 'home tuned' as the media and public discourses prefer to turn to fears of crime and violence in public spaces rather than consider violence in families.

Gendering violence

The gendered and social practices of families are neither immutable nor static but they offer roles that we constantly reflect and draw upon. The obligations between spouses, cohabiting partners, parent and child are among the strongest we encounter. Families, and family life, are considered crucial to self-identification and social identities. Yet much of what takes place in families, the practices of families, illuminates ideologies of gender, and dependency in particular (Morgan 2002). Violence can take place in gay and lesbian relationships and be committed by women against men. However, men perpetrate the overwhelming majority of incidents against women they know through intimate and familial relationships. Women and children are more likely to be killed, physically attacked or psycho-logically abused by those they know, often men in the immediate and intimate family. By contrast men are much more likely to experience the threat or realities of violence in public locations and from strangers.

A variety of sources document these trends. Nevertheless, my experience during research and policy work is that some people, among them a notable number of women, will cite the potential for women to be violent too: 'Aren't women violent too?' Why is this question posed, and so often by women? No one would deny that any human being has the potential to be violent (Kimmel, 2002). Human beings are capable of doing serious harm to both those they know as well as to strangers: 'the senseless, persistent suffering and demoralisation of violence that is the inhuman condition' (Gordimer 2003: 7). There are gendered trends in violence in families that pose contradictions to the solidarities created and pursued through blood ties, marriage and intimate relationships such as parent, child, grandparent and grandchild. All too often women bear the brunt of the immediate impact and longer-term consequences of violence. Some women seem almost apologetic about this. Some would appear to want to achieve gender parity by citing the potential for women to be violent too. Whatever the reasoning or motives of those who pose these questions, the trends in the gendered nature of violence make frightening reading. Women have a long way to go if they are to attain familial, social and economic equality.

Gender remains a significant marker of individuals, family roles and identities. Nevertheless, it is important to avoid perceiving irreconcilable differences between men and women as signified in broad and commonly-held perceptions of masculinities as dangerous and femininities as nurturing and harmless. There are multiple masculinities and femininities and these are best considered in terms of 'umbrellas' that signify a set of social relations. In most cultures and economic systems those social relations are premised on a hierarchy based on the subordination of women, albeit to varying degrees across social class, ethnicities and economic systems. Gender is not a fixed assignment but notions of hegemonic masculinities are strongly implicated in heterosexuality and the idea of the aggressive man prepared to use violence to protect and sustain a privileged position relative to women, children and other men. This poses a dilemma for sociology. Much research on violence in families, in particular violence between adult members of families, appears to support the notion that violence is a characteristic of masculine behaviour. But 'men are not simply the passive embodiments of the masculine ideology' (Brittan 1989: 68) and identities are defined, moulded and constrained through societal structures and engagement.

If the word 'perpetrator' is associated with masculinities, the word 'victim' invokes a range of meanings that draw upon femininities. Victims are perceived as helpless and hapless women, cowering in a corner unable to exert any sense of agency. Many governments, professionals and individuals promote women's safety and their ability to leave violent relationships as the best way to deal with domestic violence. The policies and practices connected with this violence become gendered in so far as women are conceptulized as those who should act; they must leave and take legal action against perpetrators. There are dangers in these presumptions of female victimhood and responses to violence, just as there are in presumptions that men will necessarily utilize their physical strength to perpetrate violent acts against intimate partners. Yes, there is evidence that demonstrates gendered trends in the experience of violence in intimate relationships. And it would seem that for a range of reasons associated with the working of power, gender and culture, this violence is under-reported. However, there is little to be gained from the personification of an entire gender.

Many of those who experience violence are aware that in reporting or acknowledging violence the focus may, ironically, shift to them and what professionals, friends and family feel they should do. For example, if women do not leave a violent relationship their children may be taken into care or placed on a supervision order, and they may be considered as potentially placing their children in danger. Thus, women can feel that reporting violence can result in a chain of events in which they may have little choice about how to establish a future for themselves and any dependants. Further, research and literature document many cases where those experiencing violence were desperate to be asked how they gained their physical or psychological injuries (McWilliams and McKiernan 1993). Fear, embarrassment, shame or the presence of a partner or family member inhibits disclosure. It may take years to tell another. This suggests there are social practices impacting on the decision about when or how to disclose violence, and these in turn have an impact on those experiencing violence and staffing relevant services.

Moving between and across the roles of mother, sister, daughter, friend and worker draws upon gender identities, among others, and these are forged through societal and economic structures. The concept of 'gender projects' makes it possible to recognize and explore the agency of people forging and shifting their identities within the frames of familial and global gender structures (Connell 2002: 82): within the processes afforded by the licence and mandate of being family members (Hughes 1971).

Underpinning the social universe of families and relationships is unpaid domestic labour. The word 'domestic' is, technically, gender neutral. Commonly used to refer to work that takes place in the home, it has attained a gendered construction in so far as much of the emotional and physical labour associated with this term is gendered. Discourses concerned with domestic labour evoke gendered images and ideas on roles and responsibilities. This is all too evident in the ways that specific skills and tasks are embedded in femininities (the daily tasks of cooking, washing and ironing) and masculinities (the irregular tasks of car maintenance or electrical repairs). While there are changes in the amount and nature of domestic caring work undertaken by men, especially in middle-class households and when both parents work full-time, it remains the case that women are often scripting and organizing care and domestic work. These trends are largely borne out by recent research on the negotiation of the amount and nature of housework undertaken by men and women (Baxter 2000).

Notions of families continue to focus on the intimate adult partnership as the hub around which family networks and familial and friendship relationships revolve. Thus in many societies, not least contemporary western societies, same-sex relationships continue to be viewed with suspicion, appearing by some to pose a challenge to the institution of marriage and 'the family'. Same-sex relationships that form the basis to families do not accrue the same legal rights as heterosexual partnerships (Card 2002; Mason 2002; Moran *et al.* 2004). The emphasis on heterosexuality as a supposed 'ideal type' of relationship around which to form families reinforces presumptions that violence is less likely to occur in these than same-sex relationships. What research there is, is inconclusive. The contractual basis to marriage and obligations in marriage and parenthood allow for a level of discretion that can render accountability for violence problematic (Card 2002). To what extent do societal structures enable, encourage and enhance the social practices that sanction and silence violence in families?

Discovery and denial

'I didn't exist. I was a ghost. I walked around in emptiness. People looked away; I wasn't there. They stared at the bruises for a split second, then away, off my shoulder and away' (Doyle 1998: 186).

While services have improved and violence in families is acknowledged through a range of policies and services, there remain silences and taboos that create opacity regarding violence in families. Many abused women speak of feelings of invisibility. Their bodies, physical and verbal interactions with others can offer many signs and symptoms for others to respond or react to. Discovery of violence may not necessarily lead to disclosure. Sexual violence is especially hard to discuss and disclose given taboos in all cultures, and customs and religious practices in some countries and locations. Silences can present the survivor with a situation of double jeopardy, namely of suffering ongoing physical or psychological harm, coupled with inhibitions on speaking out for fear of further indignities, violations and even death.

Global data provide evidence of suffering and violations across diverse cultures. Can we bear responsibility for things that happen in families that are not ours, and reside in other countries? The tensions between the public and the private, our family and their family, my state and their state, create a series of dialectics that can be creative in so far as it helps us to avoid oversimplification and too atomistic an approach. The duty to know, and to acknowledge, requires more than laws and policies:

Most people, at most times, in most societies, are more interested in 'making life' than 'making history'. Their sustaining ideology is ... keep a low profile and don't let yourself get too bothered by big problems ... But surely social justice deserves more than law. There are states of being such as good citizenship, which are less than heroic but more than mere law-abiding. They do not demand extraordinary heroism, but they do discourage silence.

(Cohen 2001: 277)

Family members have a great capacity to 'ignore or pretend to ignore what happens in front of their eyes, whether sexual abuse, incest, violence, alcoholism, craziness or plain unhappiness' (Cohen 2001: 64). This may be partially explained by images of family life that determine which aspects can be shared or must remain private, even denied.

Unwelcome and potentially dangerous situations are denied. This may be illustrated through the example of the Warsaw Ghetto from 1940–3 (Cohen 2001: 31). With hindsight, interpretations of the future of the Jews in the Ghetto are unambiguous. They were incarcerated *en route* to death in extermination camps. However, in the midst of everyday life in the ghetto survival took centre stage. The thought that this may be part of a wider policy of extermination was in the minds of most. Yet what to do when you and your family are hungry and seek emotional solace from the horrors all around?

This may seem an extreme example to draw upon at this point, but it highlights the dilemmas posed by levels of experience and thinking. The everyday experiences of the 'victim' and the sheer effort required to survive are factors in a person's consideration of what to do next: to seek help and support, to leave, to try and work within the family and relationships to tackle violence? The anticipated and actual reactions of others may inhibit reporting and action, especially if they focus on the potential agency of those already exhausted and dispirited as a result of ongoing episodes of violence. The 1943 uprising in the Warsaw Ghetto was prompted by evidence of mass killings and death camps coupled with ongoing experiences of extreme deprivation. News that the Ghetto was to be emptied was the catalyst for violent action in self-defence. Nevertheless, for some three years many found the accumulating evidence unbearable and sought to deny that premature death was likely. Outside the Ghetto many also tried to deny what was going on. How could such mass killings take place in Europe during the twentieth century? The sheer scale of this was too vast to conceive of.

In considering the workings of denial Cohen (2001: 51) differentiates between micro and macro denial. The former refers to dissonance between physical violence and 'appropriate' reaction; for example, in drawing upon the example of domestic violence Cohen (2001: 51) suggests variance in denial could include 'you can't call that real violence' (offender) and 'he's perfectly okay without drink' (victim). Underpinning these denials are the recurring themes of accommodation, routinization, tolerance, collusion and cover-up. Macro denial refers to denial at the societal level. Continuing his use of the example of domestic violence Cohen (2001: 52) outlines what he considers to be a process from denial to acknowledgement. In the denial phase domestic violence was out of sight, contained and concealed, even normalized. The social construction of legal and police services were generated around the designation of women as property and the protection of the family as private space. Feminist activity in the 1960s, combined with the campaigning work of a number of social movements on human rights and violence, led to changes in the law, related services and wider societal attitudes.

Given recognition of domestic violence, why do silences and denials persist? Is it the persistence of myths surrounding the apparent safety and security of families and homes? Part of the contemporary human condition is to find safety and security through holding onto positive meanings of families and home, despite evidence to the contrary (Young 1997: 159).

In the novel *Mystic River*, the author tackles the issues of friendship, family and honour (Lehane 2001). The origins of the contemporary events in the book lie in the abduction of a child, one of three boys who were close friends in a downtown neighbourhood in an east coast US city. As adults their lives intersect again when the grown-up daughter of one of the friends who was not abducted is murdered. Her father suspects the friend who was abducted and sexually abused. He reasons that his childhood friend has become a socially inept adult and therefore might have sought redress for what happened to him as a child through the abduction and murder of the young woman. Seeking revenge for the death of his daughter he murders the friend. The decision to murder this man was supported by a suggestion from the friend's wife that she too thought he had murdered the young woman. Subsequently, it becomes clear that this man did not murder the daughter; rather, it was an accidental death resulting from a prank by teenagers that went wrong. Although the senior detective on the case, the third friend, has a strong suspicion that a murder has been committed he cannot bring himself to arrest his childhood friend. The detective finds himself caught up in the emotions of friendship, knowledge of the abuse many years before, and an apparent empathy for a man and friend who in his eyes was trying to avenge his daughter's death, albeit with dreadful consequences.

Towards the end of the book the wife of the man who murdered his friend tries to explain the tangled web of events to their children. She tells her husband what she said to the children:

> Daddy is a king, not a prince. And kings know what must be done –
> even if it's hard – to make things right. Daddy is a king, and he will do
> – he will do what he has to do for those he loves . . . Everyone makes
> mistakes. Everyone. Great men try to make things right. And that's all
> that matters. That's what great love is. That's why Daddy is a great
> man.
>
> (Lehane 2001: 429)

Her exposition of events draws heavily on powerful symbols and ways of displaying masculinities, family honour and pride. Her words draw upon the myths of gender and families. The death of the innocent friend is termed a 'mistake' but excused as their father, her husband, was apparently trying to right the wrong of the death of their stepsister. She goes on to speculate about the wife who shared her suspicions with her husband commenting, 'what kind of wife says those things about her husband?'

Loyalty, honour and kinship matter most and these are themes evident in many gender and family practices, family histories and stories. In most societies there remains a duality in which women are viewed as, on the one hand, fragile creatures that require protection and, on the other, as sexual and troublesome and from whom society, and men, may need protection. Women can be killed or intimidated for actual or perceived immoral behaviour.

Patriarchal ideas continue to cast men as the protectors of women. If men's protection is violated, they lose honour because either they have failed to protect a woman or to bring her up correctly. To cleanse this honour, and thus that of the family, males may be sanctioned to murder or chastise the woman. The vulnerability of women around the world to this type of violence will only be reduced when these patriarchal and cultural mindsets are challenged and effectively confronted.

To talk of honour and kinship can render problematic a realistic acknowledgement of what is taking place. After all, many individuals would do what they could to bolster their family in the face of physical harm or social and economic threats. The words chosen to speak about violence become a powerful force and lead to a perversion of violence. In the scenario cited above the apparent lack of loyalty of the wife of the victim is talked about in terms that place a level of blame on her and not the murderer. Honour killings and violence likewise call into question the actions of the woman, often the victim, rather than the violent behaviour and beliefs of perpetrators and communities.

When it comes to gendered violence there can be a tone of resignation, even acceptance, among some service providers, professionals and individuals. Might it be the case that abuses are intrinsic to some relationships? Or is violence just a part of relationships in some communities, cultures, races or occupations? Outright denial of violence in relationships has dissipated. For some it has been replaced by the notion of 'couple violence': that for some in intimate relationships there are levels of violence that partners are prepared to live with. Until violence becomes extreme, and unacceptable to one or other partner, then surely there is little reason to intervene. But violence has gendered meanings and outcomes and all too often women are left in fear of ongoing violence (Nazroo 1995). Denial of these gendered implications runs through the renaming of gendered violence as couple violence. This denial is also evident in the assertion that violence can be justified as it is *bound* to occur in intimate relationships; and in ways that need not necessarily trouble services, families or friends.

Raising the voices of the abused

There has been a welcome and notable growth in legal and service provision for those who have experienced abuse. I have argued that this does,
however, result in policies and practices of containment. The moral
imperative to support the abused is a strong and necessary one, but it does
enhance the potential for an averted gaze from governmental and broad
societal attitudes and practices on families and violence in families. Social
movements, in particular the women's movement, have campaigned long
and hard for a broad approach to violence and have achieved a number of
successes in reframing the issues and reorganizing services (Hague *et al.*
2003). One example is the revision of the definition of violence against
women in intimate relationships in Scotland, in which gender was cited
and the word violence changed to abuse. The current campaign of the
international human rights organization, Amnesty International, on violence against women combines inputs from social movements with the
politics of the pressure group (Grant 2000). The diversity of experiences
among women, across nations and cultures, offers the potential for a
broader front to the collective experience on being a woman and at risk of
violence.

Women have argued that while being mindful of diversities in experiences and situations there is much to be achieved through consciousness-
raising, networking and campaigning on topics that cut across social class
and cultures; for example, violence in intimate relationships. The early
development of refuges and Women's Aid groups sought to fit action to
values with non-hierarchical forms of organization (Hague *et al.* 2003).
Women's activism remains strong and never more so than in work on
violence against women, violence in wars and civil unrest and peace
movements. In recent years international organizations and governments
have encouraged participation in the formation and workings of policies
and services. As part of this, the public are encouraged to become involved
in consultation exercises on being or becoming a 'user' of services. The
growth in service user involvement parallels the ideas of the service user as
a consumer of public services (Grant 2000). This poses a challenge to social
movements that have as a goal change in civil society more generally,
achieved through strategies across social, economic and political policies.

With notable exceptions, such as the work of Amnesty International,
global debates and campaigns on violence give limited attention to the
experiences of women. The experience and workings of international
organizations and governments is generally conventional in so far as they
continue to be dominated by 'malestream' ways of working. The obvious
cessation of violence at the end of hostilities in wars or civil unrest generally leads to enhanced threats of violence for women in and outside the
home, especially when civil society places limited emphasis on the rights of
women and the detection of violent crimes. Rape continues to be a crime
associated with, and presumed to follow, the progress of wars and unrest.

The systematic use of rape during wars has begun to receive attention as a war crime but this is a recent development. In times of peace, allegations of rape among adults known to each other rarely lead to a conviction. This range of images and experiences frame the thinking of women and reinforce a sense of vulnerability. Violence, threats and intimidation are no respecter of class, culture or race. A fear of violence is in the minds of most women at they traverse life in gendered societies.

Women have been raising their voices about the gendered experience of violence for centuries. Given a contemporary culture of social movements and user involvement the voices of the abused might be expected to inform a broader approach to service and policy provision. Research has illuminated that women using available services do not feel safe, are unable to speak freely and become silenced. While there are examples of good participatory projects, many women feel: 'blamed, silenced and stereotyped and, far from being seen as having expertise derived from that they have gone through, they are often blocked from full participation in service delivery as volunteers or paid workers because they are seen as "still in the experience" ' (Hague et al. 2003: 3).

Evidence from a survey suggests that while almost half of the forums for inter-agency work consulted women users, 90 per cent of the refuges did so. The research team concluded that 'multi-agency forums may be underachieving and sometimes, perhaps, over claiming this' (Hague et al. 2003: 146). Women may be service users but can feel their views and experiences do little to inform the current or future provision of services and policies. Why is this? Survivors' experiences and ideas are not given the same weight as those that emerge from professional agendas. It continues to be the case that some evidence is valued more highly than others. For example, to speak from a so-called professional perspective is valued more highly in many quarters than the experiences of survivors.

Importantly, a number of studies conclude that even with increasing levels of services, enhanced policies and legislation, there is limited progress on women's sense of safety in the community and home (Hague et al. 2003; Scott et al. 2004). Women who wish to leave violent relationships and need to avoid contact with former partners continue to find that their ability to forge a new life is compromised. Men who perpetrate violence may gain access to children and be reluctant to leave the locality in which a woman has a social support network. Numerous examples exist of services and policies that are working tirelessly to tackle violence and many are working to base developments on the experiences of women. Regardless of the services available, if women cannot feel safe even after leaving relationships it is surely time to question the focus on containment and actively address the wider implications of violence in families. This will require a change in attitudes, behaviours, policies and practices on the part of all of us as human beings and citizens. At the very least we need to address the ingrained and negative attitudes to violence against women and reframe their experience of violence as relevant to all of us.

Governments, policies and violence

'In spite of the huge differences between various cultures, we do believe that there are indeed some things which ought not to be done to anybody, anywhere. Whatever the doubts about rights, we can all recognise human wrongs' (Midgley 2003: 9).

Recent research found that primary-school age children had limited understandings of common definitions of domestic violence. A number of the girls involved in this research believed they could avoid domestic violence if they remained unmarried (Mullender *et al.* 2003). These ideas persist in the context of a growing miasma of violence that is evident in the media reporting of wars and civil unrest, and gratuitous physical and sexual violence against women in films and television.

Violence seems to be everywhere. So what are governments to do? Violence may be conceptualized as a component of politics and thus a legitimate part of the power and activities of the state (Weber 2002). By contrast, others argue that violence is the opposite of power and is never legitimate (Arendt 1970; Besteman 2002: 3). Researchers have considered mass state violence (Fein 1993) and the role of governments in civil, ethnic and international conflicts (Glover 1999; Hinton 2002). Contemporary post-industrial states use direct force to establish a preferred order or assert a particular form of nationalism. Further, a range of state-directed and run activities achieve disciplinary, ideological and bureaucratic control and these have contradictory effects on families.

A central feature of society is the promotion and acceptance of discipline through the subdivision and control of space, time and bodily activities (Foucault 1976). The surveillance of these activities, the idea of being under the gaze of state-run or regulated bodies, provides further discipline; for example, the surveillance of parenting styles by social workers or teachers. These activities leave many uneasy, with calls for less rather than more scrutiny – at least until the next tragedy is reported.

There are obvious benefits to feeling secure in public places in so far as we can move across places and spaces, and between activities, with limited fear of physical attack or verbal abuse. Governments, through the police, the law and legal services, are central to the attainment and maintenance of levels of safety in public places. Part of any 'peace' process is enabling the movement of non-combatants, and generally the related policing work is undertaken by military and police forces, sometimes with the backing of international organizations such as the UN. The unhindered movement of people from and to the home, especially that of women and girls, is generally considered a marker of what might be termed a 'civilized' or peaceful society.

Commentators have noted the persistent threat of violence to women in Afghanistan. Having survived wars and institutionalized sexism based on interpretations of religious teaching, women and girls continue to find public spaces threatening. Sexual violence is now perpetrated with relative impunity, given the lack of policing and appropriate legal systems. This raises issues about when peace is actually achieved. Events in Afghanistan, South Africa and Northern Ireland illustrate the unintended consequences of achieving 'peace'. Moves to establish democratic forms of government do not necessarily lead to gender parity. Rather, they can promote opportunities for violence against women in and outside the home as policing is dominated by the so-called attainment of a 'peace process'.

Abuse and assault in the home or family context is not so readily identified, reported or discussed. Reporting suspicions of violence in families can lead to accusations that relatives, friends and neighbours, never mind governments, are 'nosy' or 'interfering'. The focus – or gaze – continues to be on those who *experience* violence, with their activities called into question: 'Why don't they move out?' A contradiction becomes evident. The perpetrators of abuse are clearly not happy to conform to the 'discipline society' (Aretxaga 2002). If services and policies focus their gaze upon victims this can place them in a double jeopardy: the uncomfortable and often judgemental gaze of state bodies and agencies can follow the harrowing experiences of violence. The gaze of governments on perpetrators can lead to the development and use of laws, and prevention and treatment services, although this may not accord with progress on gender equality in the arenas of social and public policies (Weldon 2002). All too often, the response of governments is positively associated with the campaigning activities of women's organizations as they link with sympathetic policymakers and members of government (Weldon 2002).

The pace of change can be slow. There remains a narrow focus on the part of most governments to the problem of violence in families. Does this slow and somewhat narrow process of change constitute a form of 'symbolic violence' (Bourdieu 1977)? It could be argued that the failure to address violence in families leaves women and children to face a further and long-term aspect of gendered inequity. Further, the failure of governments and international organizations to tackle a range of inequalities, including income, gender and age; discrimination on the grounds of sexualities and ethnicities; cultural images and discourses on violence in familial relationships; and abuses of human rights through the trafficking of women and children, could be perceived as a symbolic form of violence. These various dimensions of violence are coming under increasing scrutiny from a range of social movements and pressure groups, many of whom perceive the causes of violence and inequality as emerging from capitalism and the gendered workings of a free market, global economy (Besteman 2002; Kallen 2004).

Cross-national forms of organized crime such as the Mafia, and the involvement of a number of governments in trafficking in people, arms and drugs, often with links to organized crime, constitute forms of symbolic and actual violence that constrain human rights. There are ongoing gains, but a global rhetoric of human rights exists that may be called upon to justify interventions by governments or international organizations in other states (Kallen 2004). The trajectories of politically motivated violence, violence in families and violence between states interweave alongside actual and apparent gains in human rights.

What terms and concepts do governments adopt and use to inform their determination of these issues (Bacchi 1999: 164)? In earlier chapters, the terms 'the family', 'families', 'violence' and 'domestic violence' came under scrutiny. To talk of family violence or domestic violence denies the gendered social practices that are evident in most experiences of violence in intimate adult relationships. The ways in which these terms are used to describe violence help to produce the very problem. The 'problem representation' (Bacchi 1999: 165) is highlighted through changes in the terms used to describe violence among adult family members. These have ranged from 'wife battering' and 'spousal abuse' to gendered violence. As noted earlier, some appear ungendered such as 'domestic violence' while others draw upon gendered roles – for example, 'spousal abuse'. The manner in which a social problem is framed determines the groups or professionals that are asked to address it.

The moral outrage regarding the physical and sexual abuse of children stands in contrast to the attention given to violence against women in families. The moral imperative posed by the abuse of children denotes a particular challenge to social order and notions of a civilized society as one that protects children. Women's groups, feminists and other campaigners have worked hard to engage with, and shift, definitions and policies to place a focus upon the complex interaction of gender, familial relationships, home and violence among adults as well as adults and children (Bacchi 1999; Weldon 2002). Having made gains in international organizations, and policy and service developments in many states, the focus can now shift to a keener engagement with, and challenges to, this averted gaze.

Summary

The aim of this chapter has been to synthesize and develop ideas and evidence on the myths and denials that surround violence in intimate relationships. The safety and security of anyone experiencing violence is paramount. Attaining safety can mean leaving the proximity of intimate relationships and the home. Responses to violence include the statutory provision of refuge and legal services. These are necessary and generally under-resourced and overstretched. Without broadening responses and campaigns on gendered violence to seek action at both societal and individual levels, the focus will continue to be upon the agency of women. International governmental, societal and individual action is required.

The challenges are great. Awareness of violence in relationships appears not to diminish the need for images and ideas that promote romance. Few of us would deny our need for spiritual and physical space in which to escape the rigours of the outside world. Romantic views of love and intimate relationships are prevalent in many dimensions of culture. These views can lead to myths about families and partnerships, and in particular about, the ideas of safety and security in family and intimate relationships. These myths run parallel to images and ideas of homes and families as places of safety and security. For many, intimacy continues to be framed around heterosexual partnerships and family relationships. The promotion of romance creates an opacity to aspects of the everyday realities of relationships. Romance is at one end of the cultural spectrum and violence at the other. Yet both romance and violence imbue many aspects of media with classic stories based upon violence leading to romance and a happy ending.

Exploring family practices offers a conceptual framework through which to explore key dimensions of the gendering of life (Morgan 2002). Social practices are not immutable to change. Over the last 50 years, major changes have taken place in family and social life. The nuclear family is increasingly giving way to a web of networks across generations, relationships and friendships. The wish to care for others and to constitute groupings – households or families – in which to form psychological and physical relationships, remains a strong force in post-industrial societies. Technology helps to lessen geographical isolation as use of the internet, email and mobile phones helps generations to communicate and offer forms of care from a distance. Alongside change there are continuities. Women are the main champions of the ethic to care in families, employment and government. A growing number of men wish to be further involved in parenting and domestic labour but continuities in gendered practices in families are evident.

Moving between and across roles – wife, husband, daughter, son – draws upon a range of gender identities. Masculinities and femininities are umbrellas under which a range of attitudes and behaviours are situated. Men and women are not simply 'passive embodiments' of gendered ideologies. Nevertheless, violence and families are strongly associated with, respectively, masculinities and femininities. Men perpetrate most violence in families, although not all men are violent. Examining gender projects makes it possible to identify and recognize the workings of families and the notion of 'doing gender'. Women are disproportionately poor, paid on average less than men, and continue to have a range of commitments across generations and relationships. Emancipation, proffered through legislation and changes in social practices, has not brought women equality, albeit that it has improved the lives of many. For women, the last 50 years have been transformative but not necessarily redistributive.

As the expectations of women are transformed, some men have resorted to violence in an attempt to continue to control women's lives. Despite women's enhanced status and legal rights, gendered violence is prevalent. Violence in intimate relationships leaves many women with a double jeopardy. To speak of what is happening may lead to the break-up of the family and call into question their abilities to forge caring and intimate relationships. The shame and embarrassment associated with 'calling time' on a violent relationship continues and will remain as long as femininities are so strongly associated with an ethics of care that is centred upon families and relationships. The myths that can surround family and home life – of 'apple pie' and all things wholesome – encourage denial from within a violent relationship, as well as among those of us who can see but do not act. As long as masculinity is associated with violence, and the defence of the family, whether that be defence against physical threats or of family honour, then men too are caught in a web-like situation. It takes strength to disclose violence. It takes strength to say 'this should not happen to anyone'. Ultimately, words are part of the project to end violence but these words must translate into actions on the part of governments, organizations and individuals.

7

A critical social theory of families, violence and social change

Introduction

Sociology is concerned with the production and workings of society. In its construction and development it has 'been simultaneously concerned with and produced by "modernity"' (Witz and Marshall 2004: 19). Sociology can enhance our understanding of how we live in an ever-changing society and thus has much to offer in any exploration of violence. The focus of this final chapter is the potential for sociological work to aid the study of gendered violence in families.

Violence arises from a complex interaction of political, social, cultural and economic factors. Within those factors there is the interplay of individual and social relationships, and the ways in which people and relationships are embedded in communities through, for example, neighbourhoods, schools, shops, health centres and places of employment. In noting these factors I do not propose a linear relationship but rather a multiple and dialectic one. There is no one single theory or discipline that explains why some individuals or groups are violent or abusive towards others, or why violence is more prevalent in certain communities and groups than others (Hird 2002: 113).[1]

An overarching aim of this book is to propose a critical social theory of gender, families and violence, and in so doing to draw upon studies and theories that enhance the interrogation of a number of factors and issues, including:

---

[1] Other disciplines offer explanations, most notably biology and sociobiology and psychology and psychoanalysis (Gondolf 1985; Gelles and Loseke 1993). The focus of this book is upon sociological explanations, although work and ideas from philosophy (Arendt 1970; Card 2002), politics (Young 1997) and social policy (Wasoff and Dey 2000) are drawn upon.

- Ambivalence on the subject of violence against women. Some commentators and researchers suggest that many couples use low levels of violence in ways that do not have a lasting impact and that both men and women have the potential to be violent, thus attempting to diminish the evidence that much violence is gendered.
- Social, religious and cultural norms. These shift and interweave with global images of war and the violent treatment of women and children in conflicts.
- The use of force and sanctions which the police, legal and armed services can use to contain violence in public spaces. The focus on violence and dangers in public places outweighs the threats posed by being in a family.

To reprise: assessing and examining violence is a complex and multi-layered process. Given this, what can sociology offer by way of enhancing understandings and promoting change? This chapter opens with a review of sociological work on violence considering first mainstream or 'male-stream' theories and then dimensions of feminist and pro-feminist studies. Drawing this part of the chapter to a close is a review of debates on social change and social practices. Developing aspects of sociological work, and calling for theoretical pluralism, I then consider the notion of the averted gaze further through the concept and processes of denial. Some explanatory critiques are then offered. In the conclusion the potential of a sociological gaze to inform research, policy and practice is explored.

Mainstream/malestream theories: an absence of gender and families

There remains a dearth of mainstream sociological theorization on violence and this is particularly so on the topic of violence in families (Ray 2000). Theory remains a high status component of sociological work and much of this work is rightly concerned with the production of society and relations therein. Early studies of the family concentrated on the relationship of the family to the economy and the (re)production of workers and responsible citizens – 'systems' theories (Parsons 1949). Critical studies of families and relationships followed but few addressed violence until the late 1960s (Bernardes 1987).

Earlier sociological theories were not so much concerned with violence *per se* but rather with the development of legitimate forms of social control, consensus and cohesion (Durkheim 1976) or sources of division, exclusion and conflict (Marx [1867] 1970). Thus when violence was recognized and considered, this generally reflected interests in the wider workings of authority and power (Arendt 1970). Theories that might be broadly premised upon notions of conflict have a long history, originating in philosophical ideas on the distinctive nature of the social in human life. For example, Hegel's assertion that man produces himself may seem naïve given the complexities of the social and economic forces we now engage with, but it gave prominence to the individual and her or his engagement with their world (Hegel 1953). For Marx, Hegelian ideas offered a framework for tenets of his theories, namely that the need to engage with capitalism and labour produces the person (Marx [1867] 1970). Marx did not theorize violence *per se* and perhaps this results from what may have seemed the distance between consciousness and revolution. Subsequently, Marxist approaches to social order have devoted a lot of time to the concepts of, for example, ideology and class relations (Ray 2000). However, the recourse to revolution, hard to realize without conflict and violence, remains relatively under-theorized although well documented (Arendt 2002: 21).

The work of Weber (2002) is indicative of a focus, in classic aspects of sociology, on the state and state-sanctioned conflicts. The role of the state has been defined as a 'human community that (successfully) claims the *monopoly of legitimate use of physical force within a given territory*' (Weber 2002: 13, original emphasis). Weber asserts that the state is the only social institution that can claim legitimacy to engage in violence in national and international law. In this analysis, for a given social order to persist for any length of time, it would need to be based on non-violent and what are considered normative and legitimate forms of domination operating through the state.

In contrast, others argue that violence is never legitimate, and that it is not about the operation of legitimate forms of power but the destruction of power: 'Power and violence are opposites; where the one rules absolutely, the other is absent. Violence appears where power is in jeopardy, but left to its own course it ends in power's disappearance' (Arendt 1970: 56). Citing the example of Stalin's regime in the former Soviet Union, Arendt (1970: 55) goes on to assert that the 'climax of terror is reached when the police state begins to devour its own children and yesterday's executioner becomes today's victim'.

This focus on conflict, authority and social order is furthered through the study of politics and power: 'all politics is a struggle for power; the ultimate kind of power is violence' (Mills 1959: 171). In contrast, theories of consensus and solidarity emphasize norms and values as basic tenets of social life and cooperation. Early origins of these theories are embodied in the notion of 'organic solidarity'. This proposes that consensus and solidarity would generally emerge through individuated means of the sacred embodied in, for example, human rights (Durkheim 1976).

A number of contemporary theorists offer possibilities for theoretical development on conflict and consensus (Habermas 1984, 1987; Bhaskar 1989; Giddens 1996). The 'lifeworld' is a conceptual frame to define and explore the 'symbolic space' within which culture, social integration and personality are sustained and reproduced (Habermas 1984, 1987). In this conceptual frame the private lifeworld – families – (re)produce a committed labour force, while in the public spheres the state establishes economic institutions such as private property and contract law as well as promoting and influencing consumption patterns. The broadly-framed traditions of conflict and consensus theories, respectively, highlight differing and overlapping aspects of social realities.

The book, *The Nation State and Violence*, Anthony Giddens (1996) considers violence. The focus is, as the title suggests, on the state, military power and the monopoly of violence, with limited attention paid to violence in families. The diverse experiences of violence in what are termed 'pacified' civil societies are worthy of detailed attention. The theory of structuration proposes a 'duality of structure' to describe the dynamic relationship between the person and society; the fluid relationships between structure and agency (Giddens 1984, 1994, 1996). Social structures are constituted by human agency and yet those social structures are the medium for that very constitution of activities. People who draw upon ideas, norms, rules and resources of social structures produce society and their actions have a range of consequences, 'one of which is to reproduce society ... but not in circumstances of their choosing' (Williams and May 1996: 88).

The methodology of 'retroduction' (Bhaskar 1979: 15) proposes the separation of the meaning of an act and its intention; meaning is social, intention is personal: 'Social scientists are in the business of discovering social reality and this will have antecedents in individual realities, themselves shaped by social meanings' (Williams and May 1996: 86). This offers interesting opportunities for the analysis of families and violence, proposing as it does that social structures and phenomena only exist because they determine certain activities and cannot be identified independently of them (Bhaskar 1989: 78). Families may be considered as 'an objective social category (a structuring structure)' and 'as a subjective social category (a structured structure)' (Bourdieu 1996: 21). Society cannot be identified independently of its effects, nor does it exist independently of them. People do not work to reproduce the wage labour economy 'any more than they marry to sustain the nuclear family' (Scambler 2002: 42) but these are unintended and inexorably related consequences.

Feminist and pro-feminist perspectives

Feminist theories and research have been at the forefront of questioning established methods of research, in particular the relationship between the researcher and the researched and the ethical implications of research (Letherby 2003: 144). The production and reproduction of gendered identities in families have been examined from a range of feminist perspectives. Women's and gender studies, and the study of masculinities, have all contributed to the breaking down and blurring of boundaries within the social sciences to offer alternative paradigms on families and family life.

In considering violence in families, a number of feminist and pro-feminist perspectives argue that mainstream theories, and many family violence researchers, have disregarded the interweaving and influence of gender and power, and the dominance of heterosexuality in families. For example, in Chapter 2 I discussed some of the studies that have failed to consider gender and violence. It was noted that some argue that 'violence is used by the most powerful family member as a means of legitimising his or her dominant position' (Straus 1990: 193). This assertion is based upon the idea that either a woman or a man can hold power equally. It implies that heterosexual partnerships operate on an equal footing.

Asserting equality is problematic. With differentials in employment, domestic labour, caring work, leisure time and lifetime income that favour men, especially men in heterosexual partnerships, equality is rarely evident. Power is not gender neutral and to argue so is to ignore the global patterns and workings of sexism. Further, what has been termed the recent 'backlash' against the progress of feminism has provoked renewed and keen debates on the role of families and women (Fauldi 1991), and a number of academics are contributing to a welcome growth in the study of masculinities (Jokinen 2000; Hearn 2002). Despite this, few commentators or policy makers have done any radical thinking about the role of men (Kimmel 1995). It would seem that in the arena of families, men remain consigned to roles dominated by their engagement with the labour market and the evolving role of parenting. Some positive shifts have been noted, especially in the sharing of domestic labour in middle-class households. Yet with only a small number of men interested in pro-feminist theories and ideas, or in a critical engagement with masculinities, it is the case that women work to accommodate the everyday realities of working and caring.

There is a large body of work that analyses violence as being expressive of dimensions of coercive control. Drawing on a range of theories and data, these studies have been at the forefront of a shifting emphasis to focus on perpetrators and the workings of power and oppression. Explaining that violence does 'not arise in a vacuum' and violence in families is often patterned, a number of studies point to entrenched social relations (Ray 2000: 147). Studies from feminist perspectives have contended that violence, especially men's violence to known women and girls, may be analysed as part of structured power and patriarchal social relations (Hester et al. 1997). These studies often interlink and offer explanations of violence in terms of social divisions in class, sexualities, race, religion and age.

Men's control of women and violence towards them has, in the past, been sanctioned by legal systems (Dobash and Dobash 1979). With increased equality, and changes in legislation to outlaw violence in intimate relationships, some men have actually resorted to violence to legitimize and maintain positions of privilege. Even if a woman is not experiencing violence she will be aware (unconsciously) of the dynamic but ever-present range of threats posed by patriarchy. The theory of the normalization of violence for women furthers these ideas by proposing that the avoidance of and/or the experience of violence and abuse frames the lives of all girls and women (Pylkkanen 2001). Women and girls negotiate rules of engagement with others, recognizing that without adhering to these, they may themselves be blamed for experiencing violence or harassment. Equally, men, and in particular young men, must negotiate masculinities and violence in public spaces.

The constructions, and operation of, men and masculinities with regards to violence have been charted by a number of sociologists (Hearn 2002). The role of violence in the childhood and upbringing of men has been a particular concern (Jackson 1990). It has been argued that such violence is behaviour *chosen* by men, and is the product of choice within a *structural* context of hierarchical power arrangements (Kirkwood 1993). Violence provides many men with a clearly understood mechanism to demonstrate masculinities and (re)create inequalities between genders (Jokinen 2000).

Images of masculinities and violence abound in sport, film, television, advertising, media and fiction. The celebration of machismo is epitomized in cultural phrases such as 'a man's gotta do what a man's gotta do' and is evident in series of films, such as *Die Hard* and *Terminator*. In the *Die Hard* series of films, a 'good family man' used violence to seek what is framed as redemption for violent acts perpetrated against immediate family members and friends. These are prominent examples of the cultural transmission of attitudes and ideas that uphold notions that violence can be used by men, and in a positive manner. At times these images are also used to reiterate and bolster patriotism, particularly in times of war and conflict when the state sanctions men to take part in military service and action. For example, Arnold Schwarzenegger called US soldiers the 'real terminators' in a speech made during a visit to Iraq. This assertion received popular acclaim among media and military groups.

Structural analyses have highlighted the varied and dynamic impact of masculinities and offer a complex and differentiated notion of patriarchies (Hearn 1998; Connell 2002). As noted earlier, not all men are violent and any focus on studies premised upon a structural analysis of patriarchy must avoid an oversimplified explanation: 'men's violence within patriarchies, although persistent, is also variable and specific, rather than monolithic' (Hearn 1998: 32). Most autonomous women's organizations and sympathetic policymakers argue for responses that combine structural and contextual approaches; sympathetic services and protection and prevention campaigns on violence in families and violence in general.

Work on social movements, considered in the previous chapter, has explored how individuals unify in struggles about common causes (Sorel 1961; Gouldner 1976). In these struggles, violence can clarify and mark the limits of issues and act as a form of social binding, promoting the conduct of, or condoning, the act of violence – for example, the Klu Klux Klan in the US or paramilitary groups that have formed around sectarianism in Ireland. It can also bind those who are concerned to tackle violence and campaign for services, support and preventive programmes – for example, Women's Aid, Amnesty International and Human Rights Watch. These groups or movements are associated with the politics of identity in so far as they also create a politics of identification (Hetherington 1998: 38). Women's Aid valorizes ideas and work based upon feminist and non-hierarchical principles that seek to tackle stereotypes of violence against women and children. This work raises important questions and runs campaigns about violence across services, organizations and politics. Identification with gender politics and activities links to international work and organizations through, for example, the potential offered by the declarations and activities of international organizations such as the UN or the World Health Organization. Social movements offer identifications through practices that are 'situated in spaces that actually matter to the performance' (Hetherington 1998: 38).

Contemporary analyses have also charted the growth in patriarchal organizations with cross-state and territorial links yet without a territorial base themselves – for example, the UN, the International Monetary Fund and the EU. These are both gendered and gendering organizations and thus 'there are significant features of the gender order which cannot be understood locally, which *require* analysis on a global scale' (Connell 2002: 108). Considering gender as a structure of world society illuminates the ways in which economics, politics and cultural norms achieve and promote patterns of gender and sexuality. These vary, but the domination of women by men is very evident in most aspects of life. Thus it is notable that the World Health Organization (2002) has undertaken a review of studies originating from across the globe on the topic of violence, and that the final report places emphasis on gender inequities and the role of cultural norms in determining social roles and attitudes to violence. While welcome, the World Health Organization (an agency of the UN) carries limited influence in global politics. This is certainly the case on health issues that are predominantly social in origin (rather than infectious conditions). Global activities depend on the involvement of governments, agencies and groups. The impact of this report has been patchy, with it receiving a welcome reception from those already active on the topic, while there has been a muted response from many other quarters.

Gender, women's studies and social policies have highlighted diverse impacts of violence (in terms of race, age, disability and social class), emphasizing multiple and reflexive interconnections between, among others, power/resistance, discourse/knowledge and agency/identity (Bhatti-Sinclair 1994; Pringle 1995). These theoretical frames offer explanations that are multiple and varied, and consider the context characteristics of immediate and ongoing acts of violence. Here, studies have the potential to transcend divisions between individuals, groups and structures.

The arrival of feminist and pro-feminist studies and theories presents a series of challenges to mainstream/malestream sociological theories as well as to the analysis of social practices and change. Critical perspectives on gender, families and violence are no longer the focus of a sub-discipline, the sociology of families. Today the workings of gender, families and violence are considered across a number of sub-themes in sociology such as gender and women's studies, autobiography and health and illness. However, there remain struggles and tensions in the battle to ensure gender is featured in any analysis or explanation (Young 1997).

Social worlds, social practices and social change

It might be fair to conclude that families and violence have not come centre stage in classic and mainstream sociological theory. While 'violence is a persistent feature of social life ... (with a few exceptions) it has not been central to sociological concerns' (Ray 2000: 145). Sociological theory has tended to focus on social cohesion and consensus, with the study of violence largely seen 'as a residual category of power' (Ray 2000: 145). While this may be the case in mainstream sociological theory, many have worked on violence from other perspectives – not least of which are gender, sexualities and power – exploring violence as structured gendered oppression supported by cultural norms (Hearn 1998; Kelly 1999). In the past, such approaches have been more concerned with the analysis of collective conflicts (war and civil strife) and crime, with, by contrast, a contemporary emphasis on gender, families and violence largely evolving through gender and women's studies.

This reflects the 'taken for grantedness of families', the hierarchical and gendered nature of sociological work, especially on theory, combined with an earlier marginalization of women and gender in the social sciences. While it is not the purpose of this book to critique the historical development of sociological theory, research and policy work on families and violence has evolved alongside critical debates on the masculinist nature of classical texts and theories (Marshall and Witz 2004). The boundaries between public and private have been conflated with a masculine/feminine distinction 'with most sociological interest directed towards the former' (Witz and Marshall 2004: 20). The conflation of the public with the masculine has led to presumptions that social action and agency are in a generic sense male. When women, or the concept of gender, appear they may be conceptualized with respect to the masculine. To move on necessitates a major rethink and shift in analysis:

> An integral part of feminist sociology's aim to rethink – and perhaps reshape – the social must be to excavate the gendered erasures and inclusions that shaped the concept of social in the first place. A feminist politics of interrogation also necessitates that we rework the concept of the social in such a way that it erases less and includes more, rather than simply reasserting its continued salience.
>
> (Witz and Marshall 2004: 33)

Sociological theories and explanations that address the above (albeit that in post-industrial societies cultural activities have acquired greater significance), offer frames for exploring both the ongoing acceptance of, and also challenges to, violence in families. Sociologists have grappled with changes to aspects of social and economic life at the end of the twentieth century, with some asserting that there is something uniquely distinctive about this period in history. Postmodernism has offered much in the way of critique, arguing that there are no universal theories or any one reality. From this perspective there are no overarching truths, only fragmented knowledges, which come together with the specificities of time and place. Central to postmodernism is the treatise that asserts that knowledge is part of power and that power is ubiquitous (Williams and May 1996: 157; Letherby 2003: 52). Drawn from this premise there is not one truth but many: 'there are a variety of contradictory and conflicting standpoints, of social discourses, none of which should be privileged' (Millen 1997: 7.7). Taken literally, postmodernism suggests that all we can do is to present various accounts and to query and challenge these. This attack on 'grand theory' or meta-analysis proves to be self-defeating when considering families and violence as it undermines the need to address the breadth and depth of material, structural and social inequalities.

Commentators suggest we are living with an increased pace of social change, denoted by some as a period of 'high modernity' or 'post-traditional society' (Giddens 1994). Others have proposed that contemporary times might be considered 'reflexive modernity' (Beck 1994) while for some this is simply a particular phase of modernity (Bauman 1990). Issues of difference and diversity have achieved prominence through poststructural and postmodernist studies. In general these theories argue for the existence of a multiplicity of identities produced discursively through the dynamics of structural determination and choice.

The continuing (re)formation of families poses hazards and insecurities that for some threaten the very existence of the family (fission) and for others are a manifestation of the fusion of potentially competing identities. Structural changes are resulting in social agents who construct their own biographies in a society where material and social inequalities restrict information and choices. Inequalities persist but seem hidden from view until disrupted; an obvious example is continuing inequities between men and women despite gains in the labour market by women. Examining the continued ascription of roles on the basis of gender and age, in the context of a wage economy, family life seems half industrial (the engagement with the labour, market) and half feudal (needs for care and interdependence) (Beck 1994). Certainly, violence in families poses hazards and insecurities but these have not just 'emerged'. Increasingly, sociological studies and explanations are illustrating the obviousness of dangers in family life while many groups and agencies are challenging attempts to silence or ignore violence through the collection and distribution of evidence.

The challenges are monumental. As an example: research in three high schools in Edinburgh with young people aged 12–16 explored their knowledge and attitudes to violence against women (Zero Tolerance 1994). Findings indicate high levels of tolerance for violence between men and women particularly when the perpetrator is married to the victim. The majority of young people interviewed expressed some likelihood of using violence in their future relationships.

From an averted to a sociological gaze

Emotions can change according to our proximity to acts of violence, and the relationship, if any, with those experiencing or perpetrating violence. We tend to empathize most readily with the suffering of those we feel close to. Yet bystanders, relatives, friends, victims and perpetrators can deny suspicions or knowledge of violence. The notion of the averted gaze embodies the outcomes of these denials, namely the failure to act upon the sight of violence. This involves knowing about violence and yet choosing not to act. And as 'much human suffering takes place in private, invisible to any outside observer' (Cohen 2001: 15), denial can involve those who are the nearest relatives, living in the same household or with access to intimate knowledge. How might denial manifest itself? Cohen (2001: 7) proposes three possibilities:

- *Literal*: this refers to factual or blatant denial. Within families this might be illustrated by the mother who denies her daughter is being abused by her son-in-law. She may prefer to live with implausible explanations from her son-in-law and daughter. Refusing to acknowledge the evidence, for whatever reason, leads to denial. This may result from ignorance, lies or may work as a defence mechanism against the consequences of acceptance.
- *Interpretive*: evidence is given a different meaning. For example, ethnic cleansing might be perceived as people choosing to move to avoid violence, and domestic abuse as everyday marital conflict and stresses. The evidence is not denied but is interpreted in such a way that action is not necessary by those who are aware of, or observing, the violence.
- *Implicatory*: what is denied or minimized are the *implications* of the violence. So while the evidence is not denied, the witness to the beating of a child might say 'What can I do? After all he's the parent', the witness to the mugging, 'They might turn on me' or the person who becomes aware of the long-term economic abuse and neglect of an older person, 'It's worse in other countries you know.' It may be that the observer genuinely does not consider the violence to be 'that bad'.

These categories offer a continuum from the almost apologetic (if I don't deny violence I might make things worse) to the cynical, 'I'm all right Jack' approach (let them get on with it as long as it's not affecting my family). States of denial may be infused with the unbearable weight of knowledge, self-deception, and an inability to grasp the evidence or acknowledge moral realities (Arendt 1970; Glover 1999; Cohen 2001). More often, explanations for ignoring or not taking violence in families seriously will draw from all three 'states of denial'. At issue is how to explore responses with regards to available evidence and theories. To care does not necessarily involve being vocal and visibly active. It is important to differentiate between being a witness in close proximity to violence and being aware of the need to act to change attitudes, policies and practices. Denial spans a number of realms (Cohen 2001: 9):

- cognition (not acknowledging the facts);
- emotion (not feeling, not being disturbed);
- morality (not recognizing responsibility);
- action (not taking steps in response to knowledge).

And it can take place at various levels: individual/personal, official and cultural.

International and national organizations can, and do, ask us to consider suffering, but violence against women and children has taken some time to achieve a place on mainstream policy and legal agendas. The recognition of violence in legislation and services has been a long-term and discursive project (Hearn and Parkin 2001: 43). While the law and services began to acknowledge violence in families over 150 years ago with the 1853 Act for Prevention and Punishment of Aggravated Assaults on Women and Children and the 1861 Offences Against the Person Act, interpretations and responses were patchy and did little to tackle assumptions about men's authority over women and children. Even today historical legacies and the continued workings of patriarchy result in contradictory meanings and activities in so far as the law and related services increasingly recognize violence but do so in a manner that is limited and with inadequate consideration of power and gender.

Attitudes towards rape, and particularly rape in marriage, further illuminate the workings of various dimensions and aspects of denial. The common presumption that rape is only 'real and valid' if perpetrated by a stranger is one that continues to be promoted through images and ideas in various forms of media and culture. Most societies reserve specific abhorrence for the rapist who abducts a woman or girl from a public place. But these form a minority of cases. Reported allegations of rape are increasing while convictions in the UK decline. Many of those involved in these cases are known to each other through a past or current relationship. While some of the increase in reporting originates from enhanced confidence that legal and other services will be sympathetic, sexually motivated violence is ongoing and, some argue, increasing. Some assert that sexual crimes are perpetrated by men challenging women's growing strength in economic and social terms (Viner 2003). In times of war, ethnic and civil unrest, rape (sometimes of a neighbour or friend) continues to be viewed as a weapon and trophy of conflict.

In most of the incidents reported, the potential for legal action rests upon the contested nature of consent to sexual acts and the use of women's sexual history by defence lawyers (Lees 2002). Many women and girls do not report sexual violence, or withdraw allegations, especially if they know, and have reason, to fear the perpetrator. If the perpetrator is a relative, spouse or partner, or close family friend, it can provoke disbelief – he is in a position of trust and so surely would not do this; she must be inventing this claim – combined with an apportioning of blame – she probably led him on. A continued presumption that men have a stronger sex drive than women may be used to excuse sexual abuse. But why do men sexually violate female relatives when often they have other relationships? An obvious factor is the opportunities afforded in family relationships and life, leading to abuses of power and trust through violence and violation.

It is especially difficult to achieve a conviction from allegations of sexual violence. Marriage or heterosexual cohabitation is still imbued with notions of rights to sexual activity. In the case of rape and sexual violence by a man known to the victim, societal denial works in a number of ways. For example, evidence may not be acknowledged by the media, and legal systems persist with images and practices based on stranger rape as the most appropriate type of rape to be brought before the courts. Morality works here through the denial of responsibility for what goes on in the context of families: 'after all these are generally safe places and any perpetrator must be abnormal in some way'. The 'ordinariness' of those who perpetrate violence may be well known to police and the courts but to many people, someone 'must look like a violent type' – whatever that is!

When governmental action is taken on sexual violence, this is usually hard fought for and often a consequence of the campaigning of women's and human rights groups. Legislative and policy changes are under constant scrutiny in case they prove to be too radical a challenge to the nuanced but nevertheless global norms and working of families. Women and children may have achieved greater recognition in legislation and socially, but it can appear that their experiences are silenced or taken less seriously than they might be. Globally, attitudes to violence against women and girls are illustrated in the manner in which rape in war and civil unrest is tolerated as part of a soldier's behaviour. Rape in war was outlawed in the Geneva Conventions of 1949 (Card 2002: 120). It was only in 1996 that the International Criminal Tribunal of The Hague first served indictments for sexual assault, and those were against eight Bosnian Serbs. This was the first indictment for rape as a war crime in any international court or tribunal. That it has taken so long to have sexual violence against women (or men for that matter) considered a war crime suggests that there has been a level of acceptance and silence surrounding the ongoing and systematic abuse of women and girls during and after wars and civil unrest.

Rape and sexual violence are acts of domination. Women note the threat in both the public and private spheres of life. They seek to limit the threat of violence through their actions and responses and live with the 'normalization of violence'.

Explanatory critiques

One of the aims of this book is to explore the potential for sociological perspectives to offer a critical theory on the continued denial of many aspects and dimensions of violence in families. Sociology, as C. Wright Mills (1959) proposed, should consider the interrelated workings of 'personal troubles' and issues of social structure and social practices. Denial, for example, may be considered a personal activity, but it is also operating at various levels including families, governments, agencies and international organizations. It comprises ideas that include assertions that 'something did not happen, does not exist, is not true or is not known about' (Cohen 2001: 3). A critical theory should therefore explore the complex and discursive relationship between violence in families, social structures and states of denial.

Violence in families is a source of increasing concern and activity and so at one level it is evidently not denied; it does exist and this is acknowledged. However, allegations of violence can challenge taboos that imbue families and lead to stigma. Further, among family members there can be an:

> astonishing capacity to ignore or pretend to ignore what happens in front of their eyes, whether sexual abuse, incest, violence, alcoholism, craziness or plain unhappiness ... The family's distinctive self-image determines which aspects of shared experience can be openly acknowledged and which must remain closed and denied. These rules are governed by the meta-rule that no one must either admit or deny that they exist.
>
> (Cohen 2001: 64)

These 'meta-rules' create a contradiction with the idea of a 'civilized' society premised upon notions of democracy, freedom of speech and respect for human rights. Some family members cannot, or do not, say anything. When something is said those words can be treated with disbelief, suspicion and a sense of disloyalty. Further, few talk of the miseries of family life that all too many women and children experience. The family is a way of organizing human relationships and life and remains fundamental to the organization of wider social and economic practices and worlds. To talk of families in less than positive terms can be viewed in some political and social quarters as a form of heresy.

The upbringing of children, the longer-term well-being of citizens, the sustainability of neighbourhoods and communities, are tasks and aims fundamental to everyday life. In short, domestic and caring labour is critical to the cohesion and working of societies. Much of a care economy is centred upon families and social networks. Women exchange their labour power on the basis of accepting that equality evidently does not exist but that they are sustaining and nurturing relationships, achieving satisfaction along with a sense of exploitation. A study of men's and women's perceptions of fairness in relation to the domestic division of labour found that 60 per cent of women respondents reported that the division of labour in the home was fair even though they were doing far more: in this study women reported spending 24 hours per week on housework in comparison to 9 hours per week for men: 'This suggests that fairness is not calculated in terms of an equal distribution of time and tasks. Rather the balance is tipped decidedly in men's favour . . . men agree that women have a much heavier domestic labour load. This suggests that men hold quite biased views about what is considered a fair distribution of household labour' (Baxter 2000: 625). Women's perceptions of fairness were based on men's involvement in specific types of task. If men became involved in tasks strongly associated with women, such as cleaning, cooking and shopping, then their input, however limited, enhanced women's perception of fairness.

Unpaid domestic labour is perceived as non-work (no matter how valuable) and for many women the option is to employ someone else to undertake such work so as to avoid conflicts in families. This has created a mobile, global and often exploitative market in domestic and caring labour (Ehrenreich and Hochschild 2002). The avoidance of dealing with the realities of inequities in these divisions of labour, coupled with the social and economic pressures to form and maintain families, especially for the raising of children, gives rise to false beliefs about fairness and satisfaction in family life.

Feminists and pro-feminists would argue that their critiques of families and promotion of diversities in living arrangements offer alternatives to false beliefs about the sanctity and security of family life. For most of us, the overall benefits of family life outweigh the realities – as long as psychological and physical well-being are not challenged to the point of disillusionment, self-harm or violence.

Conclusions

In the section 'Discovery and denial' in Chapter 6, the tenets of sociological and philosophical work on denial were outlined (Cohen 2001; Card 2002). Differentiating between micro and macro denial offers the potential to analyse how individuals (micro) and societies (macro) can acknowledge domestic violence. Yet this 'acknowledgement' has led to responses that are individuated in ways that focus upon those experiencing abuse. These responses can be, and often are, indifferent to repertoires of violence associated with masculinities, governments and global organizations. There are 'cultural interpretations and neutralizations . . . [which] . . . encourage a dulled, passive acceptance of violence: this is what men are like, this is the fate of women, there's no point in telling anyone, these things should be kept in the family' (Cohen 2001: 52).

Continued levels of violence in families, the slow pace of change in gender roles and discourses, the limited acceptance of the need for care work and dependency over our lives, and images of violence in various dimensions of culture interweave to ensure that there is an acknowledgement of violence in families and yet limited attempts to explore and challenge the causes. There is denial of the need to tackle causes – namely, the workings of families (family practices), ideas about family values and solidarities, the social and economic predicaments of those who are not worker citizens and have limited access to finance and social networks, and the continued prominence afforded to families as places of sanctity from the perils and strains of modernity (secondary denial). The gap that exists between 'concern and action' moves us beyond treating physical symptoms and economic consequences to address the longer-term psychological abuses and the varied and interrelated causes (Cohen 2001: 289). Certainly the threshold in public opinion for the toleration of violence in families has lowered. Services and the law have followed, reinforced and enhanced these trends. I would never wish to suggest anything other than support for services, institutions and social movements working to identify violence and support those experiencing it. However, the continued focus on the victim leads to processes of containment that allow for the averted gaze with many convinced that if women are supported and can leave, then that is another social problem addressed. Failure to tackle the causes of violence against women is evident in the workings of many societies. The continued dominance of masculine notions of privacy, coupled with fears on the part of governments and commentators that further intervention in families could pose unacceptable challenges to solidarities, present barriers to debates and action.

In international law, and in most but not all states, men and women are defined as citizens with equal rights. However, sexual and cultural codes define men and women as opposites and seek to avoid any ambiguities on gender roles and sexualities. Ideas of gendered roles continue to define women and men in terms of their engagement, or otherwise, with domestic or paid work (Connell 2002: 56). This notion of a 'social contract' is, as Pateman (1988) comments, underpinned by a 'sexual contract', that is, the private subordination of women to men. This gives liberal democracies the smokescreen of equality alongside the everyday realities of a 'fraternal social contract' (Pateman 1988).

As considered in earlier chapters, the basis to many families is the heterosexual partnership, whether marriage or cohabitation. Marriage is seemingly a 'contractual' arrangement but differs greatly from contracts that might be signed for the purposes of a loan or employment (Card 2002: 157). Many of the obligations in marriage, and for that matter parenting, are highly informal. On the ending of the 'contract' (e.g. divorce or separation) obligations do not dissolve as they would when a loan is paid off or a house sold. Given that these intimate relationships are underpinned with the processes of power and the exercise of judgement and discretion, services and legal systems may find it 'difficult to hold a spouse, or a parent, accountable for abuse' (Card 2002: 156).

Violence is a social choice and 'a clear intention to do harm, for which men are individually responsible' (Hearn 1998: 210):

> The reproduction of feelings of powerlessness and being out of control can easily be one mode of maintaining power and control. And yet while men are certainly engaged, through the doing of violence, in maintaining and elaborating power and control, in another sense some men are also not fully in control of themselves – whether through drink or drugs, through rage, through the lure and excitement of violent movement. That sense of not being in control of themselves is, however, still knowable and to an extent predictable.
>
> (Hearn 1998: 220)

Accounts of violence may include justifications and excuses and many are drawn from cultural repertoires that may prove acceptable – for example, 'I didn't mean that. It was an accident' or 'I had to hit her to calm her down. She was hysterical.' Through such accounts perpetrators can aim to neutralize the violence and appeal to well-established ideas that violence is uncontrollable, unpredictable and sometimes necessary, if unfortunate.

Much mainstream or 'malestream' sociological work on the topic of violence has been concerned with the analysis and explanation of violence and violations between strangers or communities in wars, civil unrest and criminal acts. Underlying these studies has been an interest in social conflict, social cohesion and practices, and the interaction of groups within differing, and sometimes competing, social and economic structures. By contrast the study of gender and families, and families, violence and social change has been viewed as a sub-discipline of sociological theory; a domain of the less powerful and less prestigious.

Dimensions of sociological work have addressed violence in families, most notably, gender and women's studies. Much of this sociological work, as well as most policy and practice developments, has focused upon those who are experiencing or have survived violence. Important as this theoretical and empirical work is, it gives limited attention to the broader social, cultural and economic contexts that sanction and silence violence in families. Ironic then that sociological work on social relations affords limited time and attention to the social practices and structures that would appear to sanction or silence violence. With regards to violence it would seem there are two broad sociologies; one concerned with meta-analysis with a focus on the workings of societies, social cohesion and conflict while other sociologies – a grouping of sub-disciplines – critically consider the (everyday) practices of people, families and relationships, and violence.

As Witz and Marshall (2004: 34) assert, we need to 'grapple with the ambivalent legacy of classical sociology' and reconceptualize what we mean by the term 'social' to include the private as well as the public.

In the worlds of policy and politics there is further distinction with limited linkage between violence in national and international conflicts as personified in wars and terrorism, and individual acts of violence in families. There are silences and denials in both settings. A range of discourses in politics and the media glorify war in ways that are not dissimilar to images of families in so far as we have the notion of the 'good and just' war and the 'good and nurturing' family. Governments promote both images as key to securing social order and cohesion. They may proffer war as a means of securing a social order in which the retention and promotion of positive notions of family and everyday life are the goal; the 'just' war for the 'good' family life. When violent acts in time of war or civil unrest are considered unacceptable – for example, mass rape or mutilation – they tend to be explained through the actions of isolated and unusual individuals. At times the word 'evil' is used to denote these acts as beyond the necessary comprehension of individuals, societies or governments. On the cessation of war or conflict the search for reconciliation can encourage avoidance of the practices of violence. There is a cultural aversion to seeing this violence and violations as emerging from social and gendered practices. Violence, whether rape in war, or domestic abuse in families, is about the belief by some, usually men, that power and control is both desirable and justifiable in certain circumstances.

A starting point is to challenge key terms such as 'the family', 'families' and 'family violence'. These terms, and the conceptual frame they offer in the analysis of social problems, form opacity to a critical gendered analysis. Concepts are 'proposals about how we ought to proceed from here' (Tanesini 1994: 207). The use of these conceptual terms frames the manner in which problems are determined, explained and tackled:

> 'the problem ... is not *just* the particular phrase which is used to describe the issue, but the ways in which a particular descriptor is deployed in a specific policy proposal to produce a particular problem representation' (Bacchi 1999: 165, original emphasis).

The terms 'the family', 'family policy' and 'family violence' frame the problem of violence in a manner that renders the perpetrator invisible. Women's Aid, campaigning groups and empathetic politicians, policy-makers and practitioners have had to work consistently to ensure gender and gendered violence are on the agenda and move centre stage.

The development of *alternative concepts* might evolve through the application of the dynamic concept of the lifeworld (Habermas 1987) and, within that, family practices, namely the identification and analysis of activities associated with and undertaken by family members (Morgan 2002). Family practices invoke a sense of 'flow and fluidity', and interdependence, while enabling both description and sociological analysis. Of course, with regards to violence among adults in families, gender and the processes of gendering family practices would come centre stage. The social meaning of acts, and thus the determination of 'What is the problem?' evokes the notion of 'retroduction' (Bhaskar 1979), that is, 'what sort of process, mechanism, agency, and so on ... would have this phenomenon as its consequences?' (Benton and Craib 2001: 185). Thus, the response to 'What is the problem?' would be drawn from an analysis of data collected within the conceptual frame of family practices, and retroduction, in response to the overarching question of what sort of process, mechanisms, agency, and so on have gendered violence as its consequences.

We cannot stop at the recognition of domestic violence within government policies (Radford and Tsutsumi 2004). The globalization of violence against women is increasingly evident. Men in better-off areas of the world can respond to growing risks associated with perpetrating violence at home through the exploitation and abuse of migrant women and children, or by travelling to other countries. As long as women from ethnic groups and countries are viewed as the most disposable of people then the realities and risks of these violations will gain little attention in debates on violence (Radford and Tsutsumi 2004: 10). The current emphasis on the containment of gendered violence limits work on the 'elimination of the injustice of violence and abuse' in the 'broader project for global justice and women's rights' (Radford and Tsutsumi 2004: 10). We must work across the micro (individual) and macro (societal) levels of denial, listen to the voices of the abused and ensure the individualization of a social problem. Here I assert that to move beyond containment we must accept some responsibility for the ambiguities and contingencies that surround violence in families and violence *per se*.

Theoretical pluralism can create a bridge between 'two sociologies' – namely, meta-narratives and theories, and sociological work on the everyday. Sociological theories can offer explanatory potential on gender, families, violence and social change. The false beliefs and the moral relativism that clearly surround discourses and activities on gender, families and violence may be examined through feminist and pro-feminist perspectives. Their focus upon gender and workings of coercive power encourage an analysis of the sociocultural processes that combine to create and reinforce diversities and specificities. Considered within a global context, theoretical pluralism offers a more useful explanatory project (Eagleton 2003).

In all of this work the *questions to pose* should reflect a critical analytical approach to the problem. Cohen (2001) demonstrates, and details, the continued workings of denial. Yet this presents a grey zone for research, policy and practice as the continued calls for a specific form of privacy for families present barriers to achieving respect and equity. Sennett (2003: 263) comments, 'the nub of the problem we face is how the strong can practice respect toward those destined to remain weak'. We need to reclaim and democratize privacy so that 'a person [can] have control over access to her living space, her meaningful things and information about herself' (Young 1997: 163). Privacy is about having control and autonomy over who has access, not just to spaces and places, but also to personal information, ideas and history. This is a critical concept, and can be difficult to utilize in sociological and policy work. All too often privacy is a term, in its current definition and usage, used to establish barriers, and silence any critical engagement with the topic of families and family life. To argue for a democratization of privacy would actually make apparent the very lack of safety afforded to many women and children in their day-to-day experiences. It could also form the basis of reshaping what it meant by the term 'social'. The challenge, then, is to engage in theoretical pluralism and empirical work that renews the concept of privacy, interrogates the concept of the social and reworks the boundaries between the public and the private. This would offer potential to develop social theory and research, policies and services to form the basis for tackling the gendered nature of much violence in families.

References

Acierno, R., Gray, M., Best, C. et al (2001) Rape and Physical violence: comparison of assault characteristics in older and younger adults in the national women's study. Journal of Traumatic Stress, 14, 685–695.

Action on Elder Abuse (2002) *Analysis of Complaints*, www.elderabuse.org.uk.

Allan, G. and Crow, G. (2001) *Families, Households and Society*. Basingstoke: Macmillan.

Amnesty International (2004) *Women Confronting Violence*. London: Amnesty International.

Arber, S. and Ginn, J. (eds) (1995) *Connecting Gender and Ageing*. Buckingham: Open University Press.

Arendt, H. (1951) *The Origins of Totalitarianism*. New York: Harcourt Brace.

Arendt, H. (1963) *Eichman In Jerusalem: A Report on the Banality of Evil*. New York: Viking Press.

Arendt, H. (1970) *Hannah Arendt on Violence*. San Diego: Harcourt Brace.

Arendt, H. (2002) Reflections on violence, in C. Besteman (ed.) *Violence: A Reader*. Basingstoke: Palgrave MacMillan.

Aretxaga, B. (2002) Dirty protest: symbolic overdetermination and gender in Northern Ireland ethnic violence, in C. Besteman (ed.) *Violence: A Reader*. Basingstoke: Palgrave MacMillan.

Bacchi, C. (1999) *Women, Policy and Politics: The Construction of Policy Problems*. London: Sage.

Baehr, P. (ed.) (2000) *The Portable Hannah Arendt*. Harmondsworth: Penguin.

Baker, A. (1975) Granny bashing, *Modern Geriatrics*, 5(8): 20–4.

Barlow, A., Duncan, S. and James, G. (2002) New Labour, the rationality mistake and family policy in Britain, in A. Carling, S. Duncan and R. Edwards (eds) (2002) *Analysing Families: Morality and Rationality in Policy and Practice*. London: Routledge.

Barrett, M. (1980) *Women's Oppression Today: Problems in Marxist Feminist Analysis*. London: Verso.

Barrett, M. and McIntosh, M. (1991) *The Anti Social Family*. London: Verso.

Bartky, S.L. (1990) *Femininity and Domination. Studies in the Phenomenology of Oppression*. New York: Routledge.

Bauman, Z. (1989) *Modernity and The Holocaust*. Cambridge: Polity Press.

Bauman, Z. (1990) *Thinking Sociologically*. Oxford: Blackwell.

Bauman, Z. (1991) *Modernity and Ambivalence*. Cambridge: Polity Press.

Baxter, J. (2000) The joys and justice of housework, *Sociology*, 34(4): 609–31.

Beale, K. (2003) Because she looks like a child, in B. Ehrenreich and A. R. Hochschild (eds) *Global Woman: Nannies, Maids and Sex Workers in the New Economy.* London: Granta.

Beck, U. (1992) *Risk Society: Towards a New Modernity.* London: Sage.

Beck, U. (1994) The reinvention of politics: towards a theory of relexive modernizaton, in U. Beck, A. Giddens and S. Lash (eds) *Relexive Modernization: Politics, Tradition and Aesthetics in the Modern Social Order.* Cambridge: Polity Press.

Benn, M. (1998) *Madonna and Child: Towards the New Politics of Motherhood.* London: Jonathan Cape.

Bennett, G. and Kingston, P. (1993) *Elder Abuse: Concepts, Theories and Interventions.* London: Chapman & Hall.

Benton, T. and Craib, I. (eds) (2001) *Philosophy of Social Science: The Philisophical Foundations of Social Thought.* New York: Palgrave.

Bernardes, J. (1997) *Family Studies: An Introduction.* London: Routledge.

Berthoud, R. and Gershuny, J. (eds) (2000) *Seven Years in the Lives of British Families.* Bristol: Policy Press.

Bessant, J. (1998) Women in academia and opaque violence, paper presented at the Winds of Change and the Culture of Universities International Conference, University of Technology, Sydney.

Besteman, C. (2002) *Violence: A Reader.* Basingstoke: Palgrave Macmillan.

Bhaskar, R. (1979) *The Possibility of Naturalism.* Hemel Hempstead: Harvester Wheatsheaf.

Bhaskar, R. (1989) *Reclaiming Reality.* London: Verso.

Bhatti-Sinclair, K. (1994) Asian women and violence from male partners, in C. Lupton and T. Gillespie (eds) *Working with Violence.* London: Macmillan.

Biggs, S. (1999) *The Mature Imagination: Dynamics of Identity in Midlife and Beyond.* Buckingham: Open University Press.

Biggs, S., Phillipson, C. and Kingston, P. (1995) *Elder Abuse in Perspective.* Buckingham: Open University Press.

Blaikie, A. (1999) *Ageing and Popular Culture.* Cambridge: Cambridge University Press.

Bond, J. and Phillips, R. (2001) Violence against women as a human rights violation: international responses, in C. Renzetti, J. Edleson and R.K. Bergen (eds) *Sourcebook on Violence Against Women.* London: Sage.

Donepardh, E. and Stoper, E. (1988) *Women, Power and Policy: Toward the Year 2000,* 2nd edn. London: Pergamon Press.

Bourdieu, P. (1977) *Outline of a Theory of Practice.* Cambridge: Cambridge University Press.

Bourdieu, P. (1996) On the family as a realised category, *Theory, Culture and Society,* 13(3): 19–26.

Bowlby, J. (1952) *Maternal Care and Mental Health.* Geneva: World Health Organization.

Bowlby, J. (1965) *Child Care and the Growth of Love.* Harmondsworth: Penguin.

Brannen, J. and Wilson, G. (eds) (1987) *Give and Take in Families.* London: Allen & Unwin.

Bringa, T. (2002) Averted gaze: genocide in Bosnia Herzegovina, 1992–1995, in A. Hinton (ed.) *Annihilating Difference: The Anthropology of Genocide.* Berkeley, CA: University of California Press.

Brittan, A. (1989) *Masculinity and Power.* Oxford: Blackwell.

Brown, W. (1995) *States of Injury.* Princeton, NJ: Princeton University Press.

Burman, M., Brown, J., Tisdall, K. and Batchelor, S. (2001) *A View from the Girls: Exploring Violence and Violent Behaviour.* Glasgow: University of Glasgow Department of Sociology, Anthropology and Applied Social Sciences.

Bury, M. (1995) Ageing, gender and sociological theory, in S. Arber and J. Ginn (eds) *Connecting Gender and Ageing: A Sociological Approach.* Buckingham: Open University Press.

Butler, J. (1993) *Bodies that Matter: On the Discursive Limits of 'Sex'.* London: Routledge.

Bynner, J. and Egerton, M. (2001) *The Wider Benefits of Higher Education*. London: Higher Education Funding Council.

Bytheway, B. (1994) *Ageism*. Buckingham: Open University Press.

Card, C. (2002) *The Atrocity Paradigm: A Theory of Evil*. Oxford: Oxford University Press.

Carling, A., Duncan, S. and Edwards, R. (eds) (2002) *Analysing Families: Morality and Rationality in Policy and Practice*. London: Routledge.

Channel 4 (2003) *Cutting Edge: Behind Closed Doors*. London: Channel 4 Television.

Cheal, D. (1988) *The Gift Economy*. London: Routledge.

Cheal, D. (1991) *Family and the State of Theory*. London: Harvester Wheatsheaf.

Cheal, D. (1999) Marriage: barrier or blessing? Wives' employment in Canada, in S. Lee Browning and R. Miller (eds) *Till Death Do Us Part: A Multicultural Anthology on Marriage*. Stamford, CT: JAI Press.

Cheal, D. (2002) *Sociology of Family Life*. Basingstoke: Palgrave Macmillan.

Coates, K. and Silburn, R. (1971) *Poverty: The Forgotten Englishmen*. Harmondsworth: Penguin.

Cohen, S. (2001) *States of Denial: Knowing About Atrocities and Suffering*. Cambridge: Polity Press.

Coleman, J. and Schofield, J. (2001) *Key Data on Adolescence*. Brighton: Trust for the Study of Adolescence.

Collier, R. (1995) *Masculinity, Law and the Family*. London: Routledge.

Commonwealth Fund (1999) Violence and Abuse, www.cmwf.org/programs/women/ksc_whsurvey99_fact4_332.asp.

Connell, R.W. (2000) *The Men and the Boys*. Cambridge: Polity Press.

Connell, R.W. (2001) Bodies, intellectuals and world society, in N. Watson and S. Cunningham-Burley (eds) *Reframing the Body*. Basingstoke: Palgrave Macmillan.

Connell, R.W. (2002) *Gender*. Cambridge: Polity Press.

Council of Europe (2002) *The Protection of Women Against Violence*. Recommendation Rec. 2002/5 of the Committee of Ministers to member states on the protection of women against violence adopted on 30 April 2002 and Explanatory Memorandum. Strasbourg: Council of Europe.

Crow, G. (2002) *Social Solidarities: Theories, Identities and Social Change*. Buckingham: Open University Press.

Dalley, G. (1996) *Ideologies of Caring*, 2nd edn. London: Macmillan.

De Beauvoir, S. (1970) *Old Age*. London: Deutsch, Weidenfeld & Nicolson.

Delphy, C. and Leonard, D. (1992) *Familiar Exploitation*. Cambridge: Polity.

Denfeld, R. (1997) *Kill the Body, the Head Will Fall*. London: Vintage.

Dennis, N., Henriques, F. and Slaughter, C. (1956) *Coal is Our Life*. London: Tavistock.

Department of Health (2000) *Domestic Violence: A Resource Manual for Health Care Professionals*. London: NHS Executive.

Dobash, R.E. and Dobash, R.P. (1979) *Violence Against Wives: A Case Against Patriarchy*. New York: Free Press.

Dobash, R.E. and Dobash, R.P. (1992) *Women, Violence and Social Change*. London: Routledge.

Doyle, R. (1998) *The Woman Who Walked into Doors*. London: Vintage.

Duncombe, J. and Marsden, D. (1995) 'Workaholics' and 'whingeing women': theorising intimacy and emotion work – the last frontier of gender inequality? *Sociological Review*, 43: 150–69.

Durkheim, E. (1976) *Elementary Forms of the Religious Life*. London: Allen & Unwin.

Eagleton, T. (2003) *After Theory*. London: Penguin.

Edwards, S.S.M and Hearn, J. (2005) Working Against Men's "Dometic Violence": Priority Policies and Practical for Men in Intervention, Prevention and Societal Change. Strasbourg: Council of Europe.

Ehrenreich, B. and Hochschild, A.R. (eds) (2002) *Global Woman: Nannies, Maids and Sex Workers in the New Economy*. London: Granta.

Elias, N. (1994) *The Civilising Process*. Oxford: Blackwell.

Elman, R. (1996) *Sexual Politics and the European Union: The New Feminist Challenge*. Oxford: Berghahn.

Ermisch, J. and Franceconi, M. (2000) Patterns of household and family formation, in R. Berthoud and J. Gershuny (eds) *Seven Years in the Lives of British Families: Evidence on the Dynamics of Social Change from the British Household Panel Survey*. Bristol: Policy Press.

Estes, C.L., Biggs, S. and Phillipson, C. (2003) *Social Theory, Social Policy and Ageing: A Critical Introduction*. Maidenhead: Open University Press.

EVA (2001) *Annual Report*. Lanark: EVA Project.

Fauldi, S. (1991) *Backlash: The Undeclared War Against American Women*. New York: Crown.

Featherstone, M. and Hepworth, M. (1991) The mask of ageing and the postmodern Lifecourse, in M. Featherstone and B.S. Turner (eds) *The Body: Social Process and Cultural Theory*. London: Sage.

Featherstone, M. and Wernick, A. (eds) (1995) *Images of Aging: Cultural Representations of Later Life*. London: Routledge.

Fein, H. (1993) Revolutionary and antirevolutionary geoncides: a comparison of state murders in democratic Kampuchea, 1975–1979, and in Indonesia, 1965–1966, *Comparative Studies in Society and |History*, 35(4): 796–823.

Ferri, E. and Smith, K. (2003) Family life, in E. Ferri, J. Bynner and M. Wadsworth (eds) *Changing Britain, Changing Lives: Three Generations at the Turn of the Century*. London: Institute of Education, University of London.

Ferri, E., Bynner, J. and Wadsworth, M. (eds) (2003) *Changing Britain, Changing Lives: Three Generations at the Turn of the Century*. London: Institute of Education, University of London.

Finch, J. and Mason, J. (1999) Obligations of kinship in contemporary Britain: is there normative agreement? in G. Allan (ed.) *The Sociology of the Family: A Reader*. Oxford: Blackwell.

Fineman, M.A. and Mykituk, R. (1994) *The Public Nature of Private Violence: The Discovery of Domestic Abuse*. New York: Routledge.

Foucault, M. (1976) *Discipline and Punish: The Birth of the Prison*. Harmondsworth: Penguin

Fraser, N. and Gordon, L. (1994) Dependency demystified: inscriptions of power in a keyword of the welfare state, *International Studies in Gender, State and Society*, 4: 31.

Freedom House (1997) *The Comparative Survey of Freedom, 1995–1996: Survey Methodology*. Washington: Freedom House.

Fyvel, T. (1961) *The Insecure Offenders*. London: Chatto & Windus.

Gadd, D., Farrall, S., Dallimore, D. and Lombard, N. (2002) *Domestic Abuse Against Men in Scotland*. Edinburgh: Scottish Executive Publications.

Gelles, R.J. and Loseke, D.R. (eds) (1993) *Current Controversies on Family Violence*. London: Sage.

George, L. (1986) Caregiver burden: conflict between norms of reciprocity and solidarity, in C. Cooper (ed.) *Aging: Stress and Health*. New York: Wiley.

Giddens, A. (1984) *The Constitution of Society: Outline of the Theory of Structuration*. Cambridge: Polity Press.

Giddens, A. (1994) *Beyond Left and Right: The Future of Radical Politics*. Cambridge: Polity Press.

Giddens, A. (1996) *The Nation State and Violence*. Cambridge: Polity Press.

Glover, J. (1999) *Humanity: A Moral History of the Twenteith Century*. London: Yale University Press.

Gondolf, E.W. (1985) *Men Who Batter: An Integrated Approach for Stopping Wife Abuse*. Holmes Beach, FL: Learning Publications.

Gordimer, N. (2003) Testament of the Word, *The Guardian*, 15 June.

Goodin, R.E. and Gibson, D. (2002) The decasualization of eldercare, in E.F. Kittay and E.K. Feder (eds) *The Subject of Care: Feminist Perspectives on Dependency*. Lanham: Rowman & Littlefield.

Gorer, G. (1955) *Exploring the English Character*. London: Cresset Press.

Gouldner, A. (1976) *The Dialectic of Ideology and Technology*. London: Macmillan.

Grant, W. (2000) *Pressure Groups and British Politics*. Basingstoke: Palgrave.

Greed, C. (1994) *Women and Planning: Creating Gendered Realities*. London: Routledge.

Gullette, M.M. (1997) *Declining to Decline: Cultural Combat and the Politics of Midlife*. Charlottesville, VA: University Press of Virginia.

Habermas, J. (1984) *Theory of Communicative Action, Volume 1, Reason and Rationalization of Society*. London: Heinemann.

Habermas, J. (1987) *Theory of Communicative Action, Volume 2, Lifeworld and System: A Critique of Functionalist Reason*. Cambridge: Polity Press.

Hagerstrand, T. (1978) A note on the quality of life-times, in T. Carlstein, D. Parkes and N. Thrift (eds) *Timing Space and Spacing Time, Volume 2, Human Activity and Time Geography*. London: Edward Arnold.

Hague, G., Mullender, A. and Aris, R. (2003) *Is Anyone Listening? Accountability and Women Survivors of Domestic Violence*. London: Routledge.

Hakim, C. (2003) *Models of the Family in Modern Societies: Ideals and Realities*. Aldershot: Ashgate.

Hatty, S.E. (2000) *Masculinities, Violence and Culture*. London: Sage.

Hearn, J. (1998) *The Violences of Men: How Men talk About and How Agencies Respond to Men's Violence to Women*. London: Sage.

Hearn, J. (2002) Nation, state and welfare: the cases of Finland and the UK, in B. Pease and K. Pringle (eds) *A Man's World? Changing Men's Practices in a Globalized World*. London: Zed Books.

Hearn, J. and Parkin, W. (2001) *Gender, Sexuality and Violence in Organizations*. London: Sage.

Hegel, G. (1953) *Reason in History: A General Introduction to the Philosophy of History*. London: Macmillian Reference Library.

Heidegger, M. (1971) *Poetry, Language, Thought*. New York: Harper & Row.

Heiskanen, M. and Piispa, M. (1998) *Faith, Hope and Battering: A Survey of Men's Violence against Women*. Helsinki: Statistics Finland.

Henderson, S. (1998) *Service Provision to Women Experiencing Domestic Violence in Scotland: Summary of Key Conclusions and Recommendations*. Edinburgh: Scottish Office Central Research Unit.

Hepworth, M. (1995) Positive ageing: what is the message? in R. Bunton, S. Nettleton and R. Burrows (eds) *The Sociology of Health Promotion: Critical Analysis of Consumption, Lifestyle and Risk*. London: Routledge.

Hester, M., Kelly, L. and Radford, J. (eds) (1997) *Women, Violence and Male Power*. London: Sage.

Hetherington, K. (1998) *Expressions of Identity: Space, Performance, Politics*. London: Sage.

Hinton, A.L. (ed.) (2002) *Annihilating Difference: The Anthropology of Genocide*. London: University of California Press.

Hird, M. (2002) *Engendering Violence: Heterosexual Interpersonal Violence from Childhood to Adulthood*. Aldershot: Ashgate.

Hochschild, A. (1990) *The Second Shift*. London: Piatkus.

Holter, O.G. (1995) Family theory reconsidered, in labour of love: beyond the self-evidence of everyday life, pp. 99–129, ed. T. Borchgrevink and O.G. Holter. Aldershot: Avebury.

Home Office (1999) *Living Without Fear: An Integrated Approach to Tackling Violence Against Women*. London: Stationery Office.

Hughes, E.C. (1971) *The Sociological eye: Selected Papers*. Chicago: Aldine.

Jack, R. (1994) Dependence, power and violation: gender issues in abuse of elderly people by formal carers, in M. Eastman (ed.) *Old Age Abuse*. London: Chapman & Hall.

Jackson, D. (1990) *Unmasking Masculinity: A Critical Autobiography*. London: Unwin Hyman.

Jamieson, L. (1998) *Intimacy: Personal Relationships in Modern Societies*. Cambridge: Polity.

Jenkins, R. (1996) *Social Identity*. London: Routledge.

Johnson, M. (1995) Patriarchal terrorism and common couple violence, *Journal of Marriage and the Family*, 57: 283–94.

Jokinen, A. (2000) Cultural construction of men's violence, in L. Keeler (ed.) *Recommendations of the EU Expert Meeting on Violence Against Women*. Helsinki: Ministry of Social Affairs and Health Reports, no. 13.

Juergensmeyer, M. (2000) *Terror in the Mind of God: The Global Rise of Religious Violence*. London: University of California Press.

Jyrkinen, M. and Karjalainen, L. (eds) (2001) *Minors in the Sex Trade: Report of the European Commission STOP Project*. Helsinki: STAKES & European Commission.

Kallen, E. (2004) *Social Inequality and Social Justice*. London: Palgrave.

Katz, S. (1996) *Disciplining Old Age: The Formation of Gerontological Knowledge*. Charlottesville, VA: University Press of Virginia.

Kelly, L. (1996) When does speaking profit us? Reflections on the challenges of developing feminist perspectives on abuse and violence by women, in M. Hester, L. Kelly and J. Radford (eds) *Women, Violence and Male Power*. Buckingham: Open University Press.

Kelly, L. (1999) Violence against women: a policy of neglect or a neglect of policy, in S. Walby (ed.) *New Agendas for Women*. New York: St Martin's Press.

Kimmel, M.S. (ed.) (1995) *The Politics of Manhood: Profeminist Men Respond to the Mythopoetic Men's Movement (and the Mythopoetic Leaders Answer)*. Philadelphia, PA: Temple University Press.

Kimmel, M.S. (2002) "Gender Symmetry" in Domestic Violence. A Substantive and Methodological Research Review, *Violence Against Women*, 8, 11, 1332–1363.

Kirkwood, C. (1993) *Leaving Abusive Partners: From the Scars of Survival to the Wisdom for Change*. London: Sage.

Kurz, D. (1993) *Physical Assaults by Husbands: A Major Social Problem*, in R.J. Gelles and D.R. Loseke (eds) *Current Controversies on Family Violence*. London: Sage.

Laukkanen, M.-E. (2000) Suomalainen päivälehdistö seksikaupan foorumina, *Sosiaali- ja terveysministeriön selvityksiä*, 2200: 4.

Lee, N. (2001) *Childhood and Society: Growing Up in and Age of Uncertainty*. Buckingham: Open University Press.

Lees, S. (2002) *Carnal Knowledge: Rape on Trial*. London: The Women's Press.

Lefebvre, H. (1991) *The Production of Space*. Oxford: Blackwell.

Lehane, D. (2001) *Mystic River*. New York: Batman Press.

Letherby, G. (2003) *Feminist Research in Theory and Practice*. Buckingham: Open University Press.

Lewis, J. (2000) Family policy in the post-war period, in S.N. Katz, J. Eekelaar and M. Maclean (eds) *Cross Currents: Family Law and Policy in the US and England*. Oxford: Oxford University Press.

Lundgren, E., Heimer, G., Westerstrand, J. and Kalliokoski, A.-M. (2002) *Captured Queen: Men's Violence Against Women in 'Equal' Sweden – A Prevalence Study*. Umeå: Brottsoffermyndigheten; Uppsala: Uppsala Universitet.

Lupton, D. and Barclay, L. (1997) *Constructing Fatherhood: Discourses and Experiences*. London: Sage.

Maffesoli, M. (1996) *The Contemplation of the World: Figures of Community Style*. Minnesota: University of Minnesota Press.

Marshall, B.L. and Witz, A. (eds) (2004) Engendering the Social: Feminist Encounters with Sociological Theory. Maidenhead: Open University Press.

Marx, K. ([1867] 1970) *Das Kapital, Volume 1*. London: Lawrence & Wishart.

Mason, G. (2002) *The Spectacle of Violence: Homophobia, Gender and Knowledge*. London: Routledge.

Mathews, R., Mathews, J.K. and Speltz, K. (1991) *Female Sexual Offenders: An Exploratory Study*. Orwell, VT: Safer Society Press.

McKie, L. (2003) *Families, Violence and Social Change*, 5th Annual International Visiting Lecturer Series, Lock Haven University of Pennsylvania. Lock Haven, PA: Institute for International Studies.

McKie, L., Bowlby, S. and Gregory, S. (2001) Gender, caring and employment in Britain, *Journal of Social Policy*, 30(2): 233–58.

McKie, L., Gregory, S. and Bowlby, S. (2000) Obligations to work, duties to gcare: ender, caring and social policy, paper presented at Department of Sociology seminar series, University of Surrey.

McKie, L., Gregory, S. and Bowlby, S. (2002) Shadow times: the temporal and spatial frameworks and experiences of caring and working, *Sociology*, 36(4): 897–924.

McKie, L., Gregory, S. and Bowlby, S. (2004) Starting well: gender, care and health in a family context, *Sociology*, 38(3): 593–611.

McKie, L. and Hearn, J. (2004) Gender-neutrality and gender equality: comparing and contrasting policy responses to 'domestic violence' in Finland and Scotland, *Scottish Affairs*, 48: 85–107.

McKie, L. and Jamieson, L. (2003) Families, identities and violence: creating and violating collective memories, paper presented at the annual conference of the British Sociological Association, York.

McKie, L., Watson, N., Hughes, B. and Hopkins, D. (2003) The revolt of the pathological: medical knowledge and the challenge of new social movements, paper presented at the British Sociological Association Medical Sociology Group Conference, University of York.

McLaughlin, J. (2003) *Feminist Social and Political Theory: Contemporary Debates and Dialogues*. Basingstoke: Palgrave.

McNay, L. (2000) *Gender and Agency: Reconfiguring the Subject in Feminist and Social Theory*. Cambridge: Polity Press.

McWilliams, M. and McKiernan, G. (1993) *Bringing it out in the Open: Domestic Violence in Northern Ireland*. Belfast: Stationary Office.

Midgley, M. (2003) *The Myths We Live By*. London: Routledge.

Millen, D. (1997) Some methodological and epistemological issues raised by doing feminist research on non-feminist women, *Sociological Research Online*, 2(3): www.socresonline.org.uk/socresonline/2/3/3.html.

Mills, C.W. (1959) *The Sociological Imagination*. New York: Oxford University Press.

Ministry of Social Affairs (1997) *From Beijing to Finland: The Plan of Action for the Promotion of Gender Equality of the Government of Finland*. Helsinki: Ministry of Social Affairs.

Misztal, B.A. (1996) *Trust in Modern Societies*. Oxford: Polity Press.

Misztal, B.A. (2000) *Informality: Social Theory and Contemporary Practice*. London: Routledge.

Misztal, B.A. (2003) *Theories of Social Remembering*. Maidenhead: Open University Press.

Mitchell, R. and Hodson, C. (1983) Coping with domestic violence: social support and psychological health among women, *American Journal of Community Psychology*, 11(6): 629–54.

Moran, L. and Skeggs, B. with Tyler, P. and Corteen, K. (2004) *Sexuality and the Politics of Violence and Safety*. London: Routledge.

Moran-Ellis, J. (1996) Close to home: the experience of researching child sexual abuse, in M. Hester, L. Kelly and J. Radford (eds) *Women, Violence and Male Power*. Buckingham: Open University Press.

Morgan, D. (1996) *Family Connections: An Introduction to Family Studies*. Cambridge: Polity Press.

Morgan, D. (2002) Sociological perspectives on the family, in A. Carling, S. Duncan and R. Edwards (eds) *Analysing Families: Morality and Rationality in Policy and Practice*. London: Routledge.

Morgan Disney and Associates (2000) *Two Lives – Two Worlds: Older People and Domestic Violence*. Canberra: Partnerships Against Domestic Violence.

Mullender, A. (1997) *Rethinking Domestic Violence: The Social Work and Probation Response*. London: Routledge.

Mullender, A., Hague, G., Iman, U., Kelly, L., Malos, E. and Regan, L. (2003) *Children's Perspectives on Domestic Violence*. London: Sage.

Murdock, G.P. (1949) Social Structure. New York: Free Press.

National Statistics (2002) *British Social Trends Survey, 2002*. London: The Stationery Office.

Nazroo, J. (1995) Uncovering gender differences in the use of marital violence: the effect of methodology, *Sociology*, 29(3): 475–94.

Nordborg, G. and Niemi-Kiesiläinen, J. (2001) Women's peace: a criminial law reform in Sweden, in K. Nousiainen, A. Gunnarsson, K. Lundstrom and J. Niemi-Kiesiläinen (eds) *Responsible Selves: Women in Nordic Legal Culture*. Dartmouth: Ashgate.

Nousiainen, K., Gunnarsson, A., Lundstrom, K. and Niemi-Kiesilainen, J. (eds) (2001) *Responsible Selves: Women in Nordic Legal Culture*. Dartmouth: Ashgate.

Ogg, L. and Bennett, G. (1992) Elder abuse in Britain, *British Medical Journal*, 305: 998–9.

Pan American Health Organization (2000) *Domestic Abuse: Women's Way Out*. Washington, DC: Pan American Health Organization.

Parker, R. (1981) Tending and social policy, in E. Goldberg and S. Hatch (eds) *A New Look at the Personal Social Services*. London: Policy Studies Institute.

Parsons, T. (1943) The kinship system of the contemporary United States, *American Anthropologist*, 45: 22–38.

Parsons, T. (1949) The social structure of the family, in R. Ashen (ed.) *The Family*. New York: Haynor.

Pateman, C. (1988) *The Sexual Contract*. Palo Alto, CA: Stanford University Press.

Phillipson, C. (1998) *Restructuring Old Age*. London: Sage.

Piispa, M. and Heiskanen, M. (2001) *The Price of Violence: The Costs of Men's Violence Against Women in Finland*. Helsinki: Council for Equality, Ministry for Social Affairs and Health.

Pillemer, K. and Finkelhor, D. (1988) The prevalence of elder abuse: a random sample survey, *Gerontologist*, 28(1): 51–7.

Podnicks, E. (1992) Elder abuse, in B. Schesinger (ed.) *Abuse of the Elderly*. Toronto: University of Toronto Press.

Pringle, K. (1995) *Men, Masculinities and Social Welfare*. London: UCL Press.

Privacy International (2004) *Mistaken Identity: Exploring the Relationship Between National Identity Cards and the Prevention of Terrorism*, interim report. London: Privacy International.

Pylkkanen, A. (2001) Women's peace reform in Sweden, paper presented at Les Violences a L'encontre des Femmes at le droit en Europe, Paris.

Queen's Nursing Institute (2003) *Responding to Domestic Abuse in NHS Scotland: Guidelines for Health Care Workers*. Edinburgh: Queen's Nursing Institute and Scottish Executive.

Radford, J. and Stanko, E. (1996) Violence against women and children, in M. Hester, L. Kelly and J. Radford (eds) *Women, Violence and Male Power*. Buckingham: Open University Press.

Radford, L. and Tsutsumi, K. (2004) Gloalization and violence against women – inequalities in risks, responsibilities and blame in the UK and Japan, *Women's Studies International Forum*, 27(1): 1–12.

Rake, K. (2001) Gender and New Labour's social policies, *Journal of Social Policy*, 30: 209–31.

Ray, L. (2000) Memory, violence and identity, in J. Eldridge, J. MacInnes, S. Scott, C. Warhurst and A. Witz (eds) *For Sociology: Legacies and Prospects*. York: Sociologypress.

Renzetti, C., Edleson, J. and Bergen, R.K. (eds) (2001) *Sourcebook on Violence Against Women*. London: Sage.

Ribbens McCarthy, J. and Edwards, R. (2002) The individual in public and private: the significance of mothers and children, in A. Carling, S. Duncan and R. Edwards (eds) *Analysing Families: Morality and Rationality in Policy and Practice*. London: Routledge.

Ronkainen, S. (2001) Gendered violence and genderless gender: a Finnish perspective, *Kvinder Kon Forskning*, 10(2): 45–57.

Rose, N. (2001) The politics of life itself, *Theory, Culture and Society*, 18(6): 1–30.

Ruthven, M. (2004) *Fundamentalism: The Search for Meaning*. Oxford: Oxford University Press.

Samuel, R. (1999) Resurrectionism, in D. Bowell and J. Evans (eds) *Representing the Nation: A Reader*. London: Routledge.

Scambler, G. (2002) *Health and Social Change: A Critical Theory*. Buckingham: Open University Press.

Schneider, J. and Schneider, P. (1994) Mafia, antimafia, and the question of Sicilian culture, *Politics and Society*, 22(2): 237–58.

Scott, M., McKie, L., Seddon, E. and Wasoff, F. (2004) *Older Women and Domestic Violence in Scotland*. Edinburgh: Health Scotland.

Scottish Crime Survey (2000) *Scottish Crime Survey*. Edinburgh: The Stationery Office.

Scottish Crime Survey (2001) *Scottish Crime Survey*. Edinburgh: The Stationery Office.

Scottish Executive (2000) *National Strategy to Address Domestic Abuse in Scotland*. Edinburgh: Stationery Office.

Scottish Executive (2001) *Preventing Violence Against Women: Action Across the Scottish Executive*. Edinburgh: Stationery Office.

Scottish Executive (2002) *Social Focus on Women and Men*. Edinburgh: Stationery Office.

Scottish Executive (2003) *NHS Scotland Guidance on Domestic Abuse for Health Care Professionals*. Edinburgh: Stationery Office.

Scottish Office (1998) *Preventing Violence Against Women: A Scottish Office Action Plan*. Edinburgh: Home Department, Scottish Office.

Seaver, C. (1996) Muted lives: older battered women, *Journal of Elder Abuse & Neglect*, 8: 3–21.

Sedger, R. (2001) Is it aged abuse or domestic violence? *Australian Domestic Violence & Family Violence Clearinghouse Newsletter*: 3–4.

Sennett, R. (2003) *Respect in a World of Inequality*. London: Norton.

Sevenhuijsen, S. (1998) *Citizenship and the Ethics of Care: Feminist Consideration on Justice, Morality and Politics*. London: Routledge.

Shields, C. (2001) *Jane Austen*. London: Phoenix.

Silva, E. and Smart, C. (eds) (1999) *The New Family?* London: Sage.

Slater, P (1999) Elder Aloule: Critical Issues in Policy and Practice. London: Age Concern.

Smith, A. D. (1973) *The Concept of Social Change: A Critique of the Functionalist Theory of Social Change*. London: Routledge & Kegan Paul.

Sorel, G. (1961) *Reflections on Violence*. New York: Collier.

Spinley, B. (1953) *The Deprived and the Privileged*. London: Routledge & Kegan Paul.

Sroufe, L.A. and Fleeson, J. (1986) Attachment and the construction of relationships, in W. Hartup and Z. Rubin (eds) *Relationship and Development*. New York: Cambridge University Press.

STAKES (1998) *Programme for the Prevention of Prostitution and Violence Against Women 1998–2002*. Helsinki: National Research and Development Centre for Welfare and Health (STAKES).

Stanko, E. (1994) Challenging the problem of men's individual violence, in T. Newburn and E. Stanko (eds) *Just Boys Doing Business: Men, Masculinities and Crime*. London: Routledge.

Stanko, E., Crisp, D., Hale, C. and Lucraft, H. (1998) *Counting the Costs: Estimating the Impact of Domestic Violence in the London Borough of Hackney*. London: University of Brunel.

Stanko, E., O'Beirne, M. and Zaffuto, G. (eds) (2002) *Taking Stock: What do we Know About Interpersonal Violence?* Swindon: ESRC.

Stets, J.E. and Straus, M. A. (1990) Gender differences in reporting marital violence and its medical and psychological consequences, in M.A. Straus and R.J. Gelles (eds) *Physical Violence in American Families*. London: Transaction.

Straus, M. A. (1990) The conflict tactics scale and its critics: an evaluation and new data on validity and reliability, in M.A. Straus and R.J. Gelles (eds) *Physical Violence in American Families: Risk Factors and Adaptations to Violence in 8,145 Families*. New Brunswick, NJ: Transaction.

Straus, M., Gelles, R. and Steinmetz, S. (1980) *Behind Closed Doors*. New York: Anchor.

Sullivan, O. (2000) The division of domestic labour: twenty years of change? *Sociology*, 34(3): 437–56.

Svensson, E-M. (2001) Sex equality: changes in politics, jurisprudence and feminist legal studies, in K. Nousiainen, A. Gunnarsson, K. Lundstrom and J. Niemi-Kiesiläinen (eds) *Responsible Selves: Women in Nordic Legal Culture*. Dartmouth: Ashgate.

Swedish Government (1999) *Violence Against Women: Government Bill 1997/98: 55*. Stockholm: Division for Gender Equality.

Tanesini, A. (1994) Whose language? In K. Lennon and M. Whitford (eds) *Knowing the Difference: Feminist Perspectives in Epistemology*. New York: Routledge.

Taylor, B. (2003) *Mary Wollstonecraft and the Feminist Imagination*. Cambridge: Cambridge University Press.

Thompson, P. (1992) I don't feel old: subjective ageing and the search for meaning in later life, *Ageing and Society*, 12: 23–47.

Titmuss, R. (1958) *Essays on the Welfare State*. London: Longman.

Toolis, K. (2002) Family man, *Guardian Weekend*, 13 July.

Townsend, P. (1954) Measuring poverty, *British Journal of Sociology*, 5: 130–7.

Tulle-Winton, E. (2000) Old bodies, in P. Hancock, E. Jagger, K. Paterson, R. Russell, E. Tulle-Winton and M. Tyler (eds) *The Body, Culture and Society: An Introduction*. Buckingham: Open University Press.

Ungerson, C. (1983) Why do women care? in J. Finch and D. Groves (eds) *A Labour of Love: Women, Work and Caring*. London: Routledge & Kegan Paul.

United Nations (1991) *United Nations Principles for Older People*, Resolution 46/91. New York: United Nations, Social Policy and Development Division.

United Nations (1993) *Declaration on the Elimination of Violence against Women*, www.un.org/documents/ga/res/48/a48r104.htm.

United Nations (1995) *Human Development Report*. New York: Oxford University Press.

Van Every, J. (1995) *Heterosexual Women Changing the Family: Refusing to be a Wife!* London: Taylor & Francis.

Viner, (2003) We live in a boom time for rape – and for rapists, *Guardian*, 2 August.

Walby, S. (1990) *Theorising Patriarchy*. Oxford: Basil Blackwell.

Wallace, C. (2002) Household strategies: their conceptual relevance and analytical scope in social research, *Sociology*, 36(2): 275–92.

Wasoff, F. and Dey, I. (2000) *Family Policy*. Eastbourne: Gildredge Press.

Watson, N., McKie, L., Hughes, B., Hopkins, D. and Gregory, S. (2004) (Inter)-dependence, needs and care: the potential for disability and feminist theorists to develop an emancipatory model, *Sociology*, forthcoming.

Weber, M. (1978) *Economy and Society*. Cambridge: Cambridge University Press.

Weber, M. (2002) Politics as a vocation in C. Besteman (ed.) *Violence: A Reader*. Basingstoke: Palgrave.

Weldon, S.L. (2002) Protest, Policy, and the Problem of Violence Against Women: A Cross-national Comparison. Pittsburgh, PA: University of Pittsburgh Press.

West, C. and Zimmerman, D. (1991) Doing gender, in J. Lorber and S. Farrell (eds) *The Social Construction of Gender*. London: Sage.

Williams, M. and May, T. (1996) *Introduction to the Philosophy of Social Research*. London: UCL Press.

Wilson, G. (2000) *Understanding Old Age: Critical and Global Perspectives*. London: Sage.

Witz, A. and Marshall, B.L. (2004) The masculinity of the social: towards a politics of interrogation, in B.L. Marshall and A. Witz (eds) *Engendering the Social: Feminist Encounters with Sociological Theory*. Maidenhead: Open University Press.

World Health Organization (1996) *Violence: A Public Health Priority*. Geneva: WHO.

World Health Organization (2002) *World Report on Violence and Health*. Geneva: WHO.

Young, D. (1995) The economic implications of domestic violence in Greater Glasgow, unpublished M.Sc. thesis, University of York.

Young, I.M. (1990) *Justice and the Politics of Difference*. Princeton, NJ: Princeton University Press.

Young, I. M. (1997) *Interesting Voices: Dilemmas of Gender, Political Philosophy, and Policy*. Princeton, NJ: Princeton University Press.

Zero Tolerance (1994) *Introduction of Zero Tolerance Campaign in Scotland*. Edinburgh: Zero Tolerance Campaign.

Author index

Content index